"Christopher Holmes has already published a
this one is the best yet. With a contemplative
his sources, he engages the psalms as a guide for constructively retrieving the
Christian tradition's witness to God's goodness. Testifying to the goodness of
God, this book places Holmes among the handful of living theologians whose
books should be read by anyone doing Christian theology today."

Matthew Levering, James N. and Mary D. Perry Jr. Chair of Theology, Mundelein Seminary

"Hard to put this down. Elegant and clear in expression, charitable in exchange,
at points poetic, and always with direct application to lived Christian life. Christopher Holmes writes in a genre of deep and generous learning coupled with
keen spiritual insight. A wise look at a theme absolutely central to who God is
and how he is toward us. The Psalter is an especially well-chosen area to take us
on his journey of discovery."

Christopher Seitz, senior professor of biblical interpretation, Wycliffe College in the
University of Toronto

"Many have sought to identify the essential message of the Psalms. Christopher
Holmes ably defends his contention that it's the deceptively simple claim that
'the Lord is good.' It's deceptively simple because once he begins to expound
its meaning, he leads us to a deep understanding of the nature of God in his
being, actions, character, commands, and as Trinity. Furthermore, it leads to
a profound consideration of God's relation to his creation and to us as fallen
human creatures. Like an intrepid explorer, Holmes probes the terrain in conversation with the theological greats, from Augustine to Barth and beyond,
but especially in conversation with Thomas Aquinas. Intellectually robust and
theologically astute, this is a book that is also spiritually enriching and devotionally stimulating. Careful study of it will lead its readers to see hidden
depths in the book of Psalms and, even more significantly, to encounter the
God who is good."

Derek Tidball, former principal of the London School of Theology, author of *The Voices of
the New Testament*, series editor for the Bible Speaks Today Bible Themes Series

"God is good, but how much more can we really say once we've said that? Holmes manages to say quite a lot more about it in this unique study, an extended conceptual gloss on the Psalms with help from Augustine, Aquinas, Barth, and Sonderegger, among others. Crammed with suggestive ideas, well-resourced from the great tradition, and deeply edifying in tone and intent, this book reinstalls divine goodness at the center of theological concerns."

Fred Sanders, professor of theology, Biola University

"Biblical exegesis and speculative theology need each other. Christopher Holmes demonstrates as much in this gem of theological engagement with the Psalms. Joining the chorus of Neo-Thomist enthusiasts, Holmes offers a compelling and hopeful account of God's goodness—an account whose aim is to draw the Christian toward prayer and praise. The distinction between essential and relational attributes provides a set of theological and critical tools for coming to terms with Scripture's plain sense. Readers who desire an able guide through the terrain of classic Christian metaphysics, Barthian misgivings about this tradition, and theological interpretation will welcome this volume."

Mark S. Gignilliat, Beeson Divinity School, Samford University

"In this important book, Christopher Holmes shows us how the Psalms, especially when read with the help of St. Thomas's commentary, reveal to us the spiritual and theological necessity of reflecting on God's attributes—particularly simplicity, perfection and, above all, goodness. He shows us that such reflection is vital for a truly Christian understanding of God as Father, Son, and Holy Spirit. Thus the book constitutes a significant challenge to those criticisms of Thomas Aquinas premised on the mistaken belief that theology can only begin with God as Father, Son, and Holy Spirit, and indicates how misplaced are the related suspicions of supposedly metaphysical or natural theological accounts of God expressed variously by more than a few leading theologians since Karl Barth. This book displays not only broad and careful scholarship, intellectual rigor, and constructive resourcefulness but also is a theology for today in the tradition of Thomas himself: practiced in contemplative mode, the product of spiritual wisdom gained from prayerful reading of the sacred page, and written with the sanctification of the faithful in mind."

Nicholas M. Healy, professor of theology and religious studies, St. John's University

STUDIES IN
CHRISTIAN
DOCTRINE
AND
SCRIPTURE

THE LORD IS GOOD

Seeking the God of the Psalter

Christopher R. J. Holmes

APOLLOS (an imprint of Inter-Varsity Press)
36 Causton Street, London SW1P 4ST, England
Email: ivp@ivpbooks.com
Website: www.ivpbooks.com

First published 2018

British Library Cataloguing-in-Publication Data
A catalogue record for this book is available from the British Library

ISBN: 978–1–78359–656–0
eBook ISBN: 978–1–78359–657–7

Typeset in the United States of America
Printed and bound in Great Britain by Ashford Colour Press Ltd, Gosport, Hampshire

*Inter-Varsity Press publishes Christian books that are true to the Bible and that
communicate the gospel, develop discipleship and strengthen the church for its mission
in the world.*

*IVP originated within the Inter-Varsity Fellowship, now the Universities and Colleges
Christian Fellowship, a student movement connecting Christian Unions in universities
and colleges throughout Great Britain, and a member movement of the International
Fellowship of Evangelical Students. Website: www.uccf.org.uk. That historic association
is maintained, and all senior IVP staff and committee members subscribe to the UCCF
Basis of Faith.*

You are good and do good;
teach me your statutes.

PSALM 119:68

Contents

Acknowledgments

MY DEBTS OF GRATITUDE ARE MANY. First, I would like to thank my colleagues in the Department of Theology and Religion at the University of Otago. I have the privilege of working with good, kind, and considerate people. I would also like to thank the Division of the Humanities at Otago for a five-month research leave during the first half of 2017. This time away allowed me to finish the book. Second, one of my PhD students, Cameron Coombe, read through a first draft of the book in its entirety, offering many helpful suggestions along the way. I am grateful. Third, for Daniel Treier's encouragement of the project: his comments, on both a rough first and a penultimate draft, were much appreciated. They have made for a better book.

Fourth and last, for Reverend Professor John Webster (1955–2016), who died midway through this project. I first met John as a ThD student at Wycliffe College, University of Toronto, in the early 2000s. Though John had by that time left Toronto for Oxford, he was nonetheless a regular visitor to Toronto. He encouraged me to pursue work on the divine attributes and supervised some of that work. Regular notes to and from him followed thereafter, first to a young theologian working at Providence Theological Seminary in Manitoba, and then to Aotearoa/New Zealand, where I have happily taught for several years now. John always seemed to know what to say and how to say it. He was not only a gifted theologian but also a faithful pastor. I would have liked for him to have read this book, but he is now with his Lord, and sees clearly the things about which I write but through a glass darkly. It is to him, a servant of God in the gospel of Christ, that I dedicate this book.

Abbreviations

ACCS	Ancient Christian Commentary on Scripture
ACMW	*Anselm of Canterbury: The Major Works.* Edited by Brian Davies and G. R. Evans. Oxford: Oxford University Press, 1998.
BDAG	Bauer, Walter, Fredrick William Danker, William F. Arndt, and F. Wilbur Gingrich. *A Greek-English Lexicon of the New Testament and Other Early Christian Literature.* 3rd ed. Chicago: University of Chicago Press, 2000.
BECNT	Baker Exegetical Commentary on the New Testament
CCSS	Catholic Commentary on Sacred Scripture
CD	Barth, Karl. *Church Dogmatics.* Edited by Geoffrey W. Bromiley and T. F. Torrance. Translated by Geoffrey W. Bromiley. 4 vols. in 12 parts (I/1–IV/4). Edinburgh: T&T Clark, 1956–1975.
Compend	Thomas Aquinas. *Compendium of Theology.* Translated by Richard J. Regan. New York: Oxford University Press, 2009.
Conf	Saint Augustine. *Confessions.* Translated by Henry Chadwick. Oxford: Oxford University Press, 1992.
DBWE	Dietrich Bonhoeffer Works
DN	Thomas Aquinas. *On the Divine Names.* Translated by Harry C. Marsh in "Cosmic Structure and the Knowledge of God: Thomas Aquinas *In Librum beati Dionysii de divinis nominibus exposition*," 265-549. PhD dissertation, Vanderbilt University, 1994.
HC	The Heidelberg Catechism. In *The Creeds of Christendom: With a History and Critical Notes.* Edited by Philip Schaff and David S. Schaff. Vol. 3, *The Evangelical Protestant Creeds.* Grand Rapids: Baker, 1990.
Hebdomads	Thomas Aquinas. *An Exposition of "On the Hebdomads" of Boethius.* Translated by Janice L. Shultz and E. Synan. Washington, DC: Catholic University of America Press, 2001.

IJST	*International Journal of Systematic Theology*
In Ps	Thomas Aquinas. *Commentary on the Psalms*. Translated by various. Project coordinator Stephen Loughlin. Center Valley, PA: Aquinas Translation Project. Last updated September 4, 2012. hosted.desales.edu/w4/philtheo/loughlin/ATP/.
Psalms	Saint Augustine. *Exposition of the Psalms*. 6 vols. Translated by Maria Boulding. Hyde Park, NY: New City Press, 2000–2004.
SCG	Thomas Aquinas. *Summa Contra Gentiles*. Translated by Fathers of the English Dominican Province. 4 vols. London: Burns, Oates & Washbourne, 1923–1929.
ST	Thomas Aquinas. *Summa Theologiae*. In *Basic Writings of Saint Thomas Aquinas*. Vol. 1, *God and the Order of Creation*. Translated and edited by Anton C. Pegis. Indianapolis: Hackett, 1997.
TDOT	*Theological Dictionary of the Old Testament*. Edited by G. Johannes Botterweck, Heinz Josef-Fabry, and Helmer Ringgren. 15 vols. Grand Rapids: Eerdmans, 1981.
TNTL	The New Testament Library
Truth	Thomas Aquinas. *Disputed Questions on Truth*. Translated by Robert W. Schmidt, SJ. 3 vols. Indianapolis: Hackett, 1994.
TWOT	*Theological Wordbook of the Old Testament*. Edited by R. Laird Harris, Gleason Archer Jr., and Bruce K. Waltke. Chicago: Moody Press, 2003.

Introduction

Why Such a Book?

THIS IS A BOOK ABOUT GOD, indeed God's goodness. In the pages to come, I unfold something of how God is goodness itself. Goodness is worth contemplating because it is the preeminent claim the Psalms make with respect to God. Of course, Scripture as a whole makes many assertions about God's nature: for example, God is almighty, faithful, holy, and merciful. But I want to think through why goodness among the attributes has preeminence in the Psalter: "You are good" (Ps 119:68). Indeed, I argue that goodness's priority in the Psalter extends to all of Scripture. Goodness has a scriptural density and range that even the other great attribute—love—does not quite have.

What do I mean? There are compelling reasons to consider God's goodness as the source and basis of God's love, just as there are for God's great works of mercy and grace that his goodness as communicated accomplishes. Mercy, grace, faithfulness—these are forms of his goodness. Goodness has the character of a cause and end; goodness is causal and teleological in nature. Accordingly, I show how God's goodness is the ground of creation because it is by its very nature communicative. God loves his own goodness and therefore creates things to share in it. I also unfold how goodness is the end of creation. God wills that all things share in the goodness he is. Goodness is creation's principle and *telos*. God loves us by willing good to us, so much so that he conserves and perfects us in the good he is. The end of all creatures is goodness, and it is from love of that same goodness that God wills to communicate it to created things. It is not insignificant, then, that God's effects of nature are declared in the opening chapters of Genesis to be good. They are good because, as we shall see, all of God's works, whether they are of nature, grace, or glory, participate in their cause.

I pursue this study in a contemplative mode. My concern is God and things as they are ordered to God. This involves contemplation undertaken for the edification of the Christian community. Thus the tone of this book is at once reflective, scholarly, and doxological. In describing the great goodness of God that we are given to know in Holy Scripture, we see that Scripture's presentation is self-involving. To speak responsibly of God's goodness is to love the God who is good. The infinite goodness of God cannot be unfolded well if description and praise are isolated from one another. Thus this study will integrate a close reading of primary texts with Christian piety, involving academic rigor undertaken in a doxological spirit. I write within a frame that is at once academic and devotional.

There is another reason for writing the book, and that is to offer an account of the Psalms' preeminent attribute of God from a broadly classical and medieval, that is, Thomistic, perspective.[1] What little written on the divine attributes in the latter part of the twentieth century and into the twenty-first has largely moved with Karl Barth, in particular his profoundly christocentric approach to the attributes. My own book on the divine attributes exemplifies this, as was the case with works inspired by Barth, such as those offered by Colin Gunton and Wolf Krötke.[2] I am now less convinced than I once was about the merits of such an approach, and so I would like to explain why, largely by considering the merits of Thomas's. My aim is to think theocentrically, to present some of the gains accrued to the doctrine of God when it prioritizes goodness and distinguishes it in relationship to

---

[1]Interestingly, one commentator on Thomas notes that the *Summa Theologiae* is about one thing above all else, "[the] reception and mediation of God's goodness." See Ghislain Lafont, *Structures et Method dans la 'Somme Théologique' de Saint Thomas d'Aquin* (Paris: Éditions du Cerf, 1996), quoted in Tyler R. Wittman, "Confessing God as God: Thomas Aquinas, Karl Barth, and the Relation Between Theology and Economy" (PhD diss., University of St. Andrews, 2016), 47n88.

[2]See Christopher R. J. Holmes, *Revisiting the Doctrine of the Divine Attributes: In Dialogue with Karl Barth, Eberhard Jüngel, and Wolf Krötke* (New York: Peter Lang, 2007); Colin Gunton, *Act and Being: Toward a Theology of the Divine Attributes* (Grand Rapids: Eerdmans, 2002); and Wolf Krötke, *Gottes Klarheiten: Eine Neuinterpretation der Lehre von Gottes 'Eigenschaften'* (Tübingen: Mohr Siebeck, 2001).

God's love. There is a place, in other words, for disciplined, prayerful, scripturally concentrated analysis of God. It is good to contemplate God—how God is ordered to himself apart from the world—precisely because the Scriptures encourage such retrospection.

In this exploration of God's goodness, I repose in what Scripture assumes to be true of God. And I do so in a way that is indebted to the most enthralling publication to appear on God's attributes since the publication of Barth's *Church Dogmatics* II/1, namely, volume 1—*The Doctrine of God*—of Katherine Sonderegger's *Systematic Theology*.[3] Her efforts to think through the God/world relationship in compatibilist terms and to argue that God is his own relationship to the world have had a significant impact on my work. They have also helped me to see more of Barth's remarkable contribution to the doctrine of God as well as some of its shortcomings.

Moreover, I take up the theme of goodness not only because of the priority assigned to it by the Psalter, but because Thomas, in his synthetic works but especially in his Psalms commentary, says about it so many helpful things that need to be distilled and presented in all of their grandeur.[4] My concern is not so much with the historical-theological task of interpreting Thomas but with the kind of metaphysical inquiry promoted by careful reading of his corpus, especially his great synthetic works and scriptural commentaries. This fits with a larger and more recent scholarly concern of mine, which is to promote Thomas as a gifted reader and expositor of Holy Scripture. What I find most interesting about Thomas is his engagement with Scripture. He has helped me to see things that I could not have seen

---

[3]Katherine Sonderegger, *Systematic Theology*, vol. 1, *The Doctrine of God* (Minneapolis: Fortress, 2015).

[4]Thomas's commentary has been subject to very little scholarly scrutiny. There is one study in English that I am aware of, namely, Thomas F. Ryan's *Thomas Aquinas as Reader of the Psalms* (Notre Dame, IN: University of Notre Dame Press, 2000), and only a few articles that engage his commentary, the most recent being a helpful piece by Gabriel Torretta, OP, "Rediscovering the Imprecatory Psalms: A Thomistic Approach," *The Thomist* 80 (2016): 23-48. In addition, James R. Ginther provides an extremely helpful introduction to Thomas's commentary "as a Textbook for Theology." Ginther discusses how the Bible functioned as the basis of theological education and also "the integral role the Psalter played in medieval culture." The reason for the popularity of Psalms as a primary text for teaching theology was, not surprisingly, its comprehensiveness. Accordingly, Ginther notes that Thomas's commentary provides "an ideal test case for how a master of the sacred page utilized the Psalms as a textbook for teaching theology." See James R. Ginther, *Omnia Disce: Medieval Studies in Memory of Leonard Boyle, O.P.*, ed. Anne J. Duggan, Joan Greatrex, and Brenda Bolton (Aldershot, UK: Ashgate, 2005), 215-16.

before, most especially the depths of the majesty of God. And so I promote attention in this book to the scriptural character of Thomas's thought, showing how his pursuit of God in himself is anchored in a rigorous reading of key Old and New Testament texts. Accordingly and more specifically, there are a few key themes that animate the nine major chapters of the book. They are as follows.

GOODNESS AND THE TRINITY

It is important to separate treatment of God's attributes from discourse on who God is, the relations that distinguish and constitute Father, Son, and Spirit. Holy Scripture encourages us to praise God for what God is, who God is, and what God does. The goodness of God is common to the three, to their one, indivisible, and undivided essence. The doctrine of God's attributes—of what is common to the Father, Son, and Spirit—provides resources for and grounds discourse about the Trinity, about who the three are in relation to one another. I argue throughout the book that it is crucial to neither separate nor confuse teaching on the one God with teaching on the Trinity. Scripture says many things that are true of the one essence common to the three, and it also says many things that are true of the three in relation to one another but that are not common to them. The challenge is to follow Scripture's lead in distinguishing between what is said in a substantial or essential sense and what is said in a relational sense.

Said differently, these three things cannot be conflated: description of the attributes identical to God's essence, the originating relations whereby each of the three is, and their works of nature and grace.[5] Rather, they are for us distinguishable truths. I write this book to offer some scriptural guidance in terms of receiving along these lines the Psalter's witness to God. The task ahead is to prayerfully attend to the Psalter's remarkable portrait of God, with the help provided by Thomas Aquinas and, to a lesser extent, Augustine, and in a way that is mindful of Barth.[6] As Thomas teaches, and as we shall

---

[5]It is not far off to the mark to suggest that Thomas's treatment of the one essence of God in advance of his treatment of the Trinity of persons represents a fresh application of Augustine's teaching. Augustine argues that some things are said of God "relationship-wise," while others are said "substance-wise." See Augustine, *The Trinity*, trans. Edmund Hill, OP (Brooklyn, NY: New City Press, 1991), 5.2.

[6]I am deeply indebted to the Aquinas Translation Project, being no Latinist myself. Stephen

note, "everything in Him [i.e. God] is His essence. . . . In God what He is and that whereby he is are the same."[7]

Goodness and Creation

The second theme has to do with the relationship between God and creation, Creator and created things. The Psalter's abundant testimony to God's goodness helps us to think through how created things, as goods in themselves, participate in the Lord's original goodness, though in a radically dissimilar way. As we shall see, goodness exists in God and is God himself. And yet, God's goodness, communicated to us in God's great works of nature and grace, is compatible with us. In this study I write about how good is said of both God and creatures, not as if they were on a kind of continuum and participant in some "thing" above them, but as said of each in a quite distinctive way. The category "transcendental" provides us with a useful way for thinking about how a divine attribute—goodness—has a different meaning when said of God and of creatures who process from God. It is also helpful for thinking more broadly about the Creator/creature relationship.

You could put it this way: Goodness is a name that is supremely true of God from eternity—"even if the world had not been," as Robert Sokolowski says.[8] Neither goodness, nor truth, nor beauty, nor unity assumes a relation

---

Loughlin, the project coordinator, and his team of translators have for the most part brought Thomas's Psalms commentary into English. See hosted.desales.edu/w4/philtheo/loughlin/ATP/. I have honored the translators' wish that the copyright notice remain at the bottom of each translation to ensure that appropriate credit be given to both individual and the project. The translators used the Latin text according to the Venice edition of 1776. The Latin original is available online at www.corpusthomisticum.org. Thomas's commentary, based on the Bibles he used—namely, the Vulgate and the Douay-Rheims—and covering only the first fifty-four Psalms, was written a few months before his death in March 1274, that is, during the last few months of his teaching ministry while in Naples, from September to December 1273, while he was writing the third part of his *Summa Theologiae*. The numbering of his commentary is quite confusing. The first nine psalms of his commentary follow our numbering, but Ps 10 and onwards follow a different order. Accordingly, Ps 10 for Thomas is actually our Ps 11. Thomas did not, for reasons I am unaware of, comment on (our) Ps 10. To keep the text of my book as clean as possible, I hold to our numbering. Thus, for example, "*In Ps* 11" indicates Thomas's comments on Ps 11, though the Latin original refers to Ps 10.

[7] Aquinas, *ST* 1.28.2; 1.29.4 ad 1. I have used Anton Pegis's translation of the *Summa Theologiae*. In referring to the *ST* as above, I mean, following the second quotation: the first part, the 29th question, the 4th article, reply "to" (*ad*) objection 1.

[8] Robert Sokolowski, *The God of Faith and Reason: Foundations of Christian Theology* (Washington, DC: Catholic University of America Press, 1995), 19.

to creatures, as is the case with an attribute such as mercy or grace.[9] However, even as goodness belongs to God alone, goodness also belongs to the creatures as well who share in God's goodness by likeness. As Thomas notes in *Truth*, "some goods belong to God alone, as eternity and omnipotence; but some others, to certain creatures as well as to God, as wisdom and justice and the like."[10] Goodness is intriguing to contemplate because it belongs to God (supremely) and to creatures (derivatively). Creatures are good only because of God, whereas God is not good because of us. This is important to think about. Scripture would have us not only believe that God is good in and of himself but also that God's goodness can be truly ascribed to secondary causes. Accordingly, good is said of God and creatures neither in a univocal or equivocal but analogical sense. Goodness provides a theologically satisfying way of unfolding what is true with respect to the Creator and creature, all the while safeguarding the great difference between God and creatures, something that analogical discourse at its best does. Goodness as an attribute indicates the compatibility of the one who is infinitely good with what is good in a finite sense. Consideration of God's goodness thus enables us to see how God's created effects are contained in him and possess likeness to him, even in the midst of great dissimilarity.

Furthermore, God's goodness supplies us with the theological reason for creation. Goodness is preeminent because it is the principal ground of creation. Thomas writes, "*Because God is good, we exist.* . . . God produced creatures not because He needed them, nor because of any other extrinsic reason, but because of the love of His own goodness."[11] The "procession of love," which is, as we shall see, the procession of the Holy Spirit, is the ground of all things outside God.[12] The upshot is that God's goodness is creation's rationale. Thus the second major concern of the book is to think through how goodness functions as not only the principle of intelligibility for creation but also the explanation for God's ongoing presence in and to created things.

---

[9]See further Aquinas, *ST* 1.13.7: "*I answer that,* Some names which import relation to creatures are applied to God temporally, and not from eternity." An example of such a name is *Lord*: "God was not *Lord* until He had a creature subject to Himself."
[10]Aquinas, *Truth* 3.21.2.
[11]Aquinas, *ST* 1.19.4, 32.1 ad 1.
[12]Aquinas, *ST* 1.27.3 ad 3.

GOODNESS AND EXPERIENCE

The approach taken to these two recurring themes, cast as they are in the frame of Psalm 119:68, is that the supreme goodness of God must be lived and experienced before it can be described. Understanding of God is the fruit of prayer, praise, meditation, and contemplation.[13] Contemplation is the lens through which God's supreme goodness must be theologically addressed. This is a motif interwoven and present throughout the book. To receive something of the Psalter's testimony to God is to pray the Psalter and to have our moral bearings changed by what we pray. The Psalms demand a kind of moral and spiritual fitness. Theology assumes, I think, devotion, and it encourages a renewed morality, for God's goodness is a spiritual and moral good that must be experienced before the theology is truly understood. Thus the presentation of God's goodness in this book takes at times almost a sermonic frame. I try to write as if contemplation of, experience with, and ultimately love for the subject matter is materially decisive.

Psalm 55's trajectory is extremely helpful in understanding the need to live if one is to articulate God's great goodness. In Psalm 55:1-5, we have David's plea before God, his announcement of his intense distress: "Fear and trembling come upon me, and horror overwhelms me" (Ps 55:5). In Psalm 55:6-8, David sets down his remedy, which Thomas describes as "the earnest care of contemplation."[14] Contemplation—"I would lodge in the wilderness" (Ps 55:7)—is the form in which God is known and loved, experienced. To contemplate is "to consider sublime causes," in other words, to consider in a contemplative mode the essence of the one who is causality itself.[15] This book is the fruit of one theologian's contemplation of the cause and of how effects resemble the goodness of their cause. It is a work that, I hope, transparently demonstrates how regenerate theological intelligence assumes a deep experience of the mysteries of which it speaks.

---

[13]Thomas calls "contemplative research . . . the summit of human inquiry" because it has to do with "knowledge of God." See Aquinas, *SCG* 1.4. For the *Summa Contra Gentiles*, I have used the translation provided by the Fathers of the English Dominican Province.

[14]Aquinas, *In Ps* 55, trans. Gregory Sadler. Except for where they are part of quotations from Thomas's text, English translations of the Psalms will come from the New Revised Standard Version.

[15]Aquinas, *In Ps* 55.

GOODNESS AND INSPIRATION

This is also not so much a discrete theme as a basic assumption about what Scripture is. Scripture is inspired, meaning that it bears the voice of the triune Lord. This is the presupposition by which I read. "Sacred Scripture," as Thomas notes, "is produced through inner urging of divine inspiration."[16] The Psalms are the Word of the Lord and are to be received as such. The psalmist's voice is transparent to the voice of another, the living, speaking Lord. In other words, when we draw attention to their inspired character, we mean that the voice of the psalmist, namely, David, is compatible with the Lord's. David's voice sets forth God and God's Son, Jesus Christ, "the true David" in and by the power of the Holy Spirit.[17]

In bearing the voice of the triune God, the Psalms bear what is common to the three, preeminently, their goodness. I write so as to demonstrate how the Psalms instruct beginners and strengthen the accomplished in goodness. Indeed, we would not have this nourishment were the Lord not good. These prayers, whether they are in the form of praise, lament, or imprecation, raise the mind to God as they do because of the Lord who is good.[18]

GOODNESS AND THE ROAD AHEAD

This book contains nine main chapters. They are as follows. In chapter one, "Simplicity," I describe how "all that is in God, is God," unfolding the convertibility of God's attributes with God's essence.[19] The plenitude of the Lord encourages us to think through how he is identical with his attributes. In particular, I explain how speech works with respect to such a God, and sketch how teaching on simplicity is related to teaching on the Trinity. In so doing, I am mindful of what one recent rather sympathetic critic of traditional teaching on simplicity, namely, Barth, has indicated, respectfully

---

[16]Thomas Aquinas, "St. Thomas's Introduction to his Exposition of the Psalms of David," trans. Hugh McDonald, The Aquinas Translation Project, http://hosted.desales.edu/w4/philtheo/loughlin/ATP/Proemium.html.

[17]This turn of phrase is taken from Thomas's discussion of the preface to Ps 35. See Aquinas, *In Ps* 35. Note that *Psalms* will be capitalized when referred to as a book of the Bible and individual items in that book. However, it will not be capitalized when speaking in a generic sense—for example, the psalms of ascent.

[18]Psalms scholar James L. Mays describes "the goodness of the Lord as the attribute beyond all others that calls for and calls forth praise." See Mays, *Psalms*, Interpretation: A Bible Commentary for Teaching and Preaching (Louisville, KY: Westminster John Knox, 2011), 27.

[19]Aquinas, *ST* 1.27.2 ad 2.

stating Barth's position while distancing myself from some of the conclusions he draws.

In chapter two, "You Are Good," the focus is on the pure goodness of God as transcendent with respect to all things. I describe the pure act of being that is God, drawing attention to God as a lovable and desirable, omnipresent and transcendent good, using Psalm 135:3-5 as a kind of test case. I also take up how God is a communicative good, the sovereign basis of every created good.

In chapter three, "Goodness and Trinity," I take up more architectonic matters, arguing for the merits of treating God's unity of essence prior to the Trinity of persons. I also contemplate how God's attributes, when understood as identical to the essence common to the three, clarify thinking regarding the manner of our creaturely participation in God. I explain, among other things, the relationship between God's attributes and works toward us, using Psalm 36:9 as a test case.

In chapter four, "You Do Good," I explore the symmetry between being and act in God, averring that the good God accomplishes expresses something profoundly true about God's life. I show how the Psalter illuminates Thomistic teaching on God as pure act, one whose great acts of nature and grace accomplish his goodness among us. I conclude by contrasting my approach with that of Dietrich Bonhoeffer's.

In chapter five, "The Good Creator," I consider God's causality. I argue for some of the advantages of understanding God in causal terms and explore how God's created effects share in and receive God's goodness. Turning to the nature psalms, I show how a robust account of God the Creator furnishes us with the context for considering the generative character of the Lord's goodness and its compatibility with what he creates.

In chapter six, "Goodness and Evil," I examine the problem of evil, explaining its nothingness and its corruptive character. I discuss how the psalms of lament teach us to avoid evil, to recognize the help of the angels, and to pursue what is good, imitating thereby our cause.

In chapter seven, "Teach Me Your Statutes," I focus explicitly on the moral dimension of God's goodness via the gift of the law as God's loving instruction, conserving us in the good he is. The law teaches us of the goodness of its source so that we may tend toward him. This chapter also unfolds how compatible is the old law with the new, using Ephesians 2:15.

In chapter eight, "Goodness and Jesus Christ," I think about the relationship between goodness and Jesus Christ. In dialogue with Psalm 22:1, I contemplate how God's attributes inform an account of Jesus Christ as one Person subsisting *in* two natures.[20] In so doing, I ask this: In what sense is incarnation a work most befitting divine goodness? I also consider how, with reference to Mark 10:18, "scripture ascribes passion and death to God's one and only-begotten Son."[21] This occasions engagement with a classical christological teaching, namely, how some things said of Jesus Christ are more becoming to one of his two natures.

In chapter nine, "Perfection," I explore how God's goodness relates to our perfection. I discuss the role of experience in Christian teaching on God, how sight relates to faith, and why our eternal joy is that of attaining God's likeness. I conclude by taking up a few statements from the Psalms to show our hope is one day to see our cause and end.

I wrap things up by making some observations about the place of devotion and experience in the doctrine of God, sounding a call to a scriptural theology and to a form of discourse on God that encourages confessional expression.

---

[20] I italicize the *in* to obviate any sense in which the presupposition "through" could be used. The one person of Jesus Christ does not subsist through anything.
[21] Aquinas, *SCG* 4.34.

ONE

Simplicity

O
N THE BASIS OF THE PSALTER'S TESTIMONY, it is fitting to describe God as a simple good. One might ask, "Why begin here?" We begin with simplicity to align ourselves with the biblical testimony to God as one whose existence is utterly complete, whose attributes are one with his essence, who depends on nothing outside himself to be the one he has always been and will be.

These are truths that we speak of in a positive sense only by speaking of what notions they exclude. Thus we begin with simplicity not insofar as it is an attribute of God, but rather as an extrabiblical concept that, at its best, honors biblical patterns of speech. The Scriptures ascribe many attributes to God, and teaching on simplicity enables us to see how the many attributes of God are one with God himself.

COMPLETE EXISTENCE

Simplicity means that nothing is accidental to God; "his existing," says Thomas, "is at once whole."[1] There are good biblical reasons for thinking this. Consider, for example, David's utter delight in the law of God, as expressed in Psalm 19:7-10. "The law of the LORD is perfect, reviving the soul" (Ps 19:7). Thomas elucidates this text by highlighting the superiority of spiritual delights. Spiritual delights "are not in motion," he writes, as they "consist in loving and understanding the good that is not in motion." God is

---

[1]Aquinas, *Compend* §8.

not in motion "because the whole is possessed at once."[2] To talk in terms of God's simplicity is to talk about how God is perfect, having no future and past, because he possesses himself entirely. Put somewhat differently, God is not in motion, so as to become something he was not before. God is simple and as such possesses himself entirely, having no need of improvement. God is utterly incapable of renovation because he is entire, complete, and, as we will see, the pure act of being itself. What is said of the law in terms of, for example, its being "perfect," "sure," "right," "clear," "pure," "true," and "righteous altogether," is said of God, who is all these things at one and the same time.

Accordingly, goodness is not at arm's length from God; goodness has no reality *per se*. Indeed, God does not participate in something called goodness as if goodness were some thing existing outside God, of which God was a part. Rather, goodness is God himself. Goodness is indicative of God's "perfect existing."[3] In a statement of supreme clarity, Thomas says, "But God is whatever He has in Himself."[4] God has goodness and other "things" such as greatness in himself. These are the same in God. Goodness does not refer to one part, as it were, of God, greatness another; rather, they are identical. In this chapter I unfold something of this sublime truth: "God is whatever He has in Himself," showing how such a claim aligns nicely with the Psalter's portrait of God.

If we begin with Psalm 118:1-5—"O give thanks to the LORD, for he is good; his steadfast love endures forever!" (Ps 118:1)—we see, following Augustine, the biblical fittingness of simplicity discourse and discover one of the two fundamental truths regarding God's simplicity. Augustine writes, "I can think of nothing nobler than this terse statement ['because he is good'] of the reason for praising him. Goodness is so essentially the character of God that the Son of God himself, when addressed as *Good teacher*, replied, *Why do you ask me about what is good? None is good except one, God alone.* (Mt 19:16-17; Mk 10:18)."[5] When we talk about God's simplicity, we speak of the deep truth that the goodness the Psalter ascribes to God "is so essentially

---

[2] Aquinas, *In Ps* 19, trans. Hugh McDonald.
[3] Aquinas, *Compend* §114.
[4] Aquinas, *SCG* 1.23.
[5] Augustine, *Psalms*, 5:334. Note that Psalm 117 for Augustine is Psalm 118 for us, as Augustine's numbering follows the Vulgate.

the character of God" that it may be said to be one with God. Goodness is what God has in himself, and is himself.

This is true not only of goodness. "All the perfections in God are really one thing."[6] Although holiness and goodness, for example, mean different things to us, they are one in God; more radically, they are God himself. Scripture talks in generous terms about the fact *that* God is, about God's actual existence—that is, his attributes. Talk about God's attributes is talk about what is essential to God, not accidental: "subsistent, not accidental."[7] As the relations of Father, Son, and Spirit are subsistent—that is, internal to and identical with the essence of God—so too are the attributes of God identical to God. The language of simplicity is in the service of unfolding the truth that God's attributes are one with his undivided and complete essence.

If such is the case, then, at the beginning of our journey into understanding something of what God is as goodness itself, we affirm this fundamental notion of simplicity: goodness is proper to God, belongs to God, and is identical with the one, perfect, and undivided being of God.

WHAT ABOUT THE MANY?

The previous discussion raises several questions, one of which is whether goodness specifies exactly the same thing in God as, for example, love, given that they are distinguished for us by Scripture itself. The first thing to say is that all the attributes of God have the same subject. The attributes refer to one and the same God and are the same thing in God. "But God is whatever He has in Himself. Therefore no accident is in God. . . . God is whatever he has."[8] God is *esse subsistens*, meaning that God is unlike anyone or anything else, "one being whose essence is to exist."[9] Because existence and essence are one for God, God's being is said to be convertible with his goodness, God's attributes as identical to his being God.

---

[6]Aquinas, *Compend* §22.
[7]Aquinas, *Compend* §48.
[8]Aquinas, *SCG* 1.23.
[9]Robert Sokolowski, *The God of Faith and Reason: Foundations of Christian Theology* (Washington, DC: Catholic University of America Press, 1995), 157. Note that Sokolowski acknowledges his indebtedness to John Wippel's piece "Aquinas's Route to the Real Distinction: A Note on *De Ente et Essentia*," *The Thomist* 43 (1979): 279-95.

To say that God is good and that God is, for example, wonderful, both of which are true, is to say things that have different nuances of meaning. They draw us to different dimensions of the Psalter's testimony to the one God. The language of "wonderful," for example, bespeaks the exuberant, extroverted love of the God whose decrees direct his people's paths. The register in the case of "wonderful" is, you might say, more temporal, and not so much essential; "wonderful" is a temporal name, assuming a "relation to creatures."[10] The register of goodness, however, is essential and thus from eternity: it is said of God *in se* and of God in relationship with us. The many names of God that Scripture supplies us with are one and one with God himself, though not in the same way.

This is a key point. Some names have a more temporal rather than an essential register. Goodness has a greater density than some other names, such as wonderful, also because, as we shall see, goodness is identical with the procession of the will in God, which Thomas identifies with the Holy Spirit. This is not the case with a name like wonderful. Such a name arises in the Psalms in response to particular acts, for example, the exodus and the giving of the law. You might say that God does wonderful things because he is good.

Essential attributes or names like that of goodness are also to be distinguished from personal names of God such as Word, Love, and Gift. Love is a personal name of the Spirit, following John 17:26, and Word is a personal name of the Son, following John 1:1-18. A personal name is different from an essential name is that it refers to another: the Holy Spirit, for example, refers to the Father as his primary cause and the Son as secondary cause, whereas essential attributes are common to the three by dint of their essence and yet held by each in a manner appropriate to their person.[11] The Holy Spirit has goodness as God the Spirit. This basic distinction is important. When we are discussing simplicity, we are reflecting on what is essential to God and thus true of the three.

NEGATIVE AND POSITIVE KNOWLEDGE

How do we know what is essential to God, given that "the divine essence by its immensity surpasses every form to which our intellect reaches; and thus

---

[10]See further Aquinas, *ST* 1.13.7.
[11]There are also symbolical or metaphorical names for God, such as Rock and Refuge.

we cannot apprehend it by knowing what it is"?[12] Are we mistaken in rejoicing with the psalmist in the Lord's enduring love and goodness? Though
our finite intellects cannot know and grasp a God who is all that he is, we
are not to despair, for "we have some knowledge therefore by knowing *what
it is not*: and we shall approach all the nearer to the knowledge thereof according as we shall be enabled to remove by our intellect a greater number
of things therefrom."[13] We approach something of God's goodness by removing what it is not, which is how we grant space to a positive knowing of
his great goodness.

Further to the point, we must remain silent about "how different God is"
from us.[14] Augustine reminds us that "we can more easily state what he is
not than what he is. . . . What is he? I have not been able to say; all I could
say is what he is not."[15] Thomas deepens this insight, putting it this way:

> But we have some knowledge thereof by knowing *what it [God] is not*: and we
> shall approach all the nearer to knowledge thereof according as we shall be
> enabled to remove by our intellect a great number of things therefrom. For
> the more completely we see how a thing [i.e. God] differs from others, the
> more perfectly we know it: since each thing has in itself its own being distinct
> from all other things.[16]

As we have seen, God has his perfect being not only *in se* but per se. Accordingly, Thomas continues, "we shall not know *what* He is in Himself."[17]
This is, of course, not a counsel to despair. Rather, it is one of epistemological
humility and of right understanding of the distinction between God and
what is not God. We can know something of "what He is not, and the relations of other things to Him," but we cannot know "what God is."[18] We
cannot know one whose "simple being possesses all manner of perfections."[19]
But we know in a positive way by speaking of the difference between God
and creature, removing from our intellects ways of describing God that are

---

[12]Aquinas, *SCG* 1.14.
[13]Aquinas, *SCG* 1.14.
[14]Augustine, *Psalms* 4:232; Ps 85(86):8.
[15]Augustine, *Psalms* 4:232; Ps 85(86):8.
[16]Aquinas, *SCG* 1.14.
[17]Aquinas, *SCG* 1.14.
[18]Aquinas, *SCG* 1.30.
[19]Aquinas, *SCG* 1.31.

more appropriate to the creature than to God. Stated differently, Augustine, and Thomas following him, is not arguing that all human talk of God, insofar as it is disciplined by the scriptural testimony, remains negative. Rather, discourse on God will happily admit that there is one question that it cannot answer, the question of "What is he?" If we respond to the question with "goodness itself," our response is not false, but it is inadequate, for we cannot conceive of an uncreated goodness—"you alone are God" (Ps 86:10). If so, then, we speak positively of God by speaking of what God is not. To use a Thomistic idiom, we cannot conceive of an unparticipated goodness without the help of created goodnesses. The latter are the grounds for articulating how different is the sole great goodness of God. We cannot conceive of one whose goodness is without limits, utterly independent of us, beyond all attribution and negation, composition and division, without the assistance provided by created things.

Consider Psalm 14:1, "Fools say in their hearts, 'There is no God.'" The fool does not think that God exists. Such thought is strange, however, says Thomas, "for the concept of God is naturally implanted in all of us." The fool goes against nature, denying *that* God is, for it is inconceivable to conceive of God as not existing. And yet, the fool does. Here we see two kinds of knowing (and speaking) at work. The fool, comments Thomas, does not know God "according to himself." If the fool were to know God according to himself, he would no longer be a fool, for God "cannot be conceived of as not existing." The fool is spiritually blind, meaning that although he or she may see, he does not truly see. For example, the witness of "sensible things" to "things divine" escapes him.[20]

Put differently, existence "is included in the definition of the subject." To know God "according to himself" is to speak "of being itself." The fool's foolishness is that of misconceiving God; the fool conceives of God "as not existing." Such a judgment is against nature. The fool thinks there is no God because of the state of the world. God, he avers, is strikingly absent in the world, given the way the world is. How does the fool learn to see that the seeming absence of good in the world is not a sign of the non-existence of God? Following Romans 1, indeterminate and rather vague

---

[20] Aquinas, *SCG* 3.2.119.

knowledge of God's existence is naturally implanted in all. But, and this is the key, such knowing is "not the same thing as knowing what God is, since that is only grasped by faith."[21] Positive knowing of God—and of what God is—requires faith.

What does Thomas's discussion of Psalm 14:1 teach us? The knowledge of faith is knowledge of what God is, and such knowledge is not available naturally, though such knowledge does not contradict what is "naturally implanted" and "indeterminately known." Intrinsic to the knowledge of faith is knowledge of God according to himself. Faith knows that God "cannot be conceived of as not existing."[22] Faith knows positively. Positive identification of God, of the heights and depths of his goodness, assumes faith.

We have seen this to be true in our brief discussion of God's simplicity. In many respects, it has been prefatory, indicating things such as (1) God is undivided and not composite, which points to what is true in a positive sense, namely, that God is one and complete; (2) none of God's essential or, for that matter, personal names are accidental to God; and (3) God is not ordered to anything outside God. "For the more completely we see how a thing differs from others, the more perfectly we know it."[23] Thomas calls this way of knowing "remotion."[24]

Strictly speaking, simplicity is not an attribute. Instead, *simplicity* is an extrabiblical term that, when rightly deployed, says something true about who God is. To speak truthfully, in faith, of a God who "is whatever he has," requires us to say what this does not involve, for example, composition, and so sets us on the pilgrimage toward jubilant affirmation of what the Lord is, complete goodness itself.[25] Such knowing is indicative of the transcendence of the Lord's goodness. We are speaking of a goodness of which all "the limiting measures of our own knowledge and experience" are removed.[26] This is one of the deep truths that teaching on simplicity champions. God's simple goodness transcends and superexceeds our knowledge in such a way

---

[21] Aquinas, *In Ps* 14, trans. Ian Levy.

[22] Aquinas, *In Ps* 14.

[23] Aquinas, *SCG* 1.14.

[24] Aquinas, *ST* 1.11.3. The other two ways of knowing are via effects and via the way of excellence. They shall be further discussed in due course.

[25] Aquinas, *SCG* 1.23.

[26] Fran O'Rourke, *Pseudo-Dionysius and the Metaphysics of Aquinas* (Leiden: Brill, 1999), 48.

that we may best describe it by what it is not, by removing all "limiting measures" so as to confess the goodness of the Lord in all his glory.

Learning Simplicity

The introduction of the language of faith points to a central concern of the book, namely, the place of devotion in and the centrality of contemplation to the doctrine of God's attributes. Articulation of divine goodness is such that it "has to be lived before it can be stated."[27] Declaration of the fullness of God takes place downstream of the experience of the "sweetness of his [God's] goodness."[28] Unless we experience God's goodness, attempts to describe its simple character—that it is *of* God himself—remain unedifying. The awesome truth, that there is nothing accidental in God and that God is not ordered to anything outside God's very self, must be lived. The notion that God is not potentially good but rather complete goodness itself must be experienced. The doctrine of God's attributes is bookended by prayer and praise.

How do we experience God's goodness? We experience it by making progress in the law so as to understand metaphysical truths. An account of divine simplicity is really an act of intellectual discipleship wherein we open our mind to one of the correlatives of the lived experience of God's goodness, first and foremost that we are experiencing a goodness that does not arise in relation to us, as if God were to become good in response to something outside God. The theologian's task is to instruct the faithful in the completely realized character of his goodness, on which their experience of goodness rests. The theologian can only do this, however, to the extent that she imitates that same goodness.

Inasmuch as we live God's goodness by making progress in the statutes we are able to appreciate dimensions of the biblical testimony to God that we could not have appreciated before. We make progress, in other words, in our speculative understanding of God by responding with intellectual humility and fear to the great "I am" of Exodus 3:14. This is not to shortchange

---

[27]Sokolowski, *Faith and Reason*, 123.

[28]John Calvin, *Joshua and the Psalms*, trans. Henry Beveridge (Grand Rapids: Associated Publishers and Authors), 960; W. Norris Clarke, *The One and the Many: A Contemporary Thomistic Metaphysics* (Notre Dame, IN: University of Notre Dame Press, 2001), 84.

the practical dimension of Christian teaching, but it is to say that
goodness has a speculative and a practical dimension and that we learn
the speculative inasmuch as we make progress in the practical. We are
initiated into the metaphysics of the divine life, as it were, by the experience of his goodness.[29] We thus learn that one of the implications of our
confession of God who alone is good is that he is simple, that his perfections are one with himself.

John Calvin sheds some light on this. He says of Psalm 119:67, "Before I
was humbled I went astray, but now I keep your word," that "David protests
that he would be completely satisfied, provided he experience God to be
liberal towards him in this one particular," the one particular being making
"progress in the knowledge of the law."[30] David's response to God is not
simply a matter of the submission of his will to that of God's. David also
wants to experience God's liberality, his goodness, to have something of
what God *is* communicated, experientially, to him.

David no longer desires to glorify the flesh, though that is the usual desire
of humankind. Rather, what David hungers after in Psalm 119:67 is an experience of the goodness that is the source of the law, knowledge of whom the
law brings. The law presents God's goodness, yes, but God's goodness does
not arise in relationship to the law, for God's goodness is uncreated. We do
not say *that* God is good because God has given the law, though that is, of
course, true. Teaching on divine simplicity reminds us that God does not
make progress in goodness, that God does not become better, whereas we,
by grace, may. Put again, God is not made perfect but is perfect, and what
is perfect is good. God is the kind of good who makes those who call out to
him good. God makes good those who keep his Word.

In our pride, we like to think that God is enriched by us. Teaching on
simplicity reminds us that God gains nothing from us. Our existence as
humans created in God's image is a participation and likeness—in terms of
our intellect and will—of God's goodness. Indeed, without God we would
cease to be: God "envelops absolutely everything in a being that is in any way

---

[29]Clarke offers a nice definition of metaphysics as "the systematic study" of "*being as such*," which
he describes, following Thomas, as "the most fundamental attribute of all real things." See *One
and Many*, 2, 25. Augustine, commenting on Ps 5:8-9 in reference to Ex 3:14, describes God as
"*Being-Itself*." Augustine, *Psalms* 1:91.
[30]Calvin, *Psalms*, 993.

positive or real."[31] God is what is positive and real in us, in a profoundly supereminent way. God is, for example, intellect and will itself. The good things that God satisfies us with come from a God whose goodness is one with his essence, the good who envelops all that is good outside his essence. We use the language of simplicity to describe in part this mystery. Again, such description is an act of intellectual discipleship with regard to goodness experienced.

Commenting on Psalm 37:3, "Trust in the LORD, and do good," Calvin again shows us the way forward, providing a nice conclusion to this section. Calvin writes that in order "to show that God is the author of all good, and that by his blessing alone prosperity is to be looked for," one must live "a holy life."[32] Demonstration of God as the cause and end of all, as goodness itself, is an expression of a holy life. We come to love God because we experience the goodness that emanates from the author of all good. Knowledge of God follows God's mode of being God. We cannot know and love God—just so, "the riches of his liberality" scandalize us—unless we are "urged and encouraged to it by various motives."[33] Accordingly, what Calvin calls cheerful "meditation upon the divine life" generates systematic-theological fruit.[34] One of those fruits is an account of the first principles of God's life, to which teaching on simplicity is intrinsic.

SIMPLICITY AND THE TRINITY

In one of the most important treatments of simplicity in the tradition, §17, §18, §22, and §23 of Anselm's *Proslogion*, we receive much help in relating teaching on simplicity to teaching on the Trinity. It is important to see how closely linked are biblical affirmations of what God is with who God is, Father, Son, and Holy Spirit. In §23, Anselm notes in a very devotional tenor that the supreme good that is God "*is equally Father and Son and Holy Spirit.*" The Father is good, and so is the Word by which the Father utters himself. The Word is as good as the One who utters that Word, and is that same good as the Father. In an arresting sentence that brilliantly relates what

---

[31]Clarke, *One and Many*, 83.
[32]Calvin, *Psalms*, 399.
[33]Ibid., 410.
[34]Ibid.

God is—goodness—to the procession by which the Son is constituted and distinguished with respect to the Father, Anselm says, "And you are so simple that there cannot be born of You any other than what You are." The one born of the Father is the goodness he (the Father) is: the Son is not other than the Father, though he is different from him—that is, he is the Son, not the Father. The point is that simplicity undergirds, informs, and is the principle of the Son's procession from the Father: "Nor can there proceed from Your supreme simplicity what is other than that from which it proceeds." The Son who proceeds is not other than he from whom he proceeds, and that because of the Father's "supreme simplicity." The Son is not less than the Father, and the Father is not better than the Son because "whatever each is singly, that the whole Trinity is altogether." The upshot is that the treatment of a divine attribute is also at the same time the treatment of the whole and indivisible Trinity. Each of the three "is not other than the supremely simple unity and the supremely unified simplicity." In this, another lucid statement, Anselm prayerfully instructs us regarding "the supremely simple unity."[35]

The affirmation that God "really is all those good things"—for example wisdom, goodness, beauty, and happiness—means, as we have seen, that God does not possess these things, as if they were qualities, but is these things.[36] Furthermore, each of the three is also "the supremely unified simplicity," God being "not many but one."[37] The upshot is that "any one of them is the same thing as all of them (the same thing as all together and as each individually)."[38] Anselm brilliantly integrates prayerful description of what God is—God's attributes—with who God is, the Trinity. The Son is the same as the Father, just as truth is, in God, the same as goodness. Together, the three are what each is singly God; and goodness, beauty, and truth—to name but a few attributes—are true of the three. Again, *"this good* [God] *is equally Father and Son and Holy Spirit."* The lesson is this: we must not isolate simplicity from Trinity, but in describing the character of the former we will be describing the life of the latter. In each case—simplicity and Trinity—we are speaking of the same truth but from two different angles.[39]

---

[35] Anselm of Canterbury, *Proslogion,* in *ACMW,* 23.

[36] Anselm of Canterbury, *Monologion,* in *ACMW,* 16.

[37] Anselm, *Proslogion,* 23; *Monologion,* 17.

[38] Anselm, *Monologion,* 17.

[39] Gavin Ortlund does a nice job of unfolding how "the Trinity can and should be seen as a *resource*

One might think that such terrain is far removed from Holy Scripture, especially the Psalter.[40] Thankfully, nothing else could be further from the truth.
In *Proslogion* §18, wherein Anselm writes, "*That there are no parts in God or in
His eternity, in which He is*," there are six references to Scripture, five of which
are to the Psalter: Psalms 59:7 (2x); 24:7; 26:8; and 12:4. Anselm's question,
"What are You, Lord, what are You; what shall my heart understand You to be?"
and his answer, "You are, assuredly, life," is a confession whose source and inspiration is the Psalter. How so? First, Anselm recalls the sin in which all are
conceived, our fall in Adam, in whom we all sinned and lost God's light. Thus
we are in darkness, the only help we have being that of the Lord, who helps
because of his goodness. Hence Psalm 25:7 implores, "according to your
steadfast love remember me, for your goodness' sake, O LORD!" The good
countenance of God must be sought. In seeking God's face, Anselm prays that
he, with the psalmist, may see with the illumined eyes of his soul the extent to
which there are no parts in God. Prayer is the means by which he understands.

Articulation of God's simplicity is, for Anselm, a fruit of the healed eye of
the soul. When Anselm says that God is wholly each of these things—for
example, goodness and blessedness—his saying so is a fruit of his fervent
striving toward the Lord. Unless the "soul gather its strength again and with
all its understanding strive once more towards You, Lord" nothing profitable
may be said. To say of God that "You exist as a whole everywhere and Your
eternity exists as a whole always" is as devotional as it is systematic-theological
discourse.[41] Simplicity, thus understood, is the fruit of sustained contemplation and experience of the prayers bequeathed to us in the Psalter, most of
all the Lord who in his great mercy does not turn away those who seek him.

---

to be utilized with respect to the meaning of divine simplicity. . . . The greater interest of most
classical theologians has been to *use* divine simplicity to ground the Trinity as firmly monothe-
istic." His piece also demonstrates, quite usefully, how "classical theologians approached divine
simplicity in a devotional frame." See Gavin Ortlund, "Divine Simplicity in Historical Perspective: Resourcing a Contemporary Discussion," *IJST* 16, no. 4 (2014): 447, 448, 442.

[40]See, for example, Cornelius Plantinga Jr., "Social Trinity and Tritheism," in *Trinity, Incarnation,
and Atonement: Philosophical and Theological Essays*, ed. Ronald J. Feenstra and Cornelius Plantinga (Notre Dame, IN: University of Notre Dame Press, 1990), 39, who argues that the "simplicity theory of the Augustinian, Lateran, and Thomistic sort cannot claim much by way of biblical
support." For a recent and lucid account of the shoddy ways in which many analytic theologians
and philosophers of religion understand simplicity, see Stephen J. Duby, *Divine Simplicity: A
Dogmatic Account* (London: Bloomsbury T&T Clark, 2016).

[41]Anselm, *Proslogion*, 18.

Addressing the Naysayers: Barth on Simplicity

As should now be clear, I am endorsing a traditional Thomist account of simplicity, unapologetically so, and in dependence on Augustine and Anselm, precisely because it makes good biblical sense. The goodness of the Lord of which the Psalter speaks so abundantly is a goodness that is in God and is the same as God himself. My path toward embracing such an account has perhaps surprisingly been made possible by Karl Barth. Some might think this odd, given Barth's heavily qualified endorsement and revision of what he calls "the classical line of approach" and "the older scholastic doctrine" of simplicity.[42] Nonetheless, Barth is an excellent interlocutor at this point because he is not a naysayer in the strict sense but rather one whose nuanced—but not unproblematic—unfolding of simplicity provides a useful platform for considering the merits of a Thomist account.

This is a challenge, largely because Barth is not the most reliable reader of Thomas. That said, Barth's disagreements with "the partial nominalism of the Thomistic and orthodox Protestant tradition" are important because they clarify why the Thomistic account of simplicity championed above works best.[43] First, the bogeyman in Barth's mind throughout §29 of *CD* II/1 is Thomas, specifically Thomas's treatment of "God's being in general, then His triune nature."[44] Barth has in mind Thomas's architectonic in *ST* 1 that treats of the one essence (q 1–26) in advance of the Trinity of persons (q 27–43). Thomas does not separate them, as Barth thinks, but rather distinguishes them. Thomas considers the one God we are given to know and love in the Scripture from a "double perspective," from the side of the one essence and from the three persons, following thereby the narrative pattern of Scripture itself.[45] Similarly, Barth is averse to treatments of the attributes— or better, *perfections*, his preferred term—that handle the attributes as if they were "various predicates of a kind of general being."[46]

---

[42]Barth, *CD* II/1, 341, 350.

[43]Barth, *CD* II/1, 330.

[44]Barth, *CD* II/1, 348.

[45]Gilles Emery, OP, "Essentialism or Personalism in the Treatise on God in St. Thomas Aquinas?," in *Trinity in Aquinas* (Ypsilanti, MI: Sapientia Press, 2003), 172. Emery writes, "The double perspective of the common nature and the Trinitarian relations is imperative in order to take account fully of Trinitarian faith." See also Emilio Brito's defense of Thomas's prioritizing the one to the three over against Hegel and in accordance with the narrative pattern of Scripture itself in "Deux modèles du Dieu unique: Thomas d'Aquin et Hegel," *Église et Théologie* 21 (1990): 33-64.

[46]Barth, *CD* II/1, 338.

Accordingly, Barth's objections in to "the Thomistic and orthodox Protestant traditions" on simplicity are several. I will briefly present them and
offer what I hope are some respectful and profitable rejoinders that expand
on the points made earlier in the chapter. But before I do that, we need to
present and discuss what Barth thinks is the function or purpose of an account of the attributes. It is this: the task is to show that in revelation and in
eternity, God is the same. Though Barth generally eschews the language of
being in favor of God as "Subject," the doctrine of the attributes, he argues,
develops and confirms "the doctrine of His being."[47] We see here two distinct aims. First, the doctrine demonstrates, for Barth, that God as he is in
relationship to us and as he is in himself is the same God. There is no God
behind God's self-disclosure in Jesus. Second, the doctrine advances our
understanding of God's being by developing, Barth adjudges, an account of
God's being as identical with a multiplicity of perfections.

To what extent does my (the Thomist) approach differ? As regards the
first point, I think that the doctrine of the divine attributes unfolds, prayerfully and reverentially and in the closest possible connection to Scripture,
what God is, whereas Barth thinks the doctrine's task is to show, dialectically,
the oneness of being and act in God. Barth's doctrine of God's attributes
brings together revelation—meaning God's self-disclosure in time—and
God's being, understood as Subject in three modes of being, so as to show
they are one and the same. Barth presses this because, as he reads the tradition to which he formally adheres, he notes the revelation of God being
described as separate—not distinct, but separate from—God's eternity, his
Godhead. This is because of a nondialectical account of their relationship,
which is the only way to account, Barth argues, for their sameness. Likewise,
dialectic is, for Barth, the best way to account for how a multiplicity of perfections "exist objectively in God himself."[48]

My approach, following the Thomist one, respectfully differs from Barth's
as its aim is to unfold the attributes of God in a compatibilist and not dialectical manner. This is not to say that I intend on surrendering what dialectic secures for Barth, namely, that "in all our thinking and speaking about

---

[47]Barth, *CD* II/1, 377.
[48]Barth, *CD* II/1, 327.

Him we must never become His masters."[49] Yes and amen. What I want to do is reach deeper into the tradition than does Barth to Thomas himself—understood on his own terms—and thereby do away with Barth's architectonic, which orders the attributes along the lines of love and freedom. Indeed, I do not think "the unity of love and freedom constitutes the biblical idea of the being of God."[50] Why? Because, contra Barth, the distinction between God *in se* and God in relation to the world is more than "heuristic."[51] If we are to secure the goal of Barth's dialectic, as we must, we must strongly distinguish—without separating—God *in se* and God in relation to the world. Accordingly, the "complete reciprocity" Barth envisages between God's love and freedom is unhelpful in securing what is an edifying aim, namely, the preservation of the Creator/creature distinction.

Said another way, Barth's account of the doctrine of the attributes binds theology to economy. The doctrine of the attributes glosses, for Barth, the identity of the one disclosed therein. I am with Barth insofar as I ask "in human words and concepts what God is and is not, and in what way He is what He is."[52] Indeed, I am especially concerned with the first half of that statement. To describe God is a matter of attending to what God has done, is doing, and will do. I describe in this book God's "perfect being" not independently of his works but as the basis, ground, foundation, anchor, principle, and presupposition of his works for us and for our salvation. This means, in part, that God is eternally good, not made good or better because of the great things he has done. Barth's desire to unite revelation and eternity—and in that order—problematically brings the doctrine of revelation into the doctrine of God. Revelation concerns knowledge, how we come to know and love this God whom we cannot see and whom Jesus Christ has made known. The task of the doctrine of the attributes, I argue, is to describe eternity—the perfect being of God—with an architectonic that resists distributing the attributes into two series along the lines of love and freedom. Instead, following Thomas, I articulate what is in God, and in so doing explain what God is, all that is essential to him, respecting thereby a strong distinction between God and the world.

---

[49]Barth, *CD* II/1, 342.

[50]Barth, *CD* II/1, 343. I have my reservations about the usefulness of "freedom" language, largely because of its voluntaristic overtones.

[51]Barth, *CD* II/1, 345.

[52]Barth, *CD* II/1, 337.

If this is correct, then, what we mean by simplicity becomes even clearer. Barth proposes an account of simplicity that moves toward a "classical, and to some extent ecumenical line of theological reflection."[53] With Thomas, Barth argues that "the divine being cannot be torn asunder into a series of attributes each real and true in itself."[54] Yes and amen. Each attribute "must include in itself every other and the totality of all others"; indeed, the doctrine of the attributes repeats and develops "the doctrine of His being."[55] Where I part company from this quite promising start—which adheres, as Barth says, "to the tradition in essentials"—is in respect of the particulars.[56] Barth's embrace of Augustinian nomenclature regarding a "simple multiplicity" as a bulwark against nominalism and/or seminominalism is sound enough. We follow Barth and the tradition by not thinking of multiplicity as pertaining to God's relationship to us, the many as a reflection of our vision and thus subsequent to the essence. That is all fine and good. Moreover, with Barth, we ought to applaud "certain German theologians of the 19th century"—namely, F. H. R. Frank, Gottfried Thomasius, and Isaak August Dorner—inasmuch as they equate attributes with being and note that God's relationship to the world is made known in them.[57] Again, the basic thesis that "God is in essence all that He is," is sound, as is "He is in essence not only one, but multiple."[58] Where I think Barth errs is in his insistence that "simplicity must be understood dialectically."[59] I think it is enough to say that all God's attributes are God himself, and that they are all moral and ethical. Barth's dialectical thinking unhelpfully introduces into the doctrine of God's being a doctrine that is clearly downstream and derivative, namely, the doctrine of revelation.

To say as does Barth that "God lives His perfect being"—and all that in a multiplicity of perfections—so as to avoid the "idol of the one and absolute which is 'properly' without motion, utterance, or action" is really unnecessary, assuming, of course, that you follow Thomas's account of the pure act of being that is God.[60] Just so, it is not a matter of God living his perfect

---

[53]Barth, *CD* II/1, 337.
[54]Barth, *CD* II/1, 339.
[55]Barth, *CD* II/1, 339, 327.
[56]Barth, *CD* II/1, 348.
[57]Barth, *CD* II/1, 330.
[58]Barth, *CD* II/1, 331.
[59]Barth, *CD* II/1, 333.
[60]Barth, *CD* II/1, 345.

being as Barth would have it. Rather, because God as perfect being lacks nothing, he is completely at rest in his pure actuality, indeed in his unceasing relations of origin that subsist within the divine being itself. What is perfect does not simply have its being in God but is God. God does not live his being but is the pure act of being itself. Barth's polemics about the Thomistic "idol of the one" rest on some pretty elementary misreadings.

Though Barth is not a naysayer literally speaking, his dialectical approach provides a fruitful contrast with mine, following as I do the Thomist view. With Barth, I am thoroughly committed to honoring the absolute prevenience of God, but I depart from Barth in thinking that the dialectic he champions adequately safeguards God's aseity. Barth tethers the being of God too closely to history by incorporating revelation into the doctrine of God, whereas a compatibilist account expresses the profound intimacy of the Creator with the creature without reading back into God's being his re-velatory activity. I think it is enough to say that God's works—what the missions of Son and Spirit accomplish—express temporally the eternal processions of Son and Spirit.

SIMPLICITY AND ACTION

The Psalms are full of petitions, for example Psalm 30:8, 10: "To you, O LORD, I cried, and to the LORD I made supplication. . . . Hear, O LORD, and be gra-cious to me! O LORD, be my helper!" David's cry to the Lord is that he would be something he was not before, namely, his helper. David asks God to be gracious to him. In pleading for God to be gracious, David is not asking God to become something that he was not before, that is, gracious. Rather, David prays that God would become to him something that he was not before, his helper. This is worth considering because Barth's basic criticism of the "platonic-aristotelian idea of being," which Barth thinks Thomas and the Protestant orthodox leave largely intact, is its lack of dynamism, "motion, utterance, or action."[61] This is an account of God's being that is humanly attained, a view of God that is static, lacking motion.[62] That is not true, however. When we consider David's penitential petitions, we see how the account of simplicity I have sketched in fact nourishes our participation in David's petitions. Let me explain.

---

[61]Barth, *CD* II/1, 345.
[62]See further Barth, *CD* II/1, 334.

God is faithful. So Psalm 30:9 asks, "Will the dust praise you? Will it tell of your faithfulness?" Simplicity doctrine is not about postulating an account of God's being that removes from God the capacity to act. By no means; the reason the triune God can and does new things—for example, create, or in David's case, be to him what he was not before, his helper—is because he is goodness itself, which when turned outward takes the form of grace and help. Because God is all that he is, he is free to be what he was not before, namely, the helper of one who calls on him. Divine simplicity, understood along Thomist lines, is not an attempt to domesticate God but rather to account for how God can be all that he is in relation to what is not himself, the creature, who is so often in desperate need of his help. Because God is good and is goodness itself, God gives creatures the choice—he does not compel them—to call on him, to freely relate themselves to him in a new way, assisting them all along in this.[63] Again, the Lord God does this because he is good. What he is in himself is the ground of his action toward us in freshly relating himself to us.

That God is pure motion itself, pure actuality, is good news to the sinner in need of the help of God. Because God is so solidly Godself, God is able to be the one he has always been before the creature he creates, maintains, and perfects—creatures in desperate need of his sustenance and aid. We creatures do not cause God to be other than he has always been. Rather, we creatures are given the immense privilege of being covenantally related to one who is, as Barth says, life itself.[64] Accordingly, teaching on simplicity informs our reception of the petitionary dimensions of the Psalter. We see with renewed eyes how God is free to be all that he is in relation to created things in ever startling and edifying ways.

CONCLUSION

To wrap up this chapter, divine simplicity emphasizes three things. First, God's attributes are identical to his essence. God's goodness, together with the other names of God, does not form God into God. The "is" of God— God's existence—is one with his essence, his perfect being. It follows, then, that God's attributes—God's names, of which goodness is preeminent—are

---

[63]On not compelling, see Aquinas, *SCG* 3.2, 148.
[64]See Barth, *CD* II/1, 322.

essential, meaning that goodness is not something God acquires from what is outside God but is "all that he is at once and essentially."[65] Second, as Calvin reminds us, the only way God becomes "a sweet name in the experience of his people" is when his goodness and kindness is lived.[66] This, I argued, is not to moralize teaching on divine simplicity, but it is to resist any attempt to isolate the metaphysics of the divine life from the call to "teach me your statutes" (Ps 119:68). Calvin reminds us that a holy life is necessary to the reception of holy truths. Teaching that indicates that God's names are identical with his essence must be experienced before it can be described. Third, simplicity as a nonbiblical idiom serves to promote attention to scriptural truth regarding how the many attributes are one in God and one with God. I respectfully demurred from Barth's revisionist account of simplicity, resting as it does on his dialectical portrait of God, though not the end of Barth's account, which is that of honoring God as God. There are merits, I think, to distinguishing in an architectonic sense prayerful description of God's being God from how God is known and expresses himself as God among us.

The pastoral point about teaching on simplicity is quite plain. God does not communicate his goodness in his great acts of nature (creation and preservation) and grace (election, reconciliation, and perfection) to get something out of it. Divine goodness, because it is divine, is not a participated goodness, that is, had in relation to another. Goodness and God are one and the same, even if there were no world. The marvel of marvels is that God communicates his profound goodness to us in creation and in Christ (and the Spirit) to make us perfect, and not to make himself perfect. God is compatible with us. We become compatible with God by living in friendship and dependence on him; whereas God does not become perfect and good in relation to us, because "to be" (as a verb) God is to be good and to be all that he is. Again, we are because God is; God's goodness is not limited by his essence but is "totally correlative to the actuality that fills it."[67] This is the basic point about simplicity.

---

[65]Ivor J. Davidson, "Divine Sufficiency: Theology in the Presence of God," in *Theological Theology: Essays in Honour of John Webster*, ed. R. David Nelson, Darren Sarisky, and Justin Stratis (London: Bloomsbury T&T Clark, 2015), 67.

[66]Calvin, *Psalms*, 532.

[67]Clarke, *One and Many*, 84.

Next, we move from more prolegomenal matters to more positive ones, that is, to an unfolding of "you are good" (Ps 119:68). We shall glimpse something of the pure act of goodness that is God, how God is a transcendent and omnipresent goodness, one that is profoundly loveable and desirable.

TWO

You Are Good

I N THIS CHAPTER I UNFOLD the *are* in "you are good."[1] This is most important. Is God really good? Is God in the very depths of God's being goodness itself? The answer is yes and yes. Faithful expounding of that yes is a matter of "contemplative research."[2] Here I present the fruits of such research, drawing out what Thomas, and to a lesser extent Augustine, have concluded with respect to God's divinity in their engagement with the Psalms. What follows is a course in goodness, the goodness that the Psalms assume to be true of God in the most preeminent sense possible.

YOU ARE YOUR OWN GOODNESS

In his *Confessions,* Augustine says of God "you yourself are your own magnitude and your own beauty."[3] The same is true of God's goodness: it is proper to God; it is God's own. God, just by being God, is good. For God, being and being good are one and the same thing.

Augustine helps us to appreciate the import of this sublime truth by contrasting it with a body. He notes that "a body is not great and beautiful by being body; if it were less great or less beautiful, it would nevertheless still

---

[1]In Hebrew טוֹב, that is, "good" or "goodness" in the broadest sense, has five general areas of meaning. There is "1) practical, economic, or material good, 2) abstract goodness such as desirability, pleasantness, and beauty, 3) quality or expense, 4) moral goodness, and 5) technical philosophical good." Concerning God as good, *TWOT* notes that this "is rich with the overtones of all possible meanings of the term 'good' (1 Chr 16:34; Ps 145:9)." *TWOT*, 345-46.
[2]Aquinas, *SCG* 1.4.
[3]Augustine, *Conf,* 70.

be body."[4] A body need not be attractive to be a body, whereas you take away goodness from God and God would not be God. By virtue of God's being God, God is good. Unlike bodily goodness, God's goodness suffers neither change nor diminishment, for God is not good in relationship to anything outside God. Rather, God is perfect, lacking nothing, and the first thing that we must say, biblically speaking, about the perfect God is that he is good.

Calvin uses some arresting language, commenting on Psalm 92:1, "It is good to give thanks to the LORD, to sing praises to your name, O Most High," to describe just what kind of goodness we encounter in God. God's "goodness and his faithfulness are incessant," writes Calvin.[5] The language of "incessant" is another way of getting at the great truth described by Augustine above. Goodness is unremittingly true of God. Accordingly, we do not simply say that God's promises or benefits have the character of goodness. As Calvin notes of Psalm 119:65 ("You have dealt with your servant, O LORD, according to your word"), "his free goodness is the only cause which induces him to deal bountifully with us."[6] We do not cause God to be good. Because God is infinite perfect being itself, God neither loses nor gains goodness in relationship to created things. God communicates with us as one who is not made good by us, but who, in communicating his goodness to us, is shown to be goodness itself—because he is good, he does good; because he is good, he deals bountifully with us.

At this juncture we begin to see, following our central text, Psalm 119:68, something of the priority of the *are* in relationship to the *do* ("you do good"). God does good works, yes, but those works are recited within the context of "his supreme Deity, and dominion."[7] God's works are expressive of his divinity, which is their principle, the immanent acts (paternity, generation, and procession) whereby he is. Thomas puts it this way: God acts "by His essence."[8] Thomas's intuition is salutary because it points to what is fundamental to the Psalter's testimony to God. God does good because God is essentially good. God is what he always is, his own goodness, world without end, and thus does good. So Psalm 107:1 states, "O give thanks to the LORD, for he is good, for his steadfast love endures forever."

---

[4]Augustine, *Conf*, 70.
[5]Calvin, *Psalms*, 802.
[6]Calvin, *Psalms*, 992.
[7]Calvin, *Psalms*, 1091.
[8]Aquinas, *ST* 1.19.4.

PURE ACT

Having said a few words about the priority of the *are* in relationship to the *do*, and of their irreversibility, we need to explore more deeply what we mean by the phrase "pure act." God is pure act (*actus purus*), meaning that there is no potentiality in God, no room, as it were, for dissolution or improvement. The *are* signifies an unceasingly active goodness. Specifically, goodness consists in the action by which God delights in and enjoys himself. How does God enjoy himself and his own goodness? Here we gesture to the originating relations whereby the three are distinguished and constituted, the very heart, as it were, of "pure act" language. There is the eternal generation of the Son from the Father and the procession of the Spirit from the Father and Son. These processions are eternal, indicating unceasing acts. The Father begets the Son in a never-ending today, and the Spirit eternally proceeds as the love of the Father for the Son and the Son for the Father. This is, again, the basic meaning of pure act language. The Son receives his being from the Father, the Spirit from both Father and Son. The processions of the Son and Spirit are internal to God's being, subsisting within. God's goodness is identical to his eternal and undivided being, his essence in which the originating relations subsist.[9]

That is straightforward enough. But more needs to be said. Accordingly, we ask, does Scripture encourage us to think of an attribute as being most appropriately said of one of the three in the pure act of being in which they are, though not without for a moment detracting from its belonging equally to the three? The answer is a qualified yes. Essential attributes such as goodness are appropriated to particular persons of the Trinity, following the pattern of Scripture itself. In the case of the Father, for example, "to the Father is appropriated *power*, which is especially shown in creation; and therefore to be Creator is attributed to the Father."[10] Scripture speaks of the Father as the origin of creation, the Son as the agent, and the Spirit as the one who perfects created things. Power is appropriated to the Father. If Thomas is right, then the actions of the three toward the outside express how each has the pure act of being common to them in a unique way. Put again,

---

[9] As Thomas states, "God's being is His essence, which is common to the three Persons." Aquinas, *ST* 1.45.6.

[10] Aquinas, *ST* 1.45.6 ad 2.

essential attributes as uniquely "possessed" by Father, Son, and Spirit structure their actions outward in the works of nature and grace.

Pushing this logic further, Thomas says of the Son, for example, that to him "is appropriated *wisdom*, through which an intellectual agent acts [i.e., the Father]; and therefore it is said: *Through Whom all things were made*."[11] The Son is the wisdom of God (the Father), though the reverse is not true: the Father is not the wisdom of the Son. The Son is the agent of creation—the Father creates through him—because of an essential attribute appropriated to the Son, wisdom. This seemingly technical point is important because it tracks with the logic of the Psalter's testimony to God in terms of God's being pure act: we have first God's supreme divinity ("you are") and then God's works ("you do"). If such is the case, then, works express essential attributes as appropriate to one of the three. The works of the Father, of the Son, and of the Spirit express what is appropriated to each in the pure act of being in which they are. Accordingly, pure act discourse has two referents. It is first a matter of the originating relations (paternity, filiation, spiration, and procession), and second, a matter of how each of the three has what is common to them in a manner befitting their person.

In the case of goodness, we move, not surprisingly, into a pneumatological register. Thomas writes, "To the Holy Ghost is appropriated *goodness*, to which belong both governance, which brings things to their proper end, and the giving of life."[12] To the Holy Spirit proceeding, what Thomas calls the procession of will, there belongs an essential attribute, which is goodness, to which there belong certain effects, namely, governance and the giving of life. Effects express attributes and, even more, are reducible to attributes insofar as effects are contained in their cause. Life, common as it is to the three in the pure act of being in which they are, is appropriated to the Spirit as the Lord and life giver.[13]

The significant question remains, however, of whether is it fitting to think of attributes as the principle of created effects, of nature, or of grace. I think that it is correct to understand attributes as the principle of effects. What I

---

[11] Aquinas, *ST* 1.45.6 ad 2.

[12] Aquinas, *ST* 1.45.6 ad 2.

[13] Interestingly, Thomas argues that the effects of the Spirit reducible to goodness are related to "justification." See Aquinas, *ST* 1.45.6 ad 3. The exegetical warrant for such a view is found in New Testament texts such as 1 Cor 6:11, wherein Son and Spirit justify and sanctify.

mean is that the Spirit does not simply "decide" to be the life giver. The Spirit is the life giver as the one who proceeds from Father and Son, bringing, by virtue of his goodness, "things to their proper end." Here we see an instance of just how much the reference to the inner life of God matters. The doctrine of creation rests on God, specifically God's attributes (what God is) and the Trinity (who God is). Both dimensions of the doctrine of God are the principle of intelligibility for the works of God outward. More specifically, the giving of life is reducible to goodness, but we are not talking about a depersonalized goodness but rather the goodness of the Spirit—as per the Nicene Creed, "I believe . . . in the Holy Spirit, the Lord and Giver of life." Once again, an account of the attributes and the identity of God is necessary in order to understand the rationale for God's works outward. Talk of goodness as internal to the Trinity works then on two levels, on an essential level and a personal level. First, we speak of goodness as what is common to the three by virtue of their one perfect being and, second, as appropriated to the Spirit, who perfects things in accordance with their end. Goodness is said of the one God and of the three, but has a different register with the former (an essential register) than the latter (a relational and pneumatological register).

To sum up this quite technical section, in confessing God as good, we turn to the language of pure act to describe something of this goodness. God's acts toward the inside, the four originating relations whereby the three exist, are the heart of pure act language. Each of the three is good in the unceasing act of being in which they exist, and to each is appropriated particular attributes in light of their origin. There are two references, then, when we talk of goodness: the originating relations of the three and what is appropriated to each of the three by dint of their origin.

PURE GOODNESS

A nice place to begin thinking through the purity of God's goodness is Psalm 16:2, "You are my Lord; I have no good apart from you." The good that God is does not need any other goods. Thus God has no need of our goods, the psalmist argues, whereas we have no good other than the Lord. This is what we mean when we describe it as pure. So Thomas comments: God "is of infinite goodness and nothing can be added to him, because he is the substantial good, extending goodness to things just as the sun extends light." God cannot be made better or enriched, as it were, though he freely communicates his goodness to other things, suffering no loss of goodness in so doing. Thomas continues; God's goodness does not extend to things "through participation." God does not participate in created being, and yet what is not God does, in varying ways, participate in him. Thomas describes God's relationship to what he has made via the language of illumination, God's "illuminating all things that exist."[14] Indeed, God's goodness is so pure that it not only gives rise to creaturely goodness but illuminates those very things as good.

To put it another way, Psalm 16:2 assumes no increase of goodness on God's part, as if God could, over time, become purer. We, however, may experience increase in goodness in terms of our delight in the same. God, in delighting in his holy ones, delights without reserve, and in so doing increases their delight in him, as is Psalm 16:3, "As for the holy ones in the land, they are the noble, in whom is all my delight." God goes well without us, is pure without us, but "it cannot go well with me," says Thomas, "without you."[15] In short, a pure goodness is a goodness to which nothing can be added, a goodness that is well without us but without which we are not well. God makes himself our good; we do not make him the good he is. "Nothing is better than God," says Thomas, commenting on Psalm 16:5, "the Lord is my chosen portion and my cup."[16] This is but another way of explaining God's goodness.

Goodness is a pure perfection rather than a derivative perfection. By pure I mean that *good* expresses in a preeminent sense the nature of God (as Being) itself. Goodness, because it is true of God's being without reserve, limitation, or measure, is without any potency, and that is what renders it "pure." It cannot become other than what it is, having, as it were, no potential. The pure act of being (*esse*) that is God is good. God "is in complete act without being made at all," and is as such good, lacking nothing.[17]

Accordingly, God is not restricted by his goodness. As "the pure unlimited Act of Existence itself, in all its simple fullness," goodness is not

---

[14]Aquinas, *In Ps* 16, trans. Steve Perkins.
[15]Aquinas, *In Ps* 16.
[16]Aquinas, *In Ps* 16.
[17]Aquinas, *SCG* 1.28.

something added onto God, something that grants even more being to God.[10] Goodness, rather, indicates the "positive fullness of perfection," the purity of his perfection.[19] In Thomas's wonderful words, God, as perfect goodness, is "*completely* made," lacking nothing.[20] Accordingly, goodness is the first thing attested of "the unlimited fullness of existence itself," which we describe as pure.[21] In the idiom of the Psalter—for example, Psalm 106:1, "Praise the LORD! O give thanks to the LORD, for he is good; for his steadfast love endures forever"[22]—God is good and because God possesses his goodness in an infinite mode, his love endures forever. Its infinite purity is the basis for its endurance through the ages.

If God possesses his own goodness in an utterly infinite way, then it "can be affirmed as literally true of God, not merely metaphors."[23] A pure attribute is "literally true of God," whereas a metaphorical attribute, or, as we noted in the previous chapter, a "temporal" name, is a mixed perfection, thereby containing imperfection or finitude in its meaning. For example, Psalm 93:1, "the LORD is king," is not literally true. To be a king, one must have subjects; one cannot be king without subjects. In the case of God, he is not made the Lord in relationship to anyone or anything outside himself: he is the Lord. Kingship "cannot survive the *purifying process* [emphasis mine] so as to be applied truthfully to the divine perfection," whereas goodness can.[24] God does not need anyone or anything in order to be purely good, because goodness's reference point is the pure act of being in which God is Father, Son, and Holy Spirit.

Is there a mode of discourse that is better rather than less suited to describing the purity of the *are*? The answer is yes, and it is analogical in nature, meaning that "purified perfections applied to God are the objective correlates of the unrestricted innate dynamism of the human spirit."[25] Behind this discussion of the purity of God's goodness is the assumption that God

---

[18]W. Norris Clarke, *The One and the Many: A Contemporary Thomistic Metaphysics* (Notre Dame, IN: University of Notre Dame Press, 2001), 231.
[19]Ibid., 232.
[20]Aquinas, *SCG* 1.28.
[21]Clarke, *One and Many*, 232.
[22]The *TDOT* calls this "the central confession statement of the Old Testament." See *TDOT* 5:315.
[23]Clarke, *One and Many*, 233.
[24]Ibid., 233.
[25]Ibid., 235.

is named from his effects, a naming that gives rise to analogical speech.[26]
The human spirit, precisely because it is created in God's likeness and image,
shares in a manner appropriate to its creatureliness in God's goodness. Insofar as it simply is, the creature is good, which denotes a participatory
goodness. Creatures by virtue of their being, by virtue of their participation
in the pure act of existence itself, are good; what exists is good. Goodness,
humanly speaking, and goodness, divinely speaking, are, however, infinitely
distinct; the former is derivative, mixed (composite), and finite, whereas the
latter is original, pure, simple, and infinite. God is perfect in the good,
perfect goodness, and analogical speech is better suited than other forms of
speech in describing this goodness. In other words, when we discuss
goodness analogically, we attribute it to God in a radically purified sense.
The problem with univocal discourse is that it assumes a one-to-one correspondence, with equivocal discourse that it assumes no correspondence.
Analogical speech does denote some similarity, yes, between God's uncreated goodness and created goodness only because God wills that his creatures share in what is his.

Uncreated—pure—goodness and created goodness do not occur on opposite ends of the same continuum. The good we are by virtue of our being
caused is analogous to the good God is. But again, our goodness is a created
goodness, caused and not uncaused. The good that God does, although
causative and perfective of creaturely goodness, does not make God better.
Creation is good, indeed very good, but it is not God, and God is not made
God in relationship to it. Created goods are a different kind of good from
the pure good that is God. The point to be secured is that goodness is a pure
perfection, "co-extensive with being," true of God in an utterly preeminent
way, and true of us too in an altogether derivative, that is, participated, way.[27]
God's goodness is pure goodness and, as such, created things are compatible
with him even as he utterly exceeds them in goodness. Analogical speech is
better suited than other forms in describing this dynamic. It denotes a mode
of signifying that is utterly transcended by the purity of what is signified.[28]

---

[26]"Because we are unable to see His essence, we come to know His existence not in Himself but
in His effects." Aquinas, *SCG* 1.11.

[27]Clarke, *One and Many*, 261.

[28]Thomas develops in the *ST* 1 the triple way via the sequence of causality, remotion (or negation),
and eminence. One denies things of God in their creaturely mode so as to predicate names of

To sum up the chapter thus far, in confessing "you are good," we speak of a pure goodness common to the pure act of being that is Father, Son, and Spirit. Such goodness is true of the three, though said most befittingly of the Spirit. This is a goodness that is complete, said of God in an absolute sense and of us, too, but only in a contingent, participatory, and derivative sense. Analogical discourse is more suited to describing this than other forms of discourse, ensuring that nothing false is ascribed to the pure goodness that is God.

A Lovable and Desirable Good

The goodness of God, as a pure goodness, is also a lovable goodness: "you are good" and as such are lovable. In this section we think about why the good is lovable. The good "is in some way *lovable*," writes Norris Clarke, "the good is being as desirable, valuable, lovable."[29] The reference of goodness's desirability is, first, on the level of God *in se*. John 17:26 notes that the Spirit is the love with which the Father loves the Son, and the Son the Father. God loves himself *per se*, just as God knows and wills himself: the Father loves the Son in the Spirit, the Son the Father in the same Spirit who is their love proceeding. God is love, and what is good—God—is lovable. If such is the case, then, what is perfect is good, and what is good is desirable, indeed lovable. The good is not only loving but also lovable. Thomas writes that "what is beautiful and good is found to be pleasurable and lovable."[30] God is lovable because "He is the very essence of goodness. . . . To the extent that each one knows Him each loves Him."[31] Knowledge of God is, concomitantly, love of God. With respect to created things, there is the possibility of knowing without loving, but not with God. To know the Lord is to love the Lord, for God "is *goodness itself* and not merely *good*."[32]

Another way to put this is that the good is not simply desirable (Aristotle's point, which Thomas advances), but that the good is "ultimate and primary

---

God attributable to him in a preeminent manner. See further Fran O'Rourke, *Pseudo-Dionysius and the Metaphysics of Aquinas* (Leiden: Brill, 1999), 34-35.

[29]Clarke, *One and Many*, 262.

[30]Aquinas, *Truth* 3.22.1.

[31]Aquinas, *Truth* 3.22.2.

[32]Aquinas, *SCG* 1.38.

in itself."[33] Thus when we know God we say goodness, and such speaking is a function of love. Accordingly, it is not adequate to speak of God as being itself, although that is true. "Goodness and being are really the same," yes, but goodness said of God allows us to say more than being, for "good adds a relationship of what is perfective."[34] Goodness thus has a greater range than being. What God causes, God will undoubtedly perfect, and all that because he is desirable as the good. To know God as good is to have one's knowledge of the good perfected in the form of love.

"The essence of goodness consists in this, that it is in some way desirable," writes Thomas.[35] O'Rourke puts it this way: "*Bonum* makes explicit the note of 'desirability' not expressly pronounced in the notion of *ens* [existence]."[36] This is important because the desirability of God cannot be inferred straightaway from a doctrine of God's being as subsisting being itself, which is what you get with Aristotle. Only when we describe the perfect being of God as goodness itself do we capture the dynamics of the Psalter's testimony to God as one who is more desirable than life. The Psalter does not say "you are existence" and therefore are to be desired; no, it says that you are good and are therefore more desirable than all else. God as the good is our end, the end, and, remarkably, he perfects us in that same end (the end he is) by evoking desire and love of himself. Again, the metaphysical underpinnings of this are key: because God loves himself, is happy in himself, takes pleasure in himself, and knows himself, he conducts us to the same: "From the fact that God takes pleasure in Himself, he directs other things to Himself."[37] Exclusively identifying God with the good allows you to appreciate and in-dwell the psalmist's acclamation in Psalm 84:10, "For a day in your courts is better than a thousand elsewhere."

It would be tempting to think of love for God simply in terms of the obedient human response to the scriptural declaration of God's goodness. Although that is true, there is much more to be said, for love of God springs from the love God has for himself. God is to be enjoyed for himself, disin-terestedly, as love itself. Enjoyment of God in God, in the happiness that is

---

[33] O'Rourke, *Pseudo-Dionysius*, 85.
[34] Aquinas, *ST* 1.5.5; Aquinas, *Truth* 3.22.1.
[35] Aquinas, *ST* 1.5.5.
[36] O'Rourke, *Pseudo-Dionysius*, 87.
[37] Aquinas, *Truth* 3.22.1.

God's very nature, is an end in itself. The object of creaturely delight in this life and the life to come is God. How so? What the Psalms communicate is something of the manner in which one learns to see "the good things of the spirit." Such things "are seen not with the eyes but with the heart."[38] Augustine, mindful of his hearers' (and our) skepticism—"'I don't see them [good things]'"—pushes things even further: "Anyone who is in love sees them."[39] Unless God is loved, God cannot be seen as the good; the good things of God remain unseen, unloved, undesired. Such sight, Augustine reminds us, takes place only with the eyes of the heart, and when the eyes of the heart seek, desire, and love God, they "lack no good thing" (Ps 34:10). The greatest thing is God, a good that cannot perish and which is inherently desirable. We encounter in God a good that cannot be seen as such without being loved—loved and desired, as it were—with the heart.

Here we glimpse the deep moral and pastoral purchase of teaching on God in himself, the pure goodness of God. The one who is in love sees good things, indeed the only one who is good. God loves himself through us—through the pure act of being in which he is Father, Son, and Spirit—when we love God; similarly, God delights in himself when we delight in him. An account that unfolds God's essential goodness, its purity, is only responsible to the extent that we describe its desirability and lovability. The moral concomitant of describing the good as desirable is a life that desires, hungers, and thirsts after the good.

The heart is the faculty by which we see, if we are to desire and see the Lord at all. If the heart is corrupt, what is seen will be seen as corrupt. We cannot know the Lord as good without desiring the Lord as good. So Augustine asks, "Where is your lookout post, from where do you try to see? From what vantage point do you look out in your effort to understand? From your heart, surely. But if your heart is your lookout post, Christian, be sure you have your heart on high."[40] The Christian cannot be indifferent to the location of her heart, for if her heart is not located on high, she cannot see the deep things of God. This is a key theme of the book. Faithful articulation of the preeminent attribute of God assumes and demands, for

---

[38] Augustine, *Psalms* 2:34; Ps 33(34):10-11.
[39] Augustine, *Psalms* 2:34; Ps 33(34):10-11.
[40] Augustine, *Psalms* 3:36; Ps 52(51):4.

Augustine, as it should for us, a heart on high. The treatment of the good that God is must include discourse on its desirability and lovability, not as an afterthought but as intrinsic to is very character. As pure, it is desirable, most worthy of love. And without love we cannot see and we will, as a result, speak of a severely diminished good rather than of our one and only supreme good.

ARE WE GOOD?

The Psalter teaches that our hearts are not on high—"my sin is ever before me" (Ps 51:3). Knowledge of our sin is a fruit of God's revelation, which is an act of his goodness. God does not baptize us in our badness but shares "in our mortal nature so that mortals might become sharers in his godhead. Having promised to communicate his goodness to you, he first communicated with you in your badness."[41] Augustine reminds us that God's communication to us in our badness saves us. The assumption is that goodness— by dint of its actuality and purity—is by its very nature communicative and generative of other goods: in this case, a heart that acknowledges its badness so that it might desire and share in his goodness.

Articulation of God's goodness as a lovable goodness assumes an ascent. Time and time again, in his exposition of the Psalter, Augustine reminds his hearers that "unless we have first experienced our thirst in this desert, in this bad situation where we are, we shall never reach that good which is God."[42] If we are to reach the good that is God, we must experience thirst (desire) for God. This involves action on our part. We pray for something to transpire in us, namely, our thirsting for what we did not thirst for before, which is grace.

Knowledge of "that good which is God" begins from the place where we lack experience of it. Psalm 63:1, "My flesh faints for you, as in a dry and weary land." This perfectly describes the "bad situation" in which we find ourselves. The "dry and weary land," however, is the means by which God increases desire for and love of God's self. Augustine continues, "Sometimes it may happen that he trains us by letting us feel the pinch, but that is because he wants us to love him all the more, and to save us from becoming decadent

---

[41] Augustine, *Psalms* 3:37; Ps 52(51):4.
[42] Augustine, *Psalms* 3:236; Ps 62(63):3.

through excess, and forgetting him."[43] When we love him all the more, we recognize that "[his] steadfast love is better than life. . . . My soul is satisfied as with a rich feast" (Ps 63:3, 5). There is no object worthier of love than God. In this life, insofar as we are immersed in the church's liturgy and faithfully follow the Lord Jesus, are we able to see with the eyes of the heart our eschatological inheritance, God himself. "We are to possess him," preaches Augustine, "and be possessed by him, for all eternity."[44] To be possessed by the one loved is bliss. This love seeks us, tenderly, "before ever we began to love God! And if before we loved God we were so dearly loved by him that he made his coequal Son human for our sake, what must he be reserving for us now that we have come to love him?"[45] Our love for God is occasioned by God's love for us, that of the Father whose coequal Son became human for our sake. Again, our love for God rests on God's love of and happiness in himself. Properly speaking, God does not desire us because God has need of us. God's love of us is good because God seeks and desires us for his own sake, because God knows that there is nothing better for us than himself. Without a rich account of the pure act of being that is God, it is all too easy to conclude that God's love is not actually true, that God's love for us is the means by which God secures something for himself. Thankfully, that is not the case: God desires that we love him because God is completely and fully love *in se*. However, God cannot be loved as the good he is if our hearts are not in the right place. Indeed, the placement of our hearts is a serious matter. A clear, truthful, and disciplined unfolding of the preeminent goodness of God, especially its lovable character, will always point to the need for a holy heart. Love that is leavened by the Psalter's testimony "loves the bridegroom [Jesus Christ] alone, and loves him for himself, disinterestedly."[46]

If Augustine's teaching and preaching on the ascetical demands intrinsic to reception of God's goodness are right, then the question he poses to his congregation, "But what about you—what are you doing?" is not a secondary matter for presentation of God's goodness.[47] To be sure, it is not the

---

[43] Augustine, *Psalms* 3:237; Ps 62(63):3.
[44] Augustine, *Psalms* 3:238; Ps 62(63):3.
[45] Augustine, *Psalms* 3:238; Ps 62(63):3.
[46] Augustine, *Psalms* 3:491; Ps 72(73):28.
[47] Augustine, *Psalms* 3:491; Ps 72(73):28. In Athanasius's words, "But for the searching and right understanding of the Scriptures there is need of a good life and a pure soul, and for Christian

heart of the matter—God is. That said, Augustine's question is far from ir-
relevant. When Augustine writes, "*My good is to hold fast to God. In this
consists total goodness. Do you want more?*" he infers that holding fast is
necessary for reception of the Psalter's testimony to God's "total goodness"
as lovable goodness.[48] An account of God's goodness, if it is to track with
the Psalms' testimony, cannot be indifferent to Augustine's question "But
what about you?" Articulation of the good God that God is means that one
must hold fast to it, if its depths are to be described and declared in a manner
that honors the Psalter's patterns of speech. God loves himself and loves us
in himself, purely so, thereby desiring us in and through the abundance of
his own goodness, so that we might in turn desire him.

TRANSCENDENT GOODNESS

Having attended previously to the pure act of goodness that is God, the fittingness of analogical speech in describing the extent to which goodness is
coextensive with God's being itself, and how God's goodness is lovable and
desirable, it is fitting to step back and present two summative characteristics
of its actuality, namely, its transcendence and omnipresence. The utter transcendence of God is one of the key themes of the Psalter's testimony. "There
is none like you among the gods, O Lord, nor are there any works like yours"
(Ps 86:8). As we have observed, Israel's God is not a God who exists as a
thing in the universe, which is to say a thing that is made or caused. The
gods of the nations are human productions, whereas God is not made. "Who
could conceive an adequate idea of the difference between him who made
it, and what was made?"[49] Augustine avers that the Creator/creature distinction is so great that we cannot comprehend it; indeed, we cannot comprehend anything unmade, "his eternal power and divine nature, invisible
though they are" (Rom 1:20). That said, we may apprehend the testimony of
created things to their Creator. Such things provide us with the means by
which we may glimpse something of the Creator's transcendence, assuming,
of course, that our hearts are being set on high.

---

virtue to guide the mind to grasp, so far as human nature can, the truth concerning God the
Word." See Saint Athanasius, *On the Incarnation* (Crestwood, NY: St. Vladimir's Seminary Press,
1993), §57.

[48] Augustine, *Psalms* 3:491; Ps 72(73):28.

[49] Augustine, *Psalms* 4:232; Ps 85(86):8.

The language of transcendence reminds us that attributes, such as goodness, are predicated of God and other things, albeit in profoundly different ways. Goodness is first in God to such a degree that we, strictly speaking, cannot know the how of this. Just so, we turn to created things in order to know the one who transcends them. Just as the title "king" is meaningless without subjects, so too is transcendence meaningless without things that are transcended. The challenge is to articulate how one who is pure actuality differs from those things that are not pure act—that is, created things. Thomas writes, helpfully, that "we arrive at the knowledge of God from other things, the reality of the names predicated of God and other things is first in God according to His mode, but the meaning of the name is in Him afterwards. Wherefore He is said to be named from His effects."[50] Our intellect, finite as it is, arrives at knowledge of the transcendence of God via created effects, that is, "from other things." Goodness is "first in God," meaning that it is essential to God as cause, true of what is caused, indeed "the various perfections of creatures." Accordingly, these effects are our tutors. By them we are led to God and in turn name God.[51] We know that God is good from the things he has made, but his goodness superexceeds what we can say of it on the basis of created effects insofar as his good is an unparticipated goodness: "first in God according to His mode." God is "*goodness itself*," and "therefore nothing that is not goodness can be in Him."[52] The point is simply that God's goodness not only transcends his created effects but so radically and infinitely superexceeds them that we are unable to say what such a God is, only *that* he is.

An account of knowing God "from other things" is entirely unnatural to us in those lands whose common sense is derivative of the Enlightenment and of naturalism and its cousin materialism. We do not know the world as an enchanted place, as created, a gift by which its Creator is naturally known as such. We do not think of the world as participating in anything, as at every moment caused by the one who is present to it as its cause, really relating it to himself in abundant happiness and joy.

The extent to which God's goodness transcends straightforwardly positive and negative ways of speaking about it only intensifies as our pilgrimage

---

[50] Aquinas, *SCG* 1.34.
[51] Aquinas, *SCG* 1.34, 35.
[52] Aquinas, *SCG* 1.38, 39.

to the heavenly city unfolds. Jesus Christ is the way to the Father, and the Father "leads us in his way by leading us in his Christ."[53] The language of "way" helps us appreciate Jesus' own sense of the radical difference between goodness as we know it and his Father's supreme goodness. "Why do you call me good? No one is good but God alone" (Mk 10:18; Lk 18:19; cf. Mt 19:17). Jesus is, of course, good, but not good in the same sense as his Father, for Jesus is the way to the Father and thus to his goodness, which, of course, he shares in from eternity as the Father's only begotten. Following Augustine's idiom, the Father leads us in his goodness by "leading us in his Christ," who, of course, leads us to the Father.

Jesus' own words to the "certain ruler" and his description of himself in the Fourth Gospel as "the way" encourage recognition of how he enacts his goodness, namely, in his mission of obedience to the will of his Father. In that sense, the Father's goodness is "greater" than his Son's, for the Father sends and the Son is sent.[54] The goodness of which we haltingly speak in relation to created things is infinitely, qualitatively distinct from what we see even in Jesus' own proclamation and embodiment of the good news. Created things are good via participation, whereas he is good by nature. While we are on pilgrimage in this life, let us praise the One whose goodness is so pure and actual that it contains nothing that is not good. This is the deep truth toward which Augustine's unanswerable question "What is he?" gestures, the knowledge of praise.[55]

Regarding our knowledge and love for God and for others in God, it is possible, in this life, to make progress. We may increase in knowledge of how qualitatively distinct is God's goodness from ours as we move toward God. Christian teaching about the transcendent character of God's goodness is, as I have been arguing all along, participatory teaching. We cannot know that goodness "is first in God according to His mode," that is, in a purely actual way, without embarking on the pilgrimage of discipleship. Divine

---

[53] Augustine, *Psalms* 4:235; Ps 85(86):15.

[54] Augustine has a very important discussion in *On the Trinity* with respect to what is said of him in the "form-of-a-servant" and the "form-of-God." Augustine's "rule," as he calls is, attunes us to how the Lord Jesus is the "Father's equal by nature, by condition his inferior." Augustine, *The Trinity*, trans. Edmund Hill, OP (Brooklyn, NY: New City Press, 1991). See books 2 and 1 respectively.

[55] Augustine, *Psalms* 4:232; Ps 85(86):8.

goodness can only be received in as far as the recipient has embarked on that pilgrimage. Without that pilgrimage, we will conflate God's mode with that of our own mode of being, which is idolatry. An account of God's goodness works something like this: the more you know, the more strength you acquire to see—and thus to love—God with the eyes of the heart. Purity of heart is coterminous with seeing God in relation to other things, with recognizing that beauty, truth, goodness, and unity are first in God and therefore in other things. "Look at the birds of the air," says Jesus in Matthew 6:26. The deeply demanding and delightful task of thinking adequately of the Lord God assumes an ascetical pilgrimage the heart. It assumes ears to hear the sermon that the Lord naturally provides. The affective dimension is integral to any treatment of the metaphysics of God's life. "Only a pure heart can contemplate him."[56]

OMNIPRESENT GOODNESS

A corollary of God's pure actuality is his being everywhere present as he is—as the cause of all things. If God is seen, in this life, with the eyes of the heart, then what does the heart see as it looks toward the world he creates, sustains, and perfects in Jesus Christ, from which he is known? Is this actual, pure, lovable, desirable, and transcendent goodness of the Father, Son, and Spirit everywhere? In expounding Psalm 100:5—"For the LORD is good; his steadfast love endures forever, and his faithfulness to all generations," perhaps the greatest thanksgiving psalm in the Psalter—Augustine has a wonderful statement useful for our purposes. He writes, "It is not by spatial intervals that we approach God or distance ourselves from him."[57] The issue is not whether God is present, for God is. The issue, rather, is whether one sees the God who is invisibly present. By purity of heart, I do not move closer to God in any kind of spatial sense, but I do become "more sensitive to God."[58] If I abscond from God's Word and Spirit and am indifferent to the demands of God's love as presented in the Scriptures, then I am absent from God, unable "to perceive what is there."[59] And what is there? God, and

---

[56] Augustine, *Psalms* 5:16; Ps 99(100):2.
[57] Augustine, *Psalms* 5:16; Ps 99(100):2.
[58] Augustine, *Psalms* 5:17; Ps 99(100):2.
[59] Augustine, *Psalms* 5:17; Ps 99(100):2.

God "is present everywhere, and everywhere totally" as the cause he is.[60] It is God's presence "everywhere," moreover, that makes it possible for us to know God's via created effects. Knowledge of God is a fruit of how God exists as God.[61] Put formally, the doctrine of revelation is informed by the doctrine of the divine attributes, most especially the pure goodness of God; the doctrine of revelation is educated by and derivative of what is true of God by nature. Not only is God "present everywhere," but God is "everywhere totally." The doctrine of revelation must take this seriously. Let us recognize that God's presence—as the one he is—assumes created effects, things with an origin outside themselves. God is present everywhere as God in and through what he causes.

It is once again at this point that the profound limitations of human speech come into play. Even if I apprehend a God who "is present everywhere, and everywhere totally," how can I articulate such a mystery? Well, for Augustine, that is not quite the question to ask. The fitting and right creaturely response to the God who is "everywhere totally" is not one of articulating, indeed of speaking, but, surprisingly, of feeling "what he is, and [then] you realize that what you perceive is something than cannot be spoken."[62] If such is the case, then, the omnipresent character of God's pure goodness may be linguistically described, but only insofar as it is felt and loved. Feeling is perhaps a higher mode of knowing the one who alone is inexpressible. The Lord utters us, speaks us into being in his Word and indwells us by his Spirit, but we do not utter God, let alone cause him by our words. And yet there is a place for linguistic utterance of that omnipresent goodness downstream of feeling. The Son of God, writes Augustine, came down "to enable us weaklings to utter him in some degree, [so] the Word became weak."[63] God condescends to us in his Word that we might not be entirely silent, that we might have something positive to say, even if we get there only by speaking of what God is not, though we may feel him more in line with what he actually is. The Lord is a "passionately loving shepherd" to his people, the sheep of his pasture.[64] If Augustine is right, then there exists a subtle distinction between knowledge

[60] Augustine, *Psalms* 5:17; Ps 99(100):2.
[61] This could also be stated as God's knowledge is the ground of creation.
[62] Augustine, *Psalms* 5:18; Ps 99(100):2.
[63] Augustine, *Psalms* 5:18; Ps 99(100):2.
[64] Augustine, *Psalms* 5:27; Ps 99(100):3.

and speech. Speech (utterance) is a higher form of the knowledge of God, for it rests on the incarnation. Though we are too weak to utter "what cannot be spoken," we perceive, knowing "from other things." Utterance, however, is higher than perception. The latter requires the incarnation. What created things allow us to perceive, perhaps even feel with respect to God, the incarnation allows us to utter, to speak.

In sum, the general mode of apprehending, and not so much comprehending, the "everywhere totally" of the God who is alone good is more, in this life anyhow, a matter of awareness and feeling, indeed of being sensitive to, rather than of speaking. The object that is expressed should determine modes of expression. In giving account of the God who is not less here and more there, we do not know how God is "everywhere totally," but we can begin to feel and perceive as we journey forward toward what we do not know; having been elevated by the Word who became weak. But there is more; our "passionately loving shepherd" is not satisfied with our merely perceiving, perception being knowledge that comes from created things. God wants us to utter himself to some degree, and so the Word became flesh. Created things enable us to perceive the one who is "present everywhere," the incarnate Lord, to speak/utter the one who is "present everywhere." Perception culminates and is perfected in speech.

PSALM 135: THE GREAT GOODNESS OF THE LORD

"Praise the LORD, for the LORD is good; sing to his name, for he is gracious. For the LORD has chosen Jacob for himself, Israel as his own possession. For I know that the LORD is great; our Lord is above all gods" (Ps 135:3-5).

Psalm 135 is a profound testimony to God and to God's unwavering faithfulness toward his wayward covenant people. What is significant, in part, is how the psalmist's praise is directed first to the Lord and second to the name of the Lord, and all this on behalf of the servants of the Lord. The servants of the Lord are encouraged to praise the Lord, for he is good and gracious. Only by the time we get to Psalm 135:4 do we have reference to a work of God, namely, Jacob's election. The priority given to praise of God's name and goodness as concomitant with that name is significant and shows how identification of God takes precedence with respect to what God does. God's great work of election rests on the sheer goodness of his name.

What has been said thus far about the *are* is only profitable if it helps us to inhabit this great psalm. Augustine's comments on the psalm provide the most extended and rich account of God's goodness available to us in his *Expositions on the Psalms*. Unsurprisingly, words fail to indicate a goodness that is so exceeding, that far surpasses "the paean uttered over creation, that *God made all things exceedingly good.*"[65] More fitting is a joyful noise: "Make a joyful noise to the LORD, all the earth" (Ps 100:1). "This is our problem," writes Augustine:

> We cannot find words, but our sheer joy does not permit us to be silent; so let us neither speak nor hold our tongues. But what are we to do, if we can neither speak nor keep silence? Let us shout for joy. What does that mean: *Shout for joy?* Give vent to the inarticulate expression of your joys, belch out all your happiness to him.[66]

Augustine embraces the gastronomic metaphor precisely because it illustrates just how deeply God's goodness affects those who receive and perceive it. They may not be able to speak of it, or think of it, but they can shout for joy in praise to the God who "*satisfies your longing with good things.*"[67] The "shout" is epistemically significant.

Shouting and belching out are fitting and right because God "is himself good in the proper sense." This is what we meant earlier on in the chapter when we spoke of *pure* goodness. God makes all things exceedingly good, "but he is himself the Good whom no one made." We are talking, again, about an essential goodness, meaning that God "is good by his own goodness, not by participating in some good thing outside himself; he is good by his own self, not by cleaving to some other good." What God has created needs God "to become good," whereas God "needs no one else to make him good." This is what Augustine calls the "unique character of his goodness, yet I lack the power to state it as it deserves." Hence the superiority of shouting and belching indicates "[God's goodness] as it deserves." We see here also something of the generative character of God's supreme goodness. "Being good himself," God cannot make anything other than what is good "because that

---

[65] Augustine, *Psalms* 5:87; Ps 102(103):3-5.
[66] Augustine, *Psalms* 5:87; Ps 102(103):3-5.
[67] Augustine, *Psalms* 5:87; Ps 102(103):3-5.

is his nature, and so we know him to be essential goodness."[68] His works express his nature; created things refer us to their principle.

Augustine reminds us that the Lord does not need me or for that matter anything "else to make him good." God does not love the world because God gets something out of it; similarly, God does not love me so as "to enhance his own happiness." I need God if I am to be made perfect, but God does not need me. How then am I to speak of a love that is "more interior than myself and far above me"? I cannot speak of such a love, but I can in Jesus Christ and in the power of the Spirit shout and belch it out. However, even that shouting requires words, and the word that the Psalter supplies is the word *good*. Likewise, Augustine expounds, "When I turn to God, I think it better to attach no other word but to say simply that he is good." His goodness transcends any thoughts we may have of it because God does not depend on anything else for his goodness. Just so, we cannot speak or think of a good that is not "good by derivation from some other good" in favor of "a good that is good of itself."[69] Although we may not be able to think or even utter such a good, we can nonetheless belch and shout. The point is an important one: certain modes of "discourse" befit God's goodness better than others. Belching and shouting are more transparent to the name of the Lord than others.

Such a God is *above all gods*. Not surprisingly, Augustine refers to Exodus 3:14 in a brilliant meditation on the HE WHO IS in his commentary on Psalm 134(135):3. Goodness *per se* is not God's name: God transcends even that. God's name, rather, is "Being-Itself, as though that were his name." God's "very nature is to be, and so true is this that, when compared with him, all created things are as though they had no being." God so utterly exceeds and is so completely distinguished from what he has made—even as he is intimate with it—that compared with him it is as if it does not exist. God, unlike what he has made, "is true being, unchangeable being, and this can be said of him alone. He is being, as he is also goodness, the good of all things."[70] God is "Being-Itself"—HE WHO IS—and is as such goodness,

---

[68] Augustine, *Psalms* 6:193; Ps 134(135):3.
[69] Augustine, *Psalms* 6:193; Ps 134(135):3.
[70] Augustine, *Psalms* 6:192; Ps 134(135):3. Thomas advances Augustine's thought by speaking in terms of the perfective character of God's goodness as an end. Thomas, in other words, says things Augustine does not say; Thomas does not simply repeat Augustine but assumes his

the preeminent attribute of HE WHO IS, and who is the good of all things that derive their being from him. I do not know whether there is any better description of God available to us, outside the words of Scripture themselves, than what Augustine here supplies in relationship to Psalm 135:5, "for I know that the LORD is great."

What else is instructive in his sermon, beyond his incisive and clear comments about the metaphysics of God's goodness, is how such goodness is present to us and how we may be said to share in it. God's goodness is an *omnipresent* goodness insofar as it is present to all goods outside itself. Again, we best express this goodness doxologically. "Whatever else we praise, we praise because it is good, and no greater reason, no better or stronger motive, can be given for praising God than that he is good. *Praise the Lord*, then, *because he is good.*"[71] Importantly, praising the goodness of his works should not be spurned in favor of contemplating "him in himself."[72] This is in line with the sequence of the psalm itself. Before the first work of God is cited, there is lavish praise of God himself. That said, "we lack the capacity to contemplate him in himself." Our hearts are not pure enough to see him. Thus Augustine counsels us to "gaze upon his works, so that we many not fall silent in our praise."[73] And so Psalm 135:4-14 recalls God's works, namely, election, creation, the exodus, and the expelling of the many kings from the Promised Land. Interestingly, the psalm ends with the call to Israel, Aaron, and Levi to bless the Lord "who resides in Jerusalem" (Ps 135:21). God in his utter transcendence has accommodated himself to us, meeting us in our weakness, evoking our praise by virtue of his presence in us, compatible as it is with us, and in the works of nature around us. God does not want us to be silent but rather to sing, shout, and belch as they are the most fitting form of response to "him who gave us everything."[74] Perception of his works tends toward uttering him with the help he gives; shouting eclipses perception. The shout gives rise to a capacity—one not available otherwise—to see.

---

account of God as "Being-Itself" and speaks of this perfect being as good, not simply in causal terms but also in perfective terms, that is, as having the character of an end intrinsic to which is converting power.

[71] Augustine, *Psalms* 6:194; Ps 134(135):3.
[72] Augustine, *Psalms* 6:194; Ps 134(135):3.
[73] Augustine, *Psalms* 6:194; Ps 134(135):3.
[74] Augustine, *Psalms* 6:194; Ps 134(135):3.

The Lord is good, and we know this to be so because the Lord is good to us. The "is" is far too great for us, suitable as it is only to God, and so we must contemplate and praise the Lord in relation to his great acts for us. Scripture presents what we cannot comprehend of God and at the same time accommodates itself to us in such a way that we may by faith apprehend. Our treatment of goodness as the preeminent attribute of God is at once beyond understanding and at the same time a name adjusted to and compatible with our limited faculties. Thus Augustine comments (again) on the I AM WHO I AM: "The name I AM WHO AM is suitable to me, but the name *the God of Abraham, the God of Isaac, and the God of Jacob* is adjusted to your comprehension. If you fall back from what I am to myself, understand what I am for you."[75] Just so, our chapter has sought to treat what God is to himself, pure goodness. But the purity of his goodness is too bright to behold and so cannot remain here for long. We must consider him as he is for us. Following the pattern of Psalm 135, we must move onto what God is in relation to us, to God's great works. This we do not to depart from what God is for himself but out of faithfulness to the pattern of the psalm, which would not have us remain there too long lest we, like Moses on Sinai, be consumed by so terrible a presence.

To conclude this section, the book is an attempt to do both: to not "fall back from what I am" ("you are good") and to "understand what I am for you" ("you do good"). We understand what God is to himself by receiving what he is for us, recognizing all the while that what he is for us is adjusted to our comprehension. This chapter has taken in what cannot be taken in and so falls back, and therefore must give way, as the psalm does, to what is adjusted to our comprehension. Yes, we cannot find words, and so on the one hand this study will fail, and that is fine; and yet, nonetheless, the utter delight to be had in the one who is good encourages us to persevere in receiving what the Lord is to himself. This study is an inarticulate expression of joy, something of a belching out on page, to carry on with Augustine's gastronomic metaphor, my happiness in him.[76] Theology—the doctrine of God—represents an effort to be scripturally present to what God is to himself and in such a way as to faithfully fall back toward understanding what he is for us.

---

[75] Augustine, *Psalms* 6:196; Ps 134(135):3.
[76] See again Augustine, *Psalms* 5:86; Ps 102(103):3-5.

CONCLUSION

In this chapter we have reflected on the *are*, articulating some of the first principles of "that good to which and about which we can shout for joy, but which we can scarcely explain at all."[77] That good is, of course, God, who is "not good in any general sense but supremely good."[78] I have labored here, as in the previous two chapters, to make clear the necessity of "personal experience" for speaking the sweetness, kindness, and goodness of God.[79] To unfold God's goodness without personal experience of the same is impossible. Dogmatic theology encourages and assumes experience and is a fruit of the experience it evokes. Taste the goodness of the Lord; "belch forth in confession"; and then labor in faith with thanksgiving to say something about it which is at least not false.[80] In other words, praise is intrinsic to the systematic task. To be sure, it is not to be conflated with the systematic task itself; but the systematic unfolding of the great truths of God's being attested in Scripture itself acquires greater clarity and a more intense joy, and it more powerfully furthers advancement in our salvation when undertaken as praise of God. So Augustine explains: "We see, then, that God teaches us sweetness [i.e., goodness] by breathing delight into us, teaches discipline by sending us the right measure of tribulation, and teaches knowledge by empowering us from within to understand."[81] Goodness or "sweetness," as Augustine sometimes translates it, is true of God, "what I am to myself," and we learn God's goodness in his very goodness, by grace. Thus we cry, "Teach me your statutes."

Given that we have traced some of the first principles of God's goodness, we now proceed to think about how the good that God is relates to the Trinity. The three persons are indeed good because of the one essence that is common to them. We shall see how each of the three possesses the good in a manner appropriate to their person, and consider the way in which the particular goodness of each "structures" their work among us.

---

[77] Augustine, *Psalms* 5:86; Ps 102(103):3-5.
[78] Augustine, *Psalms* 6:215; Ps 135(136):1: "O give thanks to the LORD, for he is good, for his steadfast love endures forever."
[79] Augustine, *Psalms* 5:224; Ps 106(107):1.
[80] Augustine, *Psalms* 5:224; Ps 106(107):1.
[81] Augustine, *Psalms* 5:420; Ps 118 Exposition 17 (119):65-66.

THREE

Goodness and the Trinity

I DISCUSS IN THIS CHAPTER how the goodness of God coheres with the relations constituting and distinguishing the three persons in God. In so doing, I am following Thomas's procedure in *ST* 1. Therein Thomas distinguishes theology *de deo uno* and theology *de deo trino*, offering what Gilles Emery calls a "double perspective."[1] Though his "double perspective" has been almost uniformly rejected by Catholic and Protestant modernity, I think that there are venerable reasons for embracing it, the principle reason being that it maps nicely onto Scripture. In this chapter I unfold something of the theological rationale for the distinction with a view to how it not only promotes attention to the Psalter's witness to God but also deepens our sense of the blessed Trinity as "not someone good, but Goodness as such."[2]

To put this differently, distinguishing theology *de deo uno* and theology *de deo trino* serves us well because goodness is, first and foremost, an essential designation and only as such common to the three. "You are good"— that is, the Trinity of Father, Son, and Spirit is good. Goodness is identical to the one essence of God himself, common as it is to the three. If such is the case, then, goodness cannot be considered a relational or, more technically, a notional designation. Relational designations such as begetting, being begotten, and proceeding refer us to the three persons in relation to

---

[1]Gilles Emery, OP, "Essentialism or Personalism in the Treatise on God in St. Thomas Aquinas?," in *Trinity in Aquinas* (Ypsilanti, MI: Sapientia Press, 2003), 172. Interestingly, Thomas is not original in this as he follows Augustine's lead in distinguishing between what is said of God "substance-wise" from what is said "relationship-wise." See Augustine, *Trinity* 5.14.

[2]David Bentley Hart, "We Need to Talk About God," *Church Times* 12, no. 2 (2016): 19.

one another. Things said of the three in relationship to one another are not said of what is common to them. For example, we would not say that the one essence of God begets and is begotten, but we would say in fidelity to Scripture that the Father begets and the Son is begotten. This is why it is important to distinguish between what is common and what is proper to one (or more) of the three.[3] Scripture tells us about God and who God is but does not conflate the two spheres.[4]

The task then in this chapter is to advance metaphysical inquiry by thinking through some of the advantages of Thomas's architectonic, especially insofar as it encourages us to inhabit the Psalter. I shall pursue this task along the following lines. First, we will investigate some of the theological reasons for ascribing conceptual priority to the common in advance of the particular. Second, we shall reflect on how New Testament speech about participation in the divine nature has its register on the essential level. Third, the distinction between essential names and relative ones illustrates the concordance between nature and works in God, indeed how essential attributes structure Scripture's depiction of the works of the Trinity. Fourth and last, and most challengingly, I extend the treatment offered in the previous chapter regarding the transcendental character of goodness. When we talk about transcendentals—that is, those properties of being that jump across categories—we are talking about attributes as things said in relation to both God and creatures, though not, of course, as if God were an exemplification of these things. I explain how many of the names common to the three are the transcendentals: goodness, truth, beauty, and oneness or unity. Goodness considered as a transcendental helps us to distinguish how other descriptions of God—here I am thinking of omnipotence, omniscience, and omnipresence—refer to God in a different way from the transcendentals. The identifiers beginning with "omni" name truths particular to the divine nature without being communicable, at least in the same way as goodness is. Omniscience, for example, is not ascribed to created things, but goodness is. Goodness has a more positive and regulative resonance than does a

---

[3]I say "or more" because Father and Son both "cause" the Spirit. The Spirit originates in relation to the Father and Son, for from them the Spirit proceeds, the Father in primary sense and the Son in a secondary sense.

[4]This same is true of another important distinction, namely, the processions of the missions.

descriptive term like *omnipotence*. Both are true of God but in different ways. In this last section I think about goodness as an absolute of the Trinity that is also communicable by its very nature to what is not God.

THE CONCEPTUAL PRIORITY OF THE COMMON

Goodness is the preeminent attribute of God, whose first name is "I AM WHO I AM" (Ex 3:14). Our concern all along has been to follow Scripture's lead as we describe the goodness of the tri-personal God. The Father is good, the Son is good, and the Spirit is good—not three goodnesses but one goodness. The function of an account of the attributes of God is to describe something of what is in God, God himself, and the divine essence, and all that in accordance with God's simplicity: "All that exists in God, is God."[5] Goodness, descriptively speaking, works, as we have noted, on the essential level, indicating, in an analogical sense, God. "This is of course true of the three who are in God and are God himself," but it is not true of the relations that distinguish and constitute the three.[6] Accordingly, discourse about the originating relations by which the three are constituted themselves and distinct from one another works on a relational level, not an essential level.

This is important to contemplate because Scripture does not allow us to confuse what is said relationally of the three with what is said essentially. Scripture encourages us to speak of what is true of God himself, and it also encourages us to speak of what unites and distinguishes Father, Son, and Spirit in relation to one another. It is a matter of considering God *"under the aspect* of the essence and *under the aspect* of the distinction."[7] The advantage of Thomas's approach is that it engenders "the opportunity for a double consideration or a double approach to the God confessed by

---

[5]Aquinas, *ST* 1.27.3 ad 2. Furthermore, "there are relative properties in the persons, but in such a way that they are the persons and also the divine essence, as we say that wisdom and goodness are in God and are God himself and the divine essence." See Aquinas, *Compend* 1.67.

[6]Aquinas, *Compend* 1.67.

[7]Emery, "Essentialism or Personalism," 172, 176. Emery, following Thomas, is more subtle than is Kathryn Sonderegger on this point. Contra Sonderegger in her otherwise enthralling *Systematic Theology*, vol. 1. "The Ineffable Unicity of God" does not "govern, conform, and set forth the Triune Reality of God." See Katherine Sonderegger, *Systematic Theology*, vol. 1, *The Doctrine of God* (Minneapolis: Fortress, 2015), xv. Thomas claims less. Accordingly, the treatise on God's unicity does not "determine" what comes after it, that is, the triune reality. Rather, what comes after the account of unicity is, for Thomas, the same reality considered under a different aspect. The former is a matter of Aquinas, *ST* 1.1–26, the latter a matter of Aquinas, *ST* 1.27–43.

Christian faith."[8] Emery's point, following Thomas, is simply that there are two distinct—but not separate—spheres of talk when it comes to the mystery of God.

Thomas's architectonic points to the fullness of Scriptural testimony to God and to all things in relation to God: on the one hand God's unity (q 1–26) and on the other hand the processions internal to the divine life itself (q 27–43), and therewith the procession of creatures from God (q 44–49). Treating the essence in advance of the personal distinctions does not mean that new things are not said about God's goodness—for example, its pneumatological density—in the treatment of the distinction of persons in light of God's supernatural self-disclosure. However, an account of God's goodness is most at home in a presentation of what is essential rather than what is said relationally precisely because goodness is identical to or convertible with the divine essence. Before we set forth the goodness of any one of the three, we speak of three who are good.

Thomas avers that is it fitting to first describe what God is in advance of what is proper to a divine person because, as Emery notes, "the *proper* does not have reality without the *common*."[9] The goodness proper to each of the three assumes the goodness common to the three. That is a key point to secure, and it is why architectonics matter. The proper subsists in the common. In other words, our first task is to expound "'what concerns the essence' in order to clarify the mystery of the three divine persons."[10]

The proper order of and instruction in the doctrine of God involves us first with the essence. Accordingly, we should not rush to consider the three but linger with what Scripture teaches about God's attributes: "You are good." So Thomas in a supremely clear statement notes that "In God, to be, to live, to be wise, to be happy, and whatever else is seen to pertain to perfection and goodness, are one and the same in God, as though the sum total of His goodness were God's very being."[11] God is perfect, and as that which is

---

[8]Emery, "Essentialism or Personalism,"176. The order of Thomas's treatment in the *ST*—unlike in the *SCG*—focuses on "the order of discovery," that is, "a speculative understanding of the faith (*intellectus fidei*) which exhibits the notions, so to speak, in the inverse order in which we would find them out." See Gilles Emery, OP, *The Trinitarian Theology of Thomas Aquinas*, trans. Francesca Aran Murphy (New York: Oxford University Press, 2007), 49.
[9]Emery, "Essentialism or Personalism," 179.
[10]Ibid., 181.
[11]Aquinas, *SCG* 1–3.20.

perfect, is good and thus goodness itself. God is his life, his very being, his wisdom and happiness—these are identical to him. Theology does itself a disservice when it hurries to the works of perfect goodness without considering first their source in God and their status as works of the three who are one and the same goodness.

When we say God is good, we are speaking of a goodness that is in the essence and is the essence of God himself. This is not true of relational discourse, rooted as it is in the processions of Son and Spirit. Plurality in God, as Emery notes, refers "to relation, and not to essence in its proper formality."[12] Put differently, attributes are coextensive with the one essence and perfect being of God, while description of the three derives from relations, indeed notional attributes that are not convertible with God's essence. The gain to discourse on God's goodness, when housed in a treatment of the essence, is simple enough. Goodness does not involve us in "an analysis of relation."[13] The *is*, rather, concerns us with what is convertible with God's essence. Conversely, relations are not convertible with God's essence; so too the processions of creatures from God. What is convertible with God's essence is goodness itself, for being and being good are the same for God.[14] As Paul Griffiths notes, "the extent to which something is is also the extent to which it is good."[15] The *are*—what God is—is the focus of the doctrine of God's attributes and the very principle of intelligibility for understanding the three and their works of nature and grace.

Further to this, describing what is common in advance of what is proper encourages greater appreciation for what is "present in a unique way in each of the persons of the Trinity."[16] When Thomas thinks about goodness, he does so, as is well known, with particular reference to the Holy Spirit, who, as he says, is "goodness."[17] Goodness has a kind of pneumatological density as the very principle of God's love of all creatures.[18] As Thomas notes,

---

[12]Emery, "Essentialism or Personalism," 191.

[13]Ibid., 196-97n81.

[14]See Aquinas, *Hebdomads*, 47.

[15]Paul J. Griffiths, *Decreation: The Last Things of All Creatures* (Waco, TX: Baylor University Press, 2014), 105.

[16]Thomas Joseph White, OP, *The Incarnate Lord: A Thomistic Study in Christology* (Washington, DC: Catholic University of America Press, 2015), 264.

[17]Aquinas, *ST* 1.32.1.

[18]See Aquinas, *ST* 1.37.3 ad 3.

goodness is appropriated to a particular person, "to the Holy Ghost. . . . *Goodness*, as the nature and object of love, has likeness to the Holy Ghost, Who is Love. . . . The Holy Ghost proceeds as the love of the primal goodness whereby the Father loves Himself and every creature."[19] Ascribing conceptual priority to the one unique essence of the three indeed heightens our appreciation of the distinct ways in which of each of the three has what is common in a way befitting their origin. The Father has goodness as one who begets, the Son as one begotten, and the Spirit as one who proceeds as "the love with which you have loved me," not three goodnesses but rather one goodness (Jn 17:26).

To sum up this section, Thomas's architectonic reminds us that consideration of God's attributes involves disciplined and scripturally focused contemplation of God's essence. It is more than simply understanding "the divine attributes from within the limits of natural human reason."[20] It is, in addition, a matter of understanding—beholden to the scriptural testimony to God—what is common to the Trinity. Only when we consider the common may we consider the constitution and internal fellowship of the three by relations of origin. Again, Thomas's architectonic does not separate the two dimensions: *de deo trino* treats the essence as subsisting in each of the three. Without reflection *de deo uno*, our account of how all things relate to God in Christ through the Spirit is hamstrung. What God is in himself occupies the first place in theological inquiry because all God's works toward the outside express the ineffable reality that God is, and, by virtue of their being works, reveal God's nature and will.

GOODNESS AND PARTICIPATION

With such an account of the advantages of housing a treatment of the divine goodness in a treatise on God's essence in play, we may now consider at greater length the advantages accrued to four downstream doctrinal concerns related to trinitarian teaching, namely, these: how talk of participation works in relation to the divine essence; the relationship between attributes and acts; the concordance of nature and acts; and the relationship between what is essential and transcendentality. As I shall argue, goodness not only

---

[19]Aquinas, *ST* 1.32.1 ad 1; 39.8; 37.3 ad 3.
[20]Hart, "God," 19.

describes God's deity but also denotes the very capacity and principle of intelligibility for goodness expressed toward the outside in the missions of Son and Spirit.

First, the distinction between the essential and personal in God, as articulated by Thomas, helps us to speak with greater clarity and precision about the New Testament motif of participation in the divine nature.[21] Thomas helps us to see that while we do by grace participate in God's essential attributes, we do not participate in the processions.[22] Begetting, being begotten, spirating, and proceeding are not that in which we, by grace through faith, participate. Nonetheless, we do participate in God's nature, but only in terms of those things that are said of God in an "essential" sense. That said, we are never made participant in "a part of the divine substance."[23] As creatures made in God's likeness, we shall never have goodness as God does. Goodness is coextensive with God's being, and it is God's essence, whereas goodness is not original to us. Our goodness, rather, is had in relation to another whose goodness is from himself. Our present experience of him who causes the likeness of his goodness in us is participatory in nature—that is, by likeness.

In the life to come, however, we will no longer suffer the "manifold defects" of sin, but not because we are somehow made consubstantial with the Father, "a part of the divine substance."[24] Human beings are not from God in the same sense as the Son is from the Father.[25] Creatures that we are, we proceed from God's will, whereas the Son proceeds from the very being of the Father. Our status as adopted children of God is by grace. We are similitudes and likenesses of God, whereas the Lord Jesus is God's Son by nature, not grace. In heaven, we shall participate for all eternity in God, enjoying all things through him, who will be in all and all in all, without our being swallowed up by or collapsed into God.

Housing teaching on God's goodness and the divine attributes as a whole in the treatise on God's essence helps us to see that the bulk of participation

---

[21]The classic locus is, of course, 2 Pet 1:4, "participants of the divine nature."

[22]By grace, for example, am I declared and made righteous, righteousness being true of God from eternity.

[23]Aquinas, *SCG* 2.85.

[24]Aquinas, *SCG* 2.85.

[25]Aquinas, *SCG* 2.85.

language refers primarily to the first treatise of *ST* 1 (1–26), not the second treatise (27–43). How then do we come to participate in what is common to the three? In short, it is through their action toward the outside, the missions of the Son and Spirit—in particular, the reconciliation and redemption that those missions achieve. The works of God, understood as the fruit of the missions of Son and Spirit, confer benefits—for example, the forgiveness of sin, justification, and sanctification. The works of God among us are the means by which we participate in the divine nature, indeed God's essence. This is not to say that those who have not opened their hearts to Christ do not in some sense share in what is proper to God simply by virtue of their existence. It is to say, however, that the Christian participates in God in a different way from the non-Christian. The Christian participates in faith and thanksgiving, which is a higher form of participation in God than simply that of existence.

The works of God have a source, and that source is God's life *in se*, which is communicated to us in a specific sense in Word and sacrament. The works engender ever-greater intimacy with respect to their source; indeed, the works of reconciliation and redemption have soteriological purchase, which is different from the work of creation. His becoming for us "wisdom from God and righteousness and sanctification and redemption" (1 Cor 1:30) means that we come to share in the goodness that he is; in sharing, we become Christian. Those works communicate goodness and confer on us our status as God's adopted children. In other words, simply being a creature does not make one a Christian. Rather, a Christian is one whose life is tied to a people—"the Israel of God" (Gal 6:16)—who receive their life in relation to the Father's gift of his Son in the Spirit. Accordingly, the heart of participation language is with respect to what is said of God "substance-wise" and not what is said "relationship-wise." We do not share in the divine relations, subsistent as they are; nonetheless, we do share by grace in the essence in which they subsist—sharing in that which God is without being absorbed into God.

Another way to say this is that the second half of the treatise in the *prima pars* of *ST* (27–43) unfolds what is incommunicable. This is (again) not to undermine God's historical revelation in the form of the missions of Son and Spirit. By no means; but it is to say that the foundation of participation talk—the weight, as it were, when it comes to understanding what is participated, shared, and communicated in the economy of salvation—pertains to the first half of the treatise.

Put technically, the missions signify in a temporal sense the eternal processions. The missions signify the processions but are not the processions themselves. The missions are, rather, expressive of the processions but cannot be conflated with them. The Spirit, for example, proceeds temporally as "the gift of sanctification."[26] The Spirit as the love of the Father for the Son and the Son for the Father is poured out among us as gift. The Spirit is our sanctification, the Spirit who is goodness itself, the love of the Father for the Son and the Son for the Father.[27] Sanctification is the effect of the Spirit in which we participate by grace, and that effect (sanctification) confers goodness. This is what it means to say that we participate in what is essential to God. What is essential is communicable, not in an emanationist sense, but via effects, as received in faith.

In short, what is essential in God is what is communicable via divine effects. Effects are the result of the significations in time of what is eternally true of God. For example, the eternal Spirit who is goodness itself effects among us a gift—sanctification—that expresses what the Spirit is—goodness itself. Such an account is necessary if we are to honor the essential as what is communicable to and compatible with us rather than, say, what is notional or proper. We share by faith in the life of God, the life common to Father, Son, and Spirit.

Let us consider for a moment the third part of Psalm 24, that is, Psalm 24:7-10, insofar as it illuminates the thinking unfolded above. First, there is the literal sense of Psalm 24:7, "Lift up your heads, O gates!" This text describes how it would be if God were honored throughout the whole world. If God is to be honored throughout the world, he must be honored in our hearts. How does "the King of glory" (Ps 24:7-10) come into our hearts? Well, drawing on such New Testament texts as Ephesians 3 and 1 John 4, the king comes in, as we have said, via faith. Accordingly, the Lord begins "to be where before he was not. Therefore God enters us at that time when we

---

[26] Aquinas, *ST* 1.43 ad 7.
[27] Thomas refers to the Spirit as the "gift" of sanctification, the Word as its "author." See Aquinas, *ST* 1.43 a 7.

begin to have faith in him."[28] Though Thomas does not use the language of
"participation" to explain this, it is nonetheless helpful for unfolding the sig-
nificance of what he says. Thomas's point is that God is the active agent,
entering into us in relation to whom he was not. We are not said to enter
into God (via faith); rather, he is said to come into us when we lift up our
heads to him. God enters so as to abide in us, thereby enabling us to abide
in him, demonstrating how compatible we are with him. He created us for
fellowship with himself.

That said, in entering into us, God does not come to participate in us, as
if our being were necessary to him or he were in need of something from
us. And yet, the reverse is true; we come to share in what is true of God.
God enters us, existing thereby in a new relationship to us. God, because
he is utterly complete in himself and is only ever moved in relation to
himself, is free "to be where before he was not." Being where he was not
produces the fruit of our sharing in him. The Lord comes in, freely, as we
lift up our heads. God is present in us in a new way—not as one changed
but as one who has always been, yet begins to be the one he has always been
and will be where he was not. You may call it movement in complete rest
and repose. The Lord comes in, and we come to share in, to participate in
the life of the one who comes in, through faith. We come to share in what
is true of him, what is true of the three in their deity. What is common to
the three is that in which we share by faith, but there is more: we need to
think about how the attributes—specifically goodness—of the Trinity
structure the work of the Trinity.

Goodness and Works

Without Thomas's distinction in play, his "double perspective," we fail to see
the principle for God's works toward the outside.[29] The principle of God's
works is God's essence: God acts by his essence. Another way to say this is
that the grounds of God's acts toward the outside are God's attributes; attributes structure works. As Thomas teaches, "every effect of God proceeds
from each attribute."[30] The works of God have their ground in God's inner

---

[28]Aquinas, *In Ps* 24, trans. Stephen Loughlin.
[29]Emery, "Essentialism or Personalism," 172.
[30]Aquinas, *ST* 1.45.6 ad 3.

being; they receive their shape from God's essential names as appropriated to particular persons.

Attributes have priority in the order of systematic inquiry into God insofar as they elucidate the acts of God toward the outside. For example, power is common to the three by virtue of their essence: they are omnipotent. When we reflect on Scripture's testimony to a specific act, we often discover it as related primarily to a particular person of the Godhead. For example, creation is described for the most part with reference to God the Father, and so power is appropriated to the Father.[31] Of course, creation is a triune act: the Father creates in and through the Son by the Holy Spirit.[32] And yet, Scripture and creed assign a certain *priority* to the Father in the work of creation: the maker of heaven and earth is God, the Father almighty. A theological architectonic that treats what is essential in advance of what is true of the three in relationship to one another helps us see that God's works toward the outside express common attributes in an appropriated way. There is a perfect concordance between God's attributes and acts toward the outside. The three act as they do because of the unique way in which each possesses what is common.

Metaphysical inquiry into God's goodness reminds us that the works of God, the fruit of the missions of Son and Spirit, attest the "origin of the person who is sent."[33] The intelligibility of the missions of Son and Spirit derives from their origins; missions express, in a temporal sense, origins. And yet we recognize that the missions are not exclusively assigned to the three persons, for the missions themselves assume the divine essence and all that is in it. There is in God perfect concordance between what God is, the relations whereby God is, and what God does. The missions signify processions that are internal to God and that subsist within the essence itself. But there is more: inflected in pneumatological terms, the Spirit proceeds eternally "as the love of the primal goodness whereby the Father loves himself" and because of this "every creature."[34] The Father's love of his own goodness in the Son and Spirit has temporal expression on two levels: first,

---

[31]See Aquinas, *ST* 1.45.6 ad 2.
[32]Regarding the language of appropriation, Thomas writes, "a manifestation of the divine persons by the use of the essential attributes is called *appropriation*." See Aquinas, *ST* 1.39 ad 7.
[33]Aquinas, *ST* 1.43.5 ad 3.
[34]Aquinas, *ST* 1.37.3.

the doctrine of creation as the beginning and end of all things, and second
the Spirit's mission. "Goodness has likeness to the Holy Ghost, Who is Love
. . . Who proceeds as Love . . . [as] the gift of sanctification."[35] Attributes in
an appropriated sense structure not only the missions and the works those
missions accomplish, but even more the processions as the source of the
missions. In the case of goodness, as goodness is inherently communicative,
conservative, and perfective, goodness structures the doctrines of creation,
providence, and the last things; goodness is cause and end.[36] If such is the
case, we are in a position to extend what was said in the previous chapter
about the transcendentals—in particular, their communicable character.
The transcendentals are the point at which we may distinguish between
communicable and incommunicable attributes.

GOODNESS AND TRANSCENDENTALITY

Goodness is said of God and of all things insofar as they relate to God.
Thomas, as Jan Aertsen notes, argues that the good "is found in all categories."[37]
God is not simply the source of all that is good but is the ongoing goodness
of things, and God orders all things to his goodness. God wills that all
things—in a manner appropriate to their mode of being—be ordered to him
as God. The transcendentals are, as has been articulated, convertible with
respect to God's attributes, those attributes intrinsic to the single, infinite, and
singular reality that is God. As per chapter six, we would not say that begottenness is a transcendental, for that is to misunderstand how begottenness
language works with respect to God, but we would say that goodness is—
because it is true of the essence of God, common to the three. The divine
attributes are transcendentals; divine processions and thus notional attributes are not. The processions, God's acts toward the inside whereby each of
the three exist, do not leap across categories of being whereas goodness does;
we are created good in light of God, who is goodness itself.[38]

Aertsen deepens our thinking by noting that "because of the scope of pred-
ication, *transcendentia* are the most universal concepts that are predicated of

[35]Aquinas, *ST* 1.39.8; 43.7.
[36]See further Aquinas, *ST* 1.44.4.
[37]Jan Aertsen, *Medieval Philosophy as Transcendental Thought: From Philip the Chancellor (CA. 1225) to Francisco Suarez*, Studien Und Texte Zur Geistesgeschichte Des Mittelalters (Leiden: Brill, 2012), 696.
[38]Ibid., 9, 19.

all things."[39] What does this mean? Aertsen is suggesting, following Thomas, that the transcendentals are those properties that all things possess by virtue of their participation in God's perfection. Though universal concepts participate in their source, a robust Creator/creature distinction is not thereby compromised, for, as O'Rourke reminds us, there is an "abyss-like infinity which lies between the transcendent" and therefore, I would add, the being to whom are ascribed the transcendentals "and the beings which are the domain of our knowledge."[40] That which is essential in God is what is intellectually abstractable from creatures. What is essential in God is the cause of creatures, and is communicable, indeed compatible with them and predicated of them, in varying degrees. Created things supply us with the means by which to speak of God in accordance with the limits of natural human reason, but created things do not supply us with knowledge, for example, of the procession of the persons in God. Such knowledge is scripturally derived through and through. That said, the knowledge of God obtained through creatures does not contradict what we learn through the history of salvation, however woefully inadequate it may be in relation to revealed principles.

Another way to frame this would be to say that attributes, understood as "transcendent names," have, by their universality, a priority in relation to other attributes, like the three "omnis": omnipotence, omniscience, and omnipresence.[41] Goodness is the preeminent attribute of God, one of the reasons being that all else participates in it. God is the principle of principles by virtue of his goodness, which is manifested in many things. Sonderegger enriches our understanding of this when she writes, "metaphysical Compatibilism says that God remains who He Is, the Holy One of Israel, in His Presence to his cosmos and people."[42] She goes on to describe "such compatibilism . . . [as] the doctrine of creation."[43] Her statements lend support to our account of what is essential in God as that which is transcendental. That God remains who he is in relationship to us is the basis for

---

[39] Ibid., 20.

[40] O'Rourke, *Metaphysics of Aquinas*, 18.

[41] I am at a loss as to how to classify the "omni" attributes. They are absolute, yes, but are incommunicable, unlike other attributes. Goodness is both absolute and communicable and as such is rightly described as a transcendental.

[42] Sonderegger, *Systematic Theology*, 1:84, 87.

[43] Ibid., 108.

glimpsing how what is not God participates in him. The attributes of God—the transcendentals—are communicable and as such furnish us with the context for the doctrine of creation and God's ongoing presence to the created order.

Talk of the essential attributes as transcendentals is illuminated via the language of "compatibilism." When we describe God's attributes, we are describing, in part, God's "own Gracious Nearness" to that which is not God.[44] The Lord God is in "His nature and Person" present, which, following Sonderegger, is his "Humble Presence in all existents."[45] The Lord is not just present but present as the Lord in that which he has made; what exists, in other words, exists in him without containing him. When we talk about transcendentals, we unfold how God is present to us as God. As Sonderegger avers, God's relations to his creatures are "a form of Presence, a Transcendental Presence."[46] Put again, God does not communicate notional attributes—the attributes that distinguish and constitute the three—but his essential attributes are communicable to creatures "in their own mode and concrete life."[47] When we take Thomas's distinction between the one and the three seriously, we see the extent to which "God relates to the world through His Nature as well."[48] The transcendentals—the essential attributes—just are God's nature relating to what is not God, the created order. God indwells the world with his goodness, oneness, truth, and beauty, remaining sovereign, "always more," unparticipated and yet "admixing Its own Being and Light with our own small light."[49] Or, in Thomas's words, because "the first goodness is the effective cause of all goods, it must imprint its likeness upon the things produced; and so each thing will be called good by reason of an inherent form because of the likeness of the highest good implanted in it."[50] God makes good things because God is good, implanting his goodness in what he has made, and present to what he makes as the good by which it is made.

---

[44] Ibid., 336.
[45] Ibid., 442, 350.
[46] Ibid., 350.
[47] Ibid., 353.
[48] Ibid., 418.
[49] Ibid., 457, 462.
[50] Aquinas, *Truth* 21.4.

As a way of consolidating the insights of this dense section and of bringing it to a close, we appeal to Augustine. When Augustine considers himself in relation to God, he sees that he has nothing good in himself that is not also—and preeminently and superabundantly—true of God. All Augustine's "good qualities" are God's in utter excess. Any good, any truth, any beauty, any unity, any holiness, any righteousness, any wisdom, and any purity that he might have is God's and supremely so. "You yourself are all my good qualities."[51] If Augustine is right, as I think he is, then I suspect that we have another vantage point on the transcendentals, one that provides a nice conclusion to our discussion. The transcendentals are intelligible in relation to ourselves, but only as we prayerfully consider ourselves in relationship to God. As God's likenesses, what we have and enjoy—life, existence, being—God has without remainder. Unlike us, God is what he has. He is his own goodness, whereas the goodness we have—by virtue of being God's likenesses—is had in a participated sense. God does not have his divinity from another, but all that we have is from another, and what we have as instantiations of created goodness is God's by nature.

If such is the case, then, the attributes of God, in particular those prior by virtue of their universality, are present in what exists. The attributes—what is true of the one God in complete simplicity—provide us with a way of understanding God's relationship to creatures, especially how creatures are said to be *of* and *in* God. We turn now to Psalm 36:9 as a kind of test case whereby we see the priority of the essential and common attributes in relation to what is relation-specific and how the former structure God's relationship to creation.

PSALM 36:9 AS TEST CASE

Psalm 36:9 helps us to see something of how this works exegetically: "In your light we see light." Light is true of God's essence. God shines by the light he is, which is identical to himself, unparticipated and inexhaustible. This light is light that "a rational animal participates in . . . [via] natural knowledge; for the natural reason of a person is nothing other than the reflected gleam of divine clarity in the soul: and the [condition of being] 'after the image of

---

[51] Augustine, *Conf*, 182.

God' is an account of this clarity."[52] Thomas's dense sentence reminds us that reason, which is proper to us, participates in this light, what Thomas calls "the reflected gleam of divine clarity." Because we are created after the image of God we are able to reason naturally and to reflect the gleam of divine clarity. But there is more, including the "light of grace" and "the light of glory," which is Jesus Christ, "who is the light of light: and so is the light that is the true God."[53] Thomas's christological reading of Psalm 36:9 is instructive because it illustrates the previous section, reminding us that we see in relation to God's light. God is the primary actor by which we see what is true. The same is true of God's goodness: by virtue of it do we see what is good. And we know by faith that Jesus Christ is the very goodness of all that is good and so is the goodness that is the true God. Any light, any truth, any goodness that we may possess is the Lord's.

When we know God "by faith and hope," and see now "in light by faith" in relation to the light of light, Jesus Christ, we anticipate the day when "we will see him as he is" (1 Jn 3:2; cf. 1 Jn 4:12). The light that is God is God's own relation to us. God's goodness is his own relation to us. Because God is light, we see; because God is good, we are. The light of God is natural to us, and although at the same time it utterly surpasses us, we are, nonetheless, fit for it. Created light points us to the light that is uncreated, by which we see other lights. The uncreated light that is God lightens all things. This is demonstrated in Psalm 36:10-11 that the Lord would "continue your steadfast love" such that "the foot of the arrogant" and "the hand of the wicked" would not hold sway. The psalmist prays that God would be God in relationship to those who do not acknowledge him as God and so crush their arrogance.

Psalm 43:3 amplifies much of what Thomas has said in relation to Psalm 36:9. "O send out your light and your truth; let them lead me; let them bring me to your holy hill and to your dwelling" (Ps 43:3). *Light* and *truth* are themselves goods, indeed divine goods. But we cannot seek them without God's help and assistance; rather, we must be led to them. Not surprisingly, Thomas reminds us that these goods are taken with respect to Christ, echoing John 1:9; 14:6 respectively. According, "light" and "truth" are essential names of God; they denote what God is *in se* and are true of God in

---

[52]Aquinas, *In Ps* 36, trans. Gregory Sadler.
[53]Ibid.

a transcendent sense and of us as lesser lights and truths insofar as we are related to God. These attributes structure and clarify our relationship to God. The psalmist is asking God to send forth what he is. Incredibly, in the incarnation, light and truth dwell visibly among us in Jesus Christ. The incarnation is the answer to the psalmist's prayer. Light and truth are in Christ, said only of God in the deepest sense, but they extend from God to us, most concretely in Jesus Christ, God the Son, in and through God the Holy Spirit.

If this be so, then, we have something of a "double perspective" on offer here.[54] Light and truth are what God is, on the one hand, and they are Jesus Christ, on the other. Light and truth are said essentially and christologically and, furthermore, of the law, for example in Proverbs 6:23, "For the commandment is a lamp and the teaching a light," and Psalm 119:142, 160, "Your law is the truth. . . . The sum of your word is truth." Accordingly, the Lord is light and truth, the Lord enacts his light and truth among us in Jesus Christ, and the Lord points us to his light and truth through the light and truth of the law. Or, the Lord is good in an essentialist sense, does good in an incarnational sense, and advances us in good via the law whose very goodness he is.

Conclusion

In this chapter I have defended Thomas's treatment of the one essence of God in advance of the Trinity of persons, based on consideration of God's goodness, as a helpful way of considering the relation between what is substantial and relational in God. We have seen that Thomas's architectonic helps us, among other things, to attend to the Psalter's statements regarding what God is. Indeed, Scripture differentiates the two perspectives on God without separation and without confusion. We saw, in the case of goodness, how it is not only coextensive with God's essence but also true of goods imprinted as they are with God's likeness. Goodness is, moreover, also appropriated to the Spirit by virtue of the Spirit's procession in God, having a kind of pneumatological density.

Thomas's architectonic encourages, I argued, a faithful reading of New Testament language regarding participation in the divine nature or essence. We do not participate in the immanent processions themselves, for they are

---

[54]Emery, "Essentialism or Personalism," 172.

incommunicable. We do not share in the begetting of the Son from the Father; participation language does not work on a notional level. Instead, the language of participation in the divine nature makes best sense in relation to what is essential, absolute, and as such, transcendental. We share by nature and grace in what is God's through the saving works accomplished by the missions of Son and Spirit. Accordingly, we considered the concordance of nature and works. God does good precisely because he is good. Goodness is inherently communicable, desirable, and perfective. I explained how Thomas's architectonic illustrates how what is essential is in fact what is in transcendental. Essential and absolute attributes have a priority with respect to incommunicable attributes such as the "omnis" and a greater universality. God is, as Sonderegger avers, his own relation to the world, setting himself, as he is, in relation to us.

Thomas's arrangement is commendable based on consideration of God's goodness. He reminds us that trinitarian doctrine cannot do all the work. In fact, the treatise on the one God has systematic priority in relation to that whereby God is. All God's works in creation, providence, reconciliation, and redemption express God, the goodness that is "the same as His essence."[55] Such goodness is one with their immanent acts—that whereby each is—and is thus the very originating and perfecting cause of creation.[56] But there is an order and an asymmetry between the two spheres of discourse that I think Scripture (and the tradition) would have us take seriously. Creation, providence, and perfection: these are works supremely worthy of God's goodness. This is a goodness compatible with us and which sets forth the ineffable glory of the triune God, and is best described in advance of the distinction of persons and their missions.

Having considered goodness in a metaphysical register and with respect to the proper order of theological inquiry when it comes to the doctrine of God's attributes and the Trinity, we now move toward an account of the good God does. We think about the manner in which God wills the good, hates iniquity, and makes us, who have deflected from our supreme good, good once again. This involves paying close attention to the goodness of God's acts and how God, in manifesting his reign among us, reigns in the very goodness he is.

---

[55]Aquinas, *Truth* 21.5.
[56]Aquinas, *Truth* 21.5.

FOUR

You Do Good

T HE FOCUS OF THIS CHAPTER is the good that God does. I shall
argue that to think responsibly about this, we must think about God's
attributes, which are, as we have observed, identical with God's acts toward
the inside, the eternal processions: the Father is good, the Son is good, the
Spirit is good, not three goodnesses but one. Such mindfulness befits the
pattern of the Psalms. The Psalms very often celebrate God in advance of a
particular deed, moving from the former toward recollection of and praise
for things done. Accordingly, we discuss some of the primary acts of God
depicted in the Psalter, mindful of their inward basis and what they teach us
regarding God's goodness.

By way of anticipation of ground to be covered, the reason why "the LORD
watches over the way of the righteous" and judges "the way of the wicked"
(Ps 1:6)—two outward acts—is that, as Origen writes, unrighteousness and
evil "are unworthy of his contemplation."[1] God does not know them because
God only knows and loves in us what is of himself. What God does, in an
inward sense, is contemplate and love what is true of himself, for example,
righteousness. What God does in an economic sense, is, therefore, an
outward expression of what and who God eternally is. God knows, cares,
and watches what is not himself.

This is hard for us to grasp. When we think of God's acts, we tend to consider first what God does for us and for our salvation. This is not mistaken.

---

[1]Origen, in *Psalms 1–50*, ed. Craig A. Blaising and Carmen S. Hardin, ACCS 7 (Downers Grove,
IL: InterVarsity Press, 2008), 10.

The task ahead, I suggest, is to consider how his fellowship-creating works—his acts toward the outside—assume and point to his acts toward the inside. God's work has a foundation in God himself. In accounting for why God acts as he does, we are bound to what and who God is. It is this we need to think through first. God knows, understands, and wills what is good—that is, God's very self. Even more basically, what God knows in himself is what is coterminous with being, which is goodness itself. Thus "the way of the wicked will perish," and "the way of the righteous" is watched over. God attends to what God knows, which is, in the case of Psalm 1:6, righteousness. This is important to explain at the outset because it demonstrates how the weight of our account in this chapter remains with God *in se*. What God does is derivative of what God knows, and what God knows and loves is the good that he is. Accordingly, the way in which we account for God's doings not only utilizes the previous chapter but also amplifies it. Divine activity (again) has its inward and outward dimensions, the former functioning as the principle of intelligibility and source for the latter, the latter providing the means by which we are made over into knowers and lovers of all that the Lord is as Father, Son, and Spirit.

Put differently, God does not know what is inimical to Godself, whereas so very often we dwell on and do what is inimical to our identity as God's beloved children. So much of what we do and see bears little or no relation to our identity as the baptized. "Beloved, do not imitate what is evil but imitate what is good. Whoever does good is from God; whoever does evil has not seen God" (3 Jn 11), thus the need for a way of life—discipleship—that diminishes the gap between what we do and see and who we are in relation to God. In God there is, thankfully, no gap between being and knowledge. Because God is completely self-sufficient, God needs no help in knowing himself, whereas we, of course, do if we are to know ourselves truly. God knows the righteous in relation to Godself, indeed contemplates them in relation to what he contemplates in himself. This is to say that because God has goodness abiding in him, God does good. The acts of God cannot be detached from what is true of God *in se*. The essential attributes of God are his relation to the world. God lavishes good on us, for inherent communicability is one facet of the good that God is. God is good *per se*, and so loves created goods in the good he is. Augustine, commenting on Psalm 16:2, puts it this way: "What in any case are my goods, if not what I have been given by you? And how can the one by whom every good is given be in need of any good?"[2] This chapter explores this great truth, namely, that the good God does is the good of one who is not "in need of any good."

WILLING THE GOOD

God gives what is good. God is not only the subject and object of good but its agent and end too. Divine goodness has the character of a cause and an end, being as such continually present to what it causes. Let us dwell on this for a while. The Psalter teaches us that the good God issues blessings. We see this, for example, in Psalm 21:3, 6: "For you meet him [the king] with rich blessings. . . . You bestow on him blessings forever; you make him glad with the joy of your presence." The good that is God is not occasioned by anything outside God, in this case the king. God meets his anointed with blessings precisely because God precedes his anointed in blessing. The king cannot begin in blessing *per se* because in and of himself he has no blessing from which to begin. God precedes David in goodness, and because he precedes David, David says, "surely goodness and mercy shall follow me all the days of my life" (Ps 23:6). Indeed, the fact that God meets and precedes us in goodness itself teaches us something about God, namely, that God wills other forms—likenesses—of his uncreated goodness. God's goodness is the kind of goodness that delights in not only creating and preserving but also perfecting creaturely goodness. Thomas gets at this when he says, "Good is said to be *diffusive of self and being*."[3]

Herein lies our first key dogmatic insight with respect to God's acts. God's acts in relation to us follow on God's will, are a consequence of God's will. Now, God is his will, for God always wills himself: "the divine willing," says Thomas, "is also His being."[4] Accordingly, the Psalter does not talk about God's relationship to the world in emanationist terms; it is not fitting to talk about the good that meets the king in Psalm 21:3 as a kind of overflowing. Rather, God's relationship to his anointed and to the people as a whole is more personal, inasmuch as he wills that what he is in an essential sense be

---

[2]Augustine, in Blaising and Hardin, *Psalms 1–50*, 121.
[3]Aquinas, *SCG* 1.37.
[4]Aquinas, *SCG* 1.73.

theirs as well in a creaturely, that is, participated, sense. For example, when we pray that God's will be done, we "will" ourselves in relation to God, who in turn may then be said to will us in relation to himself.

God does good by willing that our will be subject to his goodness. "Good and upright is the LORD; therefore he instructs sinners in the way" (Ps 25:8). The goodness of God "changes what we *can* say to God, and so changes what can be said of ourselves."[5] As we speak, sing, and pray the Psalter, our voice is united with God's voice in and through Jesus Christ, allowing us to say new and better things about God and ourselves in relation to him. We learn in the Spirit to say things we could never have said before, such as "good and upright is the LORD," precisely as a fruit of divine instruction. We testify to one who accomplishes our good by teaching us the way, which is, ultimately, Jesus Christ. Herein we move beyond cognitive categories to that of taste, indeed experience. Basil, commenting on Psalm 34:8, "O taste and see that the LORD is good," puts it strikingly: "So the goodness of the heavenly Word cannot be clearly taught by doctrines, unless, examining to a greater extent the dogmas of truth, we are able to comprehend by our own experience the goodness of the Lord."[6] The good God does has to be perceived and experienced—tasted—before it can be described, doctrinally. Indeed, without experience of God's goodness, the good done by God remains inaccessible. Insofar as we taste through faith the good that God is and does, our existence itself becomes a kind of likeness to his goodness.

The first point we make, then, in this chapter, is that discourse about God's acts makes sense only in relation to God's will. The good that God does in relationship to what is not God is a matter of his will, and his will is identical to his being, goodness itself. Acts toward the outside express his will that is one with his being, which means that there is nothing God does that is not good.

HATING INIQUITY

Unlike the wicked, who do not reject evil, God is steadfast in goodness, hating iniquity. So Augustine maintains, "Hate sin and iniquity, so that you may unite yourself to God, who will hate it with you."[7] God hates what he

---

[5]Rowan Williams, "Augustine and the Psalms," *Interpretation* 58, no. 1 (2004): 18.
[6]Basil, in Blaising and Hardin, *Psalms 1–50*, 262.
[7]Augustine, in Blaising and Hardin, *Psalms 1–50*, 280.

does not do and cannot know, that is, iniquity. God does not hate the created order—what is not God. Instead, God hates what he has made insofar as it embraces iniquity and so is no longer a likeness to him. But that hatred is redemptive in nature. God refuses to know—and to thus grant being—to what has no reality, ontologically speaking. Thus God does good by turning sinners—that is, all of us—from evil. Evil can never be a sign for God, whereas we can be a sign for God insofar as we journey back to God by God. The believer can by faith reproduce "Christ's acceptance of the fallen and struggling condition to which we are without exception destined."[8] Her life can become a sign pointing to Christ; she may live in such a way that God knows her. The same, however, can never be said of evil. God does not know it, for if God did, it would have being, which it cannot possibly have. Evil is no thing; Satan by his very nature lies. In other words, God "acknowledges" the devil, but does not know—to say nothing of love—the devil. If God were to know the devil, that would be a matter of granting a kind of legitimacy to the devil that the devil simply does not have. "When he lies, he speaks according to his own nature, for he is a liar and the father of lies" (Jn 8:44). Therefore it is good news that God cannot know or see evil. That would be to grant it a status beyond the negative, to infer its (positive) being and status. So Thomas asserts, "Therefore nothing that is not goodness can be in Him: and consequently evil can in nowise be in Him."[9]

God knows and wills what is commensurate with himself, the good. This makes sense of God's hatred of iniquity, descriptions of which are prevalent throughout the Psalms. By virtue of hating evil, God acts in such a way as to refuse existence to what is opposed to God. The claim that follows is that God by grace shapes us into the kind of people who hate with him what is evil and love with him what is good.

To those who ask, God will supply them with a spirit whereby they learn and grow in his goodness. "My flesh faints for you" (Ps 63:1). Through fasting, for example, we become those sorts of people whom God loves.[10] If we do not believe God loves us and respond to his claim on us, we simply

---

[8]Williams, "Psalms," 26.

[9]Aquinas, *SCG* 1.39.

[10]This is an Augustinian way of thinking: "So we needed to be persuaded how much God loves us, and what sort of people he loves." Augustine, in *Psalms 51–150*, ed. Quentin F. Wesselschmidt, ACCS 8 (Downers Grove, IL: InterVarsity Press, 2008), 68.

exist as the sort of people whom God hates, people enthralled with iniquity and evil. Inasmuch as we are persuaded that God loves us, however, and understand what sorts of people he loves, we become good. God is the agent who makes us into the kinds of people who entreat him and love him. "Truly God is good to the upright" (Ps 73:1).

MAKING GOOD

In willing what is good, the Lord makes us worthy of receiving his goodness and love. Nonetheless, we cannot love God, who is unseen, and thus become worthy of God until the eyes of our heart are cleansed; only then do we begin to see the unseen and enjoy with the angels "that unchangeable substance."[11] Put differently, one must become morally fit so as to receive God's gifts. This is, of course, not a semi-Pelagian matter, as if we in and of ourselves could make ourselves worthy. Rather, God, working in and through us to accomplish his purposes for us, makes us into those worthy to love him. Augustine's genius lies in part in reminding us of what is abundantly clear, biblically speaking. Inasmuch as we increase in the Spirit's fruits are we made worthy to receive God's good works, thereby avoiding evil and increasing in good. Such is the noncompetitive—or compatibilist—character of God's relation to us. We sow so as to increase, yes, in the Spirit's fruit, and that we sow and increase is the Lord's doing.

God does good by keeping himself for us. Worship and love God freely, Augustine reminds us, "and you will receive God himself; God, you see, is keeping himself for you to enjoy him."[12] God does not keep himself for everyone but only for those whom he is making worthy to love himself. God is a generous and lavish giver, giving virtue and perfecting in the virtue he gives, but that is true only of those who stick to him. Augustine writes, "This will constitute the perfect and eternal wisdom, as it will constitute the truly happy life, because to attain it is to attain the eternal and supreme good, and to stick close to God forever is the sum of our good."[13] Attaining the happy life is a matter of attaining "supreme good," which is God, "the sum of our good." We see the extent, then, to which receiving the good that God gives,

---

[11]Augustine, in Wesselschmidt, *Psalms 51–150*, 112.
[12]Augustine, in Wesselschmidt, *Psalms 51–150*, 113.
[13]Ibid.

which is ultimately Godself, involves intimacy with God. What is also surprising is how things other than God may function as the means by which we who love the Lord God are made good. The Lord would have us love what he has made, but not as an end in itself, only rather in order that we might love him the more. Created goods are the means by which we enjoy God in this life. But in the life to come, that enjoyment will be immediate and uninterrupted; no longer will there be need for us to be made better.

It is unusual for us moderns to think that sticking close to God is intrinsic to making progress in speaking well of the deep things of God and of all things in relation to God. But for a premodern theologian such as Augustine, it is simply assumed. One must cling to what one speaks of if indeed the Lord God is the one spoken of. For example, in discussing the place of prudence, fortitude, temperance, and justice, Augustine reminds us of how the good itself works, thereby encouraging the traits necessary to cling to itself. God is the beginning, means, and end whereby we come to God. "The Lord will give what is good" (Ps 85:12). Prudence, fortitude, temperance, and justice are some of the goods God gives whereby we cling "to the good that cannot be lost . . . cannot be parted . . . in which there is no corruption."[14]

I think we can now begin to appreciate the main point of this section. As we describe the good that God does ("you do good") in terms of his will and its creative character, we are simply speaking about the *are* ("you are good") of the previous chapter but from a different perspective. Just by being himself, God does good, as God is his own relation to the world.[15] God wills created goodness and makes the bad good by merely being himself in relation to them. God is so secure in the good that he is that he can and does shower blessings on the just and the unjust, without, of course, condoning the unjust. Herein, we can begin to appreciate why the psalmist prays, "Do good, O Lord, to those who are good" (Ps 125:4). This is not a self-righteous prayer. Instead, it is the voice of one who has made some progress in the good and would like to be made better. God's acts are acts of will, coterminous as they are with his being, and those acts make good; they are generative of good, resting as they do on the supreme good.

---

[14]Ibid.
[15]See Katherine Sonderegger, *Systematic Theology*, vol. 1, *The Doctrine of God* (Minneapolis: Fortress, 2015), 77, wherein she writes, "God just is His own relation to the world."

God's judgments help us appreciate the severe character of his goodness. God resists the indolent, those who would hold his goodness in dispute, but gives grace to the humble. In judging our infidelity God continues to instruct us regarding the sort of goodness God is—that is, an active goodness whose relation to us is one of will. Indeed, our indolence functions as the occasion whereby God teaches us about the kind of good he is, which is a just good. God thus does good by using "any sort of occasion" to draw us to him, and God is, thankfully, able to use any sort of occasion because God "is willingly whatever he is."[16]

THE GREATNESS OF GOD'S ACTS

As I explained in the previous chapter, God's "act of being is pure."[17] God's being is neither a participated being nor a being that awaits actualization. "By his one simple act of being," God is all that he is.[18] To put this in a trinitarian idiom, God is paternity, filiation, spiration, and procession. The triune God contains no potentiality, has no appetites, lacks nothing, is self-moved, has no before and after, and is subject neither to generation nor corruption. God "is willingly whatever he is. . . . [He is] willingly eternal, unchangeable, truthful, blessed and undefeatable."[19]

The truth that God is always himself in relation to us is good news. This means, in part, that the God we come to love in Jesus and in the Spirit, and who does as he pleases, is not changed by our utter indifference to his purposes. Yes, he is grieved, but our indifference does not make him other than he is. The Lord does not manipulate to achieve the outcome of his promise. Rather, God remains happy and undefeatable despite our very best efforts to grieve him. Because God is willingly whatever he is, he is free to be and reaches out to us in the Son and Spirit, thereby achieving our salvation and redemption. Accordingly, when we talk about the acts of God toward the outside, we note acts that communicate who and what God is. When we contemplate God's acts, and when we receive their benefits in faith, we praise the one true God. All the good things God does point in this one

---

[16]Augustine, in Wesselschmidt, *Psalms 51–150*, 370, 374.
[17]Aquinas, *Truth* 3.21.5.
[18]Ibid.
[19]Augustine, in Wesselschmidt, *Psalms 51–150*, 374.

direction: "His greatness is unsearchable" (Ps 145:3). Thus our talk of God does not promise "comprehension" but rather gestures toward "a difference of unlikeness in that which is without figure, or limit, or size or quantity."[20] The unsearchable greatness of God is such that we do not have that greatness in reach. On this side of glory, we have his promises, however, the foundation of which is an unsearchable goodness and greatness.

God's acts, his works toward the outside, while they indicate God's nature and tutor us regarding who and what he is, do not bring about comprehension of that nature. As Chrysostom notes, they do not allow us to "encompass" God.[21] Attributes do indicate God's nature: goodness, as I have argued all along, is the preeminent attribute of God, convertible with God's very being. But goodness as an attribute does not express who and what is infinitely good in a manner that is entirely transparent—"for now we see in a mirror, dimly" (1 Cor 13:12). We are given to know and love a greatness that is unsearchable. In order to receive that greatness in a mode befitting us as creatures, we need to apply ourselves "to sound teaching [Titus 1:9], in other words Christian teaching."[22] Insofar as we become that "sort of person" are we able to receive sound teaching via applying ourselves to it.[23] To put this in the idiom of the Psalter, God's good Spirit must lead us "on a level path" (Ps 143:10) if we are indeed to apply ourselves to greatness so unsearchable (Ps 145:3).

THE REIGN OF GOODNESS

The Psalter is such a rich source for dogmatic reflection because it relativizes any divide between the *are* and the *do*. The Psalter refers extensively to the reign of God, to God as one who reigns. Creation and the ruling over of what he has made, especially his wayward covenant people, are the two main acts of God described in the Psalter. However, there is not a watertight distinction in the Psalter between God and his reign. While God is not

---

[20] Gregory of Nyssa, in Wesselschmidt, *Psalms 51–150*, 411.
[21] St. John Chrysostom writes, "For no pagan ever dared to set down a definition of the divine essence or to encompass it with a name." See *On the Incomprehensible Nature of God*, trans. Paul W. Harkins, The Fathers of the Church: A New Translation 72 (Washington, DC: Catholic University of America Press, 1982), 153.
[22] Augustine, *On Christian Teaching*, trans. R. P. H. Green (Oxford: Oxford University Press, 1997), 146.
[23] Ibid.

collapsed into his reign, James Mays notes the extent to which "the reign of God is God" and continues, "the very self of the Lord is all this."[24] This is "the truth for which no words are ever quite adequate."[25] Mays's useful comments remind us why it is fitting to distinguish description of God's being from God's acts toward the outside. "The reign of God is God as salvation . . . is God as life."[26] Just so, God's works can never be uncoupled from their source, God himself. God's deeds make God's reign known, something that the Psalms eloquently express. However, God's great deeds and the reign they demonstrate is *God's*. The content of the book is (again) metaphysical.[27] There is an understanding of God that undergirds the entire Psalter, intrinsic to which is this: the good that God does is his very self, and this good is, of course, unsearchably good.

The Psalms are one of the key means by which the divine rule is represented in and to us. Insofar as these ancient prayers become ours does God's rule nourish us. We are perfected by God's reign, but the same is not true for God. God's reign does not determine God, but it does form the righteous among us. The way of the righteous, not the wicked, is the way of a people who receive the Psalter's teaching about God with open arms, with praise, in the form of either lament or imprecation. Put differently, God is not enriched by his reign. God is neither expanded by the acceptance of his reign nor diminished by rejection of it. It is the righteous who learn to love a God who neither finds nor loses himself in relation to his people's lament, praise, and thanksgiving, however strong or lacking they may be.[28]

---

[24]Mays, *Psalms*, 36.
[25]Ibid.
[26]Ibid.
[27]Compare Sonderegger, who writes that the Bible "teaches content and Subject matter we can only call, 'metaphysical.'" *Systematic Theology*, 1:23.
[28]Herein lies a major objection to two recent contemporary commentaries on the Psalms, both by leading Psalms scholars. Neither acknowledges what kind of person you need to be in order to receive the Psalter's testimony to God, embedded as it is in lament giving rise to prayer and praise. One commentary is Mays's, as noted above, which provides an otherwise theologically illuminating introduction to the Psalms; the other is Brueggemann's and Bellinger's. The latter is less theologically motivated, saying things such as that the Psalms are a "vibrant expression of prayer and faith as well as vibrant portrayals of the divine and human encounter for faith communities." See Walter Brueggemann and William H. Bellinger Jr., *Psalms*, NCBC (Cambridge: Cambridge University Press, 2014), 8. While that is not false, it does not say nearly enough. The Psalms do not simply express and portray an encounter. Rather, the Psalms, by virtue of the powerful working of their object—that is, God—facilitate the encounter. One must be encountered before one can learn to speak of a God who has nothing to gain from the encounter itself. Put simply,

The human "I," united as it is to the voice of Christ and the Spirit, plays no constitutive role in God's life. The creature does not make the Creator; instead, the Creator is the principle of, the cause of, and the perfector of creatures. Whether it is King David's profoundly uneven representation of God's reign or our equally compromised reception of and witness to the one who fulfills David's reign, Jesus Christ, God is not thereby affected. So Augustine explains, "There is absolutely no way corruption can injure our God—no act of will, no necessity, no unforeseen chance—since he is God and what he wills for himself is good, and he is that same good. Whereas to be corrupted is not good."[29] Augustine's point is that the realization of God's reign among us, which is good, is what God wills for himself. The good that God is refers fundamentally to God himself. Existing and willing are one and the same for God, as is the case with being and doing. What God wills for himself is the good he is and loves, and God wills to communicate the good he is to created goods, to what is not God, most amazingly, by re-attaching us to himself in Jesus Christ.

We are not God. On this side of the fall, the gap between what we are—God's creatures—and what we will indicates how very corrupt we are. In our pride we think that we play at least some role in the constitution of our Creator, perhaps that our willing what our Creator wills for us involves a gain to our Creator. Inasmuch as we learn to love our Creator as our Creator, however, we leave such nonsense behind.

When we describe God's acts, what God does, our discourse assumes God *in se*. What God does from eternity is know, love, and will himself. Because God is God, he is always what he wills. Accordingly, God's relations with us are relations in which he wills that his reign be known and loved among us. God's relations take place (again) on the level of will. The God who wills his reign to take shape among us is, in so doing, willing himself in relation to us. Thus when Mays states, "The reign of God is God," he is pointing toward a venerable truth.[30] The Lord is king. He wills to be king over his people, to have David represent his kingship, for such a will

---

both commentaries' introductions say little about the primary purpose of the Psalter, which is to kindle love for God.

[29] Augustine, *Conf*, 114-15.

[30] Mays, *Psalms*, 36.

is exactly commensurate with his existence as the Lord. To put this in a Thomisitic idiom, his operations are never other than his substance. When we pray that God would reign among us, that activity does not bespeak newness on God's part. God always reigns. Rather, we are praying that we would be truly related to God as the one who reigns.

To put this another way, the Psalms do things to us. "Listen to the sound of my cry, my King and my God, for to you I pray" (Ps 5:2). What the Psalms do is kindle genuine love of God, a God who has no king, who cries to no one, who is not in need of prayer. Being God and being king are one and the same for God, which is not to say that Scripture confuses or conflates being God and being king of the nations—works of God are just that, works. Rather, the point is that for God to be himself is for God to be king in relation to us. There is a perfect "fit" between an essential name (goodness) and a temporal title (king).

For us, however, our being creatures and our being creatures that learn to cry out to God are not one and the same. Confession of God, though the most natural thing for us to do, does not, as absurd as this seems, come naturally to us. Our will, bound in sin, is hostile to God. In God, however, there is no hostility toward himself. Whether we confess "my King and my God" or "my God and my King," the same truth stands: God is incorruptible precisely because he is God and therefore wills for himself what is good, the same good that he is. And insofar as we will what God wills, are we said to have a will that is good.

Goodness and Mercy

We see the importance of learning to cry set forth in David's great prayer for cleansing and pardon, Psalm 51, wherein David cries out "according to your abundant mercy" (Ps 51:1). Why does David not plea according to God's abundant goodness? Why mercy and not goodness? And what is the difference? Thomas's comments are exceedingly helpful in answering these questions and for describing how God does good in relationship to things lacking his goodness. Because David knows God's nature, "he hopes on the mercy of God. . . . Whence Dionysius says that God is the very substance of goodness. And likewise Boethius [says the same] in *On the Trinity*. Whence this mercy of God is nothing other than goodness referred to the driving away of wretchedness."[31] Mercy follows on goodness; mercy is the form goodness acquires when it confronts our wickedness.

The same logic applies to Psalm 5:2, which we noted a moment ago. The rule of God is but the form his goodness acquires when it confronts our disorderliness. We confess that God is good *in se*, but we would not say that mercy or a title such as "king" has the kind of weight in God that goodness has. Mercy only needs to be had by the creature whose transgressions require mercy for their pardon; similarly, God is judge only in relation to peoples and nations who do not love and submit to his rule. Mercy is a decidedly "economic" attribute. It banishes in us what is not good. God does mercy because God is good; but we would not say the reverse. Biblically speaking, we have mercy because we have goodness. Mercy is the goodness that drives away our wretchedness, and acts of mercy indicate the utter incompatibility of God's goodness with our wretchedness.

The works of God are good. What God makes is good and is declared good. "You are good, for they are good."[32] Our declension from the goodness in and by which we are made takes the form of mercy that fills the earth. God's goodness is so excessive that it is revealed to us, in part, in the form of God's deeds of mercy. The relationship between the two is not dialectical; rather, we know and experience God as merciful, as David did, because he is good. Goodness has the most metaphysical weight.

Conclusion

I have argued in this chapter that God's activity has an inward and outward reference. The latter names the substance of God, convertible with the originating relations of the three. This is the principle for God's outward acts of nature and grace. We have noted that God's goodness is the goodness of a God who is pure act, "infinite in His actuality."[33] God is completely complete, wholly realized, the pure act of being itself, whose pure actuality is goodness itself; indeed, God is his own goodness—"God is goodness essentially."[34] Thus when we think about God's acts toward the outside,

---

[31] Aquinas, *In Ps* 51, trans. Ed Redmond.
[32] Augustine, *Conf*, 11.6.
[33] Aquinas, *SCG* 1.43.
[34] Aquinas, *Truth* 3.21.5.

whether they be of nature or grace, the principle for those acts is God's in-finite actuality, who and what God is.

I explained something of how God's relations to what is not God are those of will, the will that is the same as his substance. It is the very greatness of God's acts, specifically the accomplishment of his reign among us, that shows us the unity of what and who he is with what he does, and yet at the same time allows us to distinguish accurately between the former and the latter. God's merciful works communicate his goodness. They show us something of the expansive range of God's goodness when referred to what is lacking in it, in us who have departed from him.

In the next chapter I explore the relationship between God's goodness and creation. I step back from the three dimensions we have considered—*are* (you are good), *do* (you do good), and *teach* (teach me your statutes) in accordance with Psalm 119:68—so as to see what they imply regarding created goods more broadly. I deepen our sense that God is present to all things and has made them in such a way that they exist in him as their subject. I shall explore how created goods are the focal point for further description of the difference between the Creator and the creature and the mapping of the Creator/creature relation.

Excursus: Dietrich Bonhoeffer, a Different Approach

I have learned a great deal from Dietrich Bonhoeffer over the years. In many respects, he remains a valued conversation partner, although I find myself at times moving in a quite different direction, having, for the most part, passed through his school.

What do I mean? From the outset, the obvious needs to be said: Bon-hoeffer is not a systematic theologian. As with one of his great teachers, Martin Luther, he is an occasional theologian, having, like Luther, written in various modes so as to draw attention to the Word of God even as the world and the church imploded around him. Moreover, Bonhoeffer is not a metaphysically motivated theologian. There are many tracts of the Christian tradition that are either unknown to him or that he simply does not engage. For example, Bonhoeffer assumes the immanent Trinity but says very little about that doctrine. His concern is christological. Bonhoeffer recognizes that without the immanent Trinity, Christology is reduced to soteriology but says little more than that.[35] I mention this at the outset simply because I want to make it clear that I am not criticizing him for what he does not do: offer, again, a systematic theology. Rather, I reflect in this excursus on what is gained and lost in what I call Bonhoeffer's "relational" account of God's goodness.

Bonhoeffer's most focused treatment on the goodness of God is found in his *Ethics*, in a splendid manuscript titled "Christ, Reality, and Good." Bonhoeffer's question is simply "What is the will of God?"[36] The answer to the question has, of course, to do with God. Bonhoeffer writes, "the source of my ethical concern will be that God be known as the good [*das Gute*]."[37] The will of God is a matter of God being known as the good. What is good is what is real, and what is most real is God. "Good is the real itself."[38]

"Originally and essentially" speaking, "the good and the real," just as "the person and work," were "one."[39] Bonhoeffer equates what is good (God) with what is real (God). Insofar as God is concerned, what is real and what is good are one. "Only by participating in reality do we also share in the good."[40] When Bonhoeffer thinks of goodness, he thinks of God, and rightly so! However, Bonhoeffer's account of goodness presses more toward goodness understood "as a particular relation and not an attribute."[41] Contrastingly, Thomas writes in *ST* 1.5.3 "inasmuch as they exist, all things are good." For Bonhoeffer, this is inadequate. Indeed, Bonhoeffer discovers in Thomas's work a kind of neutrality. This is problematic, Bonhoeffer avers, for all things are good not so much as a matter of existence but as a matter

---

[35]See Bonhoeffer's fascinating "Outline on Exodus 20:2-3 as a Sermon for Trinity Sunday," in Dietrich Bonhoeffer, *Theological Education at Finkenwalde: 1935-1937*, ed. Victoria J. Barnett and Barbara Wojhoski, DBWE 14 (Minneapolis: Fortress, 2013), 635n10. Bonhoeffer notes therein in his "Outline on Exodus 20:2-3 (Student Notes) as a Sermon for Trinity Sunday" that "preaching on the economic [Trinity] rather than the immanent [Trinity] always risks turning into an outline of the entire doctrine of soteriology, and [the sermon] becomes more a report."

[36]Dietrich Bonhoeffer, *Ethics*, ed. Clifford J. Green, DBWE 6 (Minneapolis: Fortress, 2005), 45.

[37]Bonhoeffer, *Ethics*, DBWE 6:46.

[38]Bonhoeffer, *Ethics*, DBWE 6:50.

[39]Bonhoeffer, *Ethics*, DBWE 6:51.

[40]Bonhoeffer, *Ethics*, DBWE 6:51.

[41]This is Clifford's Green's judgment. See Bonhoeffer, *Ethics*, DBWE 6:50n15. It is worth noting that Bonhoeffer does not underline the first sentence but rather the latter two sentences of Pieper's three-sentence-long thesis, namely, because of his allergy to the language of "being." Pieper's thesis runs: "All obligation is based upon being. Reality is the foundation of ethics. The good is that which is in accord with reality." See Joseph Pieper, *Living the Truth: Reality and the Good: The Truth of All Things*, trans. Stella Lange (San Francisco: Ignatius, 1989), 111.

of *participation*.[42] Good, as with freedom, is understood, "as a particular relation."[43] To say, as does Thomas, that goodness and existence are one and the same is, for Bonhoeffer, not strong enough. What exists must participate in the good in order to be good. Without getting into a discussion about the origins of Bonhoeffer's less than nuanced reading of Thomas, it is important for our purposes to note Bonhoeffer's allergy to Thomas's (perceived) neutrality. For Bonhoeffer, we must participate in the good, not simply assume it.

To emphasize goodness as an attribute as I do would be, in Bonhoeffer's mind, an abstraction. My account, so he would argue, is insufficiently concrete. Bonhoeffer might ask: "Why bother talking about God's goodness *in se* when all we need to concern ourselves with is our relation to God's goodness, indeed the way in which it takes shape among us?" My response to Bonhoeffer would run like this: the claim that the good God makes on us rests on the confession that God is good *in se*, that God is indeed goodness itself. Theology should attend to and indicate the goodness of a God who is good apart from us and who has no need of us, patiently discerning the implications of divine aseity for faith and practice.

Further to the point, without describing God, we do not know to whom the great works of creation, governance, and perfection belong. The works of God whose benefits we receive in faith are just that, *works*. It is important to talk about God, in other words, without pressing immediately to God's works. This is not so as to consider a God who can be known independently of his works, but rather to describe what is true of God in light of the works God does. Bonhoeffer's concern is with the concrete reality of God in Christ, that which is really real. What I am concerned with is the articulation of the foundations of the "central message of the New Testament," foundations that the message assumes are real and that it indicates at various points.[44]

There is an edifying impulse in Bonhoeffer's great manuscript, one that he receives, surprisingly, from the great Thomistic philosopher and ethicist Josef Pieper. With Pieper, Bonhoeffer emphasizes the independence of

---

[42]That Bonhoeffer talks in these terms demonstrates the extent to which he misunderstands Thomas, for whom existence—creaturely existence—is a participated existence.

[43]Bonhoeffer, *Ethics*, DBWE 6:50n15.

[44]Bonhoeffer, *Ethics*, DBWE 6:66.

Reality and the Good—that is, God—with respect to created reality and goods, especially with regard to efforts to realize reality and the good. For Bonhoeffer, Christ is the subject and agent of reality and the good. Bonhoeffer appreciates the extent to which the Lord needs no helpers in bringing the reality and good he is into being. This is not surprisingly an emphasis that is in accord with Thomas (and Barth), and that Bonhoeffer has received from Thomas via Pieper. That said, Bonhoeffer is out of step with Thomas (and Augustine) in terms of his insistence on talking about "reality itself seen and recognized in God," rather than simply God himself and only then "reality itself seen and recognized in God."[45] There is—a more Thomist perspective would argue—a kind of reduction going on. We need to be clear about God if we are to think clearly and faithfully of reality itself seen and recognized in God.

In sum, to his credit Bonhoeffer is happy to talk about the task of ethics as attesting and participating in the God who is good. Where I move beyond Bonhoeffer is in describing the *are* (you are good) as having a priority over the *do* (you do good), not just in an architectonic sense but also insofar as the works of goodness have their principle in God's pure actuality. When it comes to God, Bonhoeffer is all about the *do*. He is a theologian of the good God does. This book is not indifferent to the *do*: after all, this excursus completes a chapter on it. Nonetheless, I explore the *do* as derivative of the *are*. We should want to distinguish between the two, while neither confusing nor separating them. Because God is essentially good and is perpetually in act insofar as he wills the good he is, God, just by being God, "bestows being and goodness on other things."[46]

---

[45]Bonhoeffer, *Ethics*, DBWE 6:53.
[46]Aquinas, *SCG* 1.37.

FIVE

The Good Creator

I N   T H I S   C H A P T E R   W E   E X P L O R E the doctrine of created goods. Not surprisingly, our approach is theocentric. We talk most faithfully about creation by talking about God. The internal basis of creation is God. The doctrine of creation is most intelligible in relation to God. There is something (and not nothing) because of God, specifically God's goodness, which is, as we have noted and shall develop further, intrinsically communicative. The doctrine of creation has one foundation, and that is the supremely good God, whose being and nature are the anchor for understanding why there is something.

Moreover, it is fitting to offer a chapter on creation because when we think about the good that God does, we are naturally led to reflect on the created order. The first thing God does with respect to his works toward the outside is create. In accounting for created goods in relation to God, we have the prime site, as it were, for the articulation of the God/world difference, specifically how goodness is said of each but in a radically different way. Is the created order a wise place to talk about such a difference? Yes.[1] This chapter will explain why, positing some of the gains accrued by thinking through the God/world difference in this way.

The Creator is present to what he has made, and he is present in a particular way, namely, as the cause of what he has made. Although God is a direct object of experience to all that he has made, we do not see God's

---

essence—how he is—in what he has made, for that is not in keeping with the character of God's communication with us, indirect as it is. Nonetheless, we consider what he has made in relation to him who is present to and in it as its cause. We learn with the eyes of faith to see that the world and all that is in it is God's and the very expression of his supreme goodness. Creation is open to its Creator, its cause—indeed, it declares its Creator; the created order shouts out that it is made and kept in relation to another, the Lord God. As we shall see, the Psalter encourages just such a train of thought.

In talking about creation in relation to God, and more specifically God's presence in and to what God he has made, we continue to pursue, with Thomas's help, a rigorous account of God's attributes. We want to understand the goodness of what God has made solely with reference to God, as having "nothing in it that is not received from the outpouring act of the creator."[2] The fundamental reason why there is anything at all is what Thomas calls the "mere bounty" of God: God "brought things into being, not as though it were due to them, but out of mere bounty," and to talk of bounty is to talk of goodness: "nothing but His goodness moves God to the production of creatures."[3] We shall explore in this chapter the goodness of God as the basic principle for understanding creation, and creation as the basic point for mapping the God/world difference. We will also examine something of the theological rationale for creation's fecundity, the relationship between being and causality, creation's openness to its Creator, and the priority of the person of the Father for thinking truthfully about creation's origin and end.

An Act of Will

Creation is an act of will on the part of God. God loves, understands, and wills himself in relation to himself—this we have seen. In loving, understanding, and willing himself, moreover, God wills other things "by His intellect and will."[4] This is important to note at the outset so as to honor the nonnecessary character of creation. God creates what is other than himself

---

[2]Thomas Joseph White, OP, *The Incarnate Lord: A Thomistic Study in Christology* (Washington, DC: Catholic University of America Press, 2015), 118.
[3]Aquinas, *SCG* 2.46.
[4]Aquinas, *SCG* 2.23.

through himself. God does this not to fill some kind of lack but rather because God's goodness is by nature communicative and generative. The language of intellect and will is also important because of its trinitarian resonances. The Father creates by the Son (his intellect) and by his Spirit (his will). Another way to say this is that God does not have being in relation to what he has made, for God is pure act, wholly actual.[5] Creation does not decide "that something accrues to God anew, and consequently that He is changed essentially or accidentally."[6] If this were the case, God would not be supremely good. Creation is radically contingent and has no other reason for being than God's great goodness.

Creation is what God wills into being through his Spirit. God is good *per se* and is not made good in relation to other things. Why is there something and not nothing? Is short, this is because God wills to share the good he is with other things. His goodness is ground of creation, and the very principle of his love for creatures. The doctrine of creation is therefore a derivative doctrine in relation to the doctrine of God's attributes. Its ground has to do with God's life. The doctrine of the divine goodness supplies the ongoing principle of intelligibility, enabling us to understand not only creation's foundation but also its teleological character "so that it participate His end."[7] Accordingly, discourse on creation is not confined to "origins" but includes "means" and "ends" as well. The created order is made, conserved, and perfected in such a way that it may participate in its source, preserver, and end. As we noted in the previous chapter, the doctrine of creation is inclusive of the doctrine of providence, and the doctrine of God's goodness is inclusive of both creation and preservation.

What does this mean for the Creator/creature distinction? God does not have a beginning and end, whereas created goods do. God is always identical to his loving, understanding, and willing, his being as Father, Son, and Spirt. These take place eternally, *in se*, whereas our willing, understanding, and loving—if we are to truly will, understand, and love—require the Lord God as their principle. Our loving, understanding, and willing refer to what lies outside us. I, for example, am unable to truly will, understand, and love

---

[5] Aquinas, *SCG* 2.18.
[6] Aquinas, *SCG* 2.12.
[7] Aquinas, *SCG* 2.35.

myself without God as subject. When I will in relation to the Lord, I will truly. But with the Lord, he wills, knows, loves, and understands himself in relation to no other. I can only truly will to be good, for example, in relation to God. He grants me the will to will what is commensurate with him and to know myself as his.

In sum, the first thing to say about the created order is that it is spoken into being by an act of will on the part of God, who in willing himself wills other things. Those other things do not exist in relationship to themselves. Human beings, who have a will by virtue of their being God's likenesses, do will but only truly in relationship to God, who is intimate to and transcendent of them. Accordingly, the Creator/creature distinction begins to take shape right away. We will rightly when we will in relationship to another, that is, God, whereas God does not and cannot will himself in relationship to other things, for God loves, understands, and wills in relationship to himself.

THE FECUNDITY OF CREATION

The proper name of God is, following Exodus 3:14, "WHO is, because it is proper to Him alone that His substance is not distinct from His being."[8] Reminding ourselves of God's completeness is important for considering creation. Unlike what is not God, God's substance and being are one; God's attributes and God's essence are identical. With creation, however, its properties, for example goodness, are participations in another who, of course, is unparticipated. God's fullness of life—aseity—is what Bruce Marshall calls "the unalterable presupposition" for what lies outside God, for created things.[9] Expressed in a Thomistic idiom, God's simplicity is the principle for the multiplicity of things.

The doctrine of God's supreme goodness helps us to see why, for example, there is "distinction in created things."[10] The reason that the one and simple God creates a world replete with distinctions has to do with what Thomas calls "God's likeness."[11] That is to say, the reason for the diversity of created

---

[8] Aquinas, *SCG* 2.52.
[9] Bruce Marshall, "The Absolute and the Trinity," *Pro Ecclesia* 23, no. 2 (2014): 152.
[10] Aquinas, *SCG* 2.45.
[11] Aquinas, *SCG* 2.45.

goods—not one species of fish but many—is "in order that they may receive God's likeness more perfectly by multiplicity than by unity."[12] The earth God has established has the multiplicity it does because of its likeness to God.[13] Likeness to the one God demands multiplicity, great variety, and unimaginable fecundity.

It is appropriate to speak of God's likeness as inclusive of all created things. Of course, we would not describe all created things as being in God's "image," for such is said only of human beings. But we would say that all created things receive God's "likeness" insofar as they have being and existence, thereby sharing in an analogical sense in the being of God. By *analogical*, we simply mean "like" their Creator insofar as they have being and they exist. That is as far as it goes, however, for God, unlike created beings, is uncreated being and existence. The dissimilarity between Creator and created is always ever greater than the similarity. To put this another way, the beauty and complexity of the created order attests and reveals the invisible nature of its maker, and in such a way as to highlight the great difference between the one who makes and what is made. Nothing that God creates is "bad," then, for the reason that goodness is what God is and is what he communicates "to other things by way of likeness to Himself."[14]

If such is the case, then, the character of the term *likeness* is not too difficult to understand. We are not talking in terms that are either univocal or equivocal but analogical. Created existences themselves—by virtue of their createdness—have, as we said above, existence in relation to another; accordingly, they are both like and unlike their maker. Existence is said of both but in a radically different way. The rocks that jut out of one of my favorite local mountains on which to run owe their existence—their sheer givenness—to God, even as God exists in a way that is supremely above their existence, that is, as their Creator. God is the perfect being for whom essence and existence are one; the same, though, is not said of the mountain, which is not the essence of mountain but an instantiation of "mountain" and whose being is had in relation to another, that is, God. God, as Thomas teaches, "exceeds all substance and nature

---

[12]Aquinas, *SCG* 2.45.
[13]E.g., Ps 119:90.
[14]Aquinas, *SCG* 2.46.

in so far as God neither participates nor is participated, but remains in God's own purity simple and undivided."[15] This is why Thomas uses the language of "likeness." The multiplicity of created things denotes a communication of his goodness but not a pure participation in it. This is key. Created things are communicated goodnesses. They do not participate in God's essential goodness by nature but rather receive his goodness by likeness. In the case of human beings, for whom it is said that they are made in God's image *and* likeness, human beings are created for a specific end, namely, that they might share in, as creatures, all that is God. We are creatures who are created in a manner compatible with our Creator and for profound intimacy with him.

Description of created things as "likenesses" goes a long way toward honoring the salience of the Creator/creature distinction. The language of "likeness" is useful, reminding us that there exists a similitude between God and creatures while resisting quite explicitly the notion of any assimilation of God to creatures, as if God and creatures were part of the same species or thing. Put simply, we do not talk about the multiplicity of creatures in relation to the one God within a common system, as if being, for example, were common to them but only in different ways. Rather than belonging to being, God is being itself. God is thus not an instance of some greater thing called *being* in which he participates in an unrestricted sense, the creature in a restricted sense.[16]

God's causal activity with respect to creation as understood along Thomistic lines maps nicely onto the biblical testimony. The great hymns to the Creator in the Psalter teach in no uncertain terms the radical dissimilarity between the Creator and what he creates. God, as Thomas teaches in his treatise on creation in *ST* 1, "alone is the most perfectly liberal giver, because He does not act for His own profit, but only out of His own goodness."[17] Hence there is no reciprocity between the Creator and the

[15] Aquinas, *DN*, 529.
[16] This is how Barth understands the analogical notion of causality. In his excursus on *causa* in *CD* III/3 §51 he argues that the Thomistic account is mistaken because it reduces God and creatures to "a single common denominator." Barth's reading of the Thomistic notion of *causa* is mistaken, though his instincts are not. Indeed, I think we have much to learn from Barth as he wrestles with this tradition of inquiry that he does not quite understand. See further John R. Betz's introduction to Erich Przywara's *Analogia Entis: Metaphysics: Original Structure and Universal Rhythm*, trans. John R. Betz and David Bentley Hart (Grand Rapids: Eerdmans, 2014), especially 58-67.
[17] Aquinas, *ST* 1.44.4 ad 1.

creature insofar as God cannot be said to create so as to gain or receive something from the act of creating. God's relations with the creature are accordingly not real "because God does not possess an identity that is in any way determined or perfected by his causation of creatures."[18] This is not to take away from either the fact that the multiplicity of creatures are really related to God or the similitude that exists between God and creatures. What it does take away is the notion that God's relations with creatures are in any way, shape, or form reciprocal. God is his own being, whereas the multiplicity of creatures are not, for they "are beings by participation."[19] The much misunderstood and maligned teaching of Thomas says quite simply this: God's relations with creatures are not real for God, meaning—only—that they do not determine God, whereas we who are determined by God are really related to God, as those who are caused by God. Thomas's point is extremely simple and biblical. Created things are willed into and conserved in being by God; God is not created and conserved by them. They are really related to God, but God is not really related to them insofar as God does not gain from them.

Psalm 24:1-2 illustrates this by testifying to the sheer givenness of things, which themselves teach us of the Lord. The Lord is not of the earth, but "The earth is the Lord's and all that is in it, the world, and those who live in it; for he has founded it on the seas, and established it on the rivers." Accordingly, Thomas comments, "The earth is of Him and of his plenitude."[20] The earth is of the Lord because the Lord is plenteous in himself. The Lord is neither founded nor established in relationship to the earth, but the earth is in relationship to him. Furthermore, by linking the act of creation and preservation to the Lord's plenitude, we see how God's acts express God, the plenitude of goodness itself. The earth is a fruit of his plenitude. There is an earth because the Lord is plenteous himself. To put it more precisely, attributes are the principle of works.[21] The work of creation, including therewith its preservation, is a work of his plenitude.

---

[18]White, *Incarnate Lord*, 189. This dimension of Thomas's thinking is hugely misunderstood by contemporary critics.

[19]Aquinas, *ST* 1.44.1.

[20]Aquinas, *In Ps* 24, trans. Stephen Loughlin.

[21]See further Aquinas, *ST* 1.45.6 ad 6, wherein Thomas states "every effect of God proceeds from each attribute."

Being and Causality

Being and causality are said of God and creatures analogically. Accordingly, being has a twofold reference. It is, first, an effect, what Thomas calls "the first and most universal" cause.[22] What exists has being, and that of and in God. What God—as cause—effects are other beings, incarnate and discarnate, animate and inanimate. Importantly, God causes what is not God in such a way that these things "know" themselves to be caused. Hence both people and "the trees of the field" join in praise of their Creator (Is 55:12).

Because God causes creatures who, as his effects, have being, his creation has likeness to him. There are resemblances, "ontological similitudes . . . that result from casual dependencies" between Creator and creature.[23] However, those resemblances are never to be understood as if there were a common something—*genus*—between the two of which each partakes. Put again, the agent (God) and what he effects (the created order) are not of the same species.[24]

The key to rightly accounting for the relationship between cause and diverse effects is to talk in nonreciprocal and compatibilist terms. The cause of creation is God—who is the pure act of being itself, in whom there is no potentiality, who is subsistent being itself. That is, of course, not true of what God causes: created things have potentiality. "In every created substance there is potentiality and act."[25] That is not true of God, for God has no potential. Creation is acted on, whereas God is not; creation is dependent and contingent, unlike God, who is independent and noncontingent. Nonetheless, created things have a kind of generic similitude to God. Creation is like God insofar as it has being, caused as it is by the perfect being of God himself. That said, creation is (radically) unlike God insofar as it is potentially corruptible, whereas that is not true of God himself. God is "more actual," indeed entirely actual, whereas creation's actuality is derivative, had only in relation to God.[26] God cannot cease to be, whereas the created order may cease to be: it is potentially corruptible. Therefore a strict nonreciprocity exists between Creator and creation. That said, such reciprocity does not preclude a compatibilist account of Creator and creature. Though

---

[22] Aquinas, *ST* 1.45.5.

[23] White, *Incarnate Lord*, 206n4.

[24] See further ibid.

[25] Aquinas, *SCG* 2.53.

[26] The "more actual" is true of intellectual substances in general. See Aquinas, *SCG* 2.56.

nonreciprocally related, the Creator is compatible with the created order; in the case of human beings, friendship with their Creator befits them as made in his image and likeness.

To rehearse what we have said so far, there is likeness (similitude) and difference (dissimilitude) between the Creator and creation. God creates as one who is being itself. What has being has existence. There is something outside God that exists only because of God, but it does not exist in like manner to God, for whom existence and essence are one, coextensive as they are with God's being. To develop this point as we must requires introduction of the notion of transcendentals, which we shall encounter and unfold in the pages to come. By way of anticipation, existence, for example, is said of God and creatures. Other transcendentals are beauty, truth, goodness, and unity. Such likeness, however—and this is key—is enfolded within exceedingly great difference. God is above and wholly other than that to which God gives existence; God is not a created existence but is existence itself. Similarly, being is a transcendental insofar as it denotes a likeness with respect to both, albeit true of both in a radically distinct way. Being is said of God without reserve and of us only by derivation and likeness, "for the fruit of the light is found in all that is good and right and true" (Eph 5:9).

I think that this helps us to understand creation's openness to its Creator, indeed to make theological sense of the many instances in the Psalms of creation's praise of its Creator. The Creator is not extrinsic to his creation but intimately present to it. "Let the sea roar, and all that fills it; the world and those who live in it. Let the floods clap their hands; let the hills sing together for joy at the presence of the LORD, for he is coming to judge the earth" (Ps 98:7-9). Texts such as this attest the natural openness of creation to its Creator, the extent to which the creation rejoices in its dependency on its Creator and looks forward to the day of his appearing. The creation is, of course, "groaning in labor pains" insofar as it suffers the effects of our sin (Rom 8:22). And yet creation's voice is not entirely vanquished by our participation in our first parents' fall. To be sure, creation does not fall, but it does suffer our fall. Even as the created order suffers our fall, however, it remains in God as its cause, and so the floods cannot but clap and the hills cannot but sing. The trees of the field know something naturally, namely, that they are made, and they delight, exuberantly so, in their being made. The hills, too, witness, naturally, to God their Creator, the judge of all the earth. Again, this witness is natural to them. The hymns of creation's praise to its Creator express the deep compatibility of what is made with him who made it.

The language of transcendentals helps us understand such compatibility. Because being is common to them, though in a radically different and asymmetrical way, there is a profound fit between Creator and created. The language of transcendentals, when rightly deployed, helps us understand something of this and of how God may be said to be found in what is good, right, and true.

At this point we need to consider further how an account of created things relates to an account of new creation. Where does the continuity and discontinuity with what precedes appear? How does the distinction between the two enrich our thinking about goodness as the principle of the created order and that order as a point of understanding the God/world difference?

Creation Versus New Creation

God is good and as such acts for the good of other things. He not only fulfills creation's purpose as the theater of his glory but is its very end "so that God may be all in all" (1 Cor 15:28). If this is so, then, we are in a better position to describe something of the relationship between creation and new creation. Creation—the doctrine of created goods—is neither to be confused with nor divided from new creation—the doctrine of reconciliation and redemption. New creation is inaugurated with Christ's resurrection, his victory over sin, death, and the devil, and manifestly consummated in relationship to all when he comes again to judge the living and the dead.

Christ is the end of this age as we know it, an age imprisoned by sin and its consequence, death; he is the subject and the agent of God's reign come to earth, the new creation. Creation suffers because of our sin but is not complicit in that sin. We sin, yes, but other created things do not sin. Instead, they suffer our fallenness and our acquiescence to and complicity with the principalities and the powers. Christ does not abolish created things, for creation has an integrity of its own, not only insofar as it attests the invisible nature of its Creator, but because it celebrates, by its very being, God its Creator (Rom 1:20). This integrity is what Susannah Ticciati describes as "the good of creation."[27]

---

[27]Susannah Ticciati, "How New Is New Creation? Resurrection and Creation *ex nihilo*," in *Eternal God, Eternal Life: Theological Investigations into the Concept of Immortality*, ed. Philip G. Ziegler (London: Bloomsbury T&T Clark, 2016), 90.

She helpfully suggests that "primordial creaturely goodness" is distinct from "goodness after sin," that is, new creation.[28] Such a way of putting things reminds us that primordial creaturely goodness is good because of its source. The goodness of the primordial creation (the creation *ex nihilo*) is of God alone. Following the cues of the Psalter, this is what the created order expresses, even subsequent to "the devastation."[29] The created order does not worship false gods as we do and thereby become corrupt but knows that it is God's and as such naturally renders praise. "Look at the birds of the air," says Jesus (Mt 6:26).

Maintaining this distinction between the good of creation (even after our failure) and the good of new creation honors the intention of Barth's orientation of creation to covenant in *CD* III. That is to say, the good of creation is only intensified in light of "the fullness of time," the time of God's sending of his Son, in whom we are chosen "before the foundation of the world" (Gal 4:4; Eph 1:4). The primordial creation, understood as the theater of God's glory, is liberated in Christ from all that would oppress its testimony to its Creator. Primordial creation's song is emancipated in Jesus Christ from all that would smother the fullness of its praise. In no way does the good of creation compete with the good of reconciliation or redemption; rather, honoring the distinct character of each good is a responsible way of revering the testimony of the Psalter to creation's praise. In a sense, the primordial creation is ahead of us insofar as it continues, even as it suffers our failure, to do what it has always done, namely, sing its Creator's praise. Much like the one person of Christ, whose divinity is neither confused with nor separated from his humanity, the created order naturally sings its Creator's praise, expresses its dependence on and love for its Creator. Similar to the man Jesus whose knowledge of God is immediate all of his days, whose life is entirely one with the Father, the created order is entirely attentive to its Creator; such attentiveness is most natural to it. It has always done what it was created to do, to declare its Creator's praise; whereas we do not do, on this side of the fall, what we were created to do, to declare and sing our Creator's praise. Put differently, the created order by its very nature participates in its Creator as

---

[28]Ibid., 107-9.
[29]The language belongs to Griffiths as found in Paul J. Griffiths, *Decreation: The Last Things of All Creatures* (Waco, TX: Baylor University Press, 2014).

its subject. This was originally true of us but not now because we have sinned; similarly, the human nature of the Son is always open to his divine nature; his human nature is always transparent to the will of his Father, even in the agony of suffering and death.

This is worth thinking about because the created order—what is not God—never ceases to be other than God, even in the day of its perfection. It is neither collapsed into nor swallowed up by God. The God/world difference, whether it be in the case of primordial creaturely goodness or goodness after sin, always remains intact, albeit in quite a different way. The good that we shall see face to face will eclipse all that we can ask or imagine, though only by degrees—transformed, yes, but not rendering invalid any continuity with what preceded it. Things made will always remain made, and they will be perfected (the new) in relation to the one from whom they are, that is, God.

CREATION'S OPENNESS

My account of the goodness of creation, of creation's principle, and of the ways in which it is similar to and dissimilar from its principle, indicates the compatibility of the Creator and the creature. This is, I think, a fair reading of the Psalter. You could say that the Psalter encourages a compatibilist account of the relationship between the Creator and the creature. In this section we consider how their compatibility bespeaks an openness on the part of created things with their Creator. Let me illustrate that via Psalm 22:25-28. The psalmist looks forward to the day when the praise he offers "from you" [i.e., the Lord] "in the great congregation" shall extend to "all the ends of the earth." Indeed, "the ends of the earth shall remember and turn to the LORD; and all the families of the nations shall worship before him." The word *remember* is key. What is to be remembered is not something foreign to the earth, summoned as it is to remember. What men and women forget "through sin" is what is natural to us, namely, "a certain knowledge of God." Just so, "some knowledge of God" is inserted into "all the families of the nations." What the apostles do—Thomas cites Jeremiah as an apostle—is lead us "back to the remembrance of natural knowledge."[30] They

---

[30]Aquinas, *In Ps* 22, trans. Stephen Loughlin.

do not lead us back to knowledge that is alien to us but rather to the one whom we have forgotten to worship due to our sin. The Lord who rules over the nations is compatible with those nations ruled, though the nations ruled are not compatible with him because of their forgetfulness. One day, however, all those who constitute them will bow down to him: "Posterity will serve him" (Ps 22:30).

Thomas, as with Paul, does not claim too much for this knowledge. It cannot be confused with the knowledge of faith derived from revealed principles. Nonetheless, it is natural, though again we forget that through sin. Sin, however, does not negate the thrust of Psalm 22:27, that "all the ends of the earth shall remember and turn" to the one we have forgotten.

What is also important to note is the place of "worship" (Ps 22:27) as remembrance's fruit: we remember and thus worship. In an example of a reading that modern historical-critical exegetes would abhor, Thomas says that the turning envisaged in Psalm 22:27 occurs "through love" and pertains "to the sacrament of the altar, since it is a kind of memorial of the Lord's passion.... And so he [David] says *They will remember*, since the conversion of the soul to God is an effect of the sacrament of the altar." The nations will remember "in spiritual worship—John 4." In addition, the good they receive in worship is "a two-fold good, namely, participation in sacred things, and veneration of God in worship."[31] In worship, "carnal people" are converted to the one whom they have forgotten, the one whom they disbelieved through their sin. Worship shows how a rough and fairly scattershot knowledge of God is transformed into a reverence for God through the sacrament as received in faith. It is natural to us to know God and to revere and worship God; however, it is also supernatural, through faith from above, indeed through the soul of Christ, who, in the Spirit, spiritually regenerates us. We see here how any "openness" we might have is utterly obscured by our forgetfulness, which is why "the trees of the field" (Is 55:12), unlike the nations, are intuitively open. We are not, however, because we rarely remember and therefore do not worship. When we do turn to the Lord by his grace, we see how good and natural is memory and worship of him.

---

[31] Aquinas, *In Ps* 22.

The Psalter's teaching does not overturn conclusions about the "eternal power and divine nature" of God's "invisible" nature arrived at naturally (Rom 1:20). And yet, it does present truths inaccessible to natural reason. Created existence declares its source—such a declaration is natural to it by virtue of its created character—and, as a result, we are "without excuse" by virtue of that which is seen. However, you and I do not, on this side of the fall, naturally see and declare our Creator in relation to created things. Although it is true that we know of God through what God has made, following Calvin's *sensus divinitatus* and Romans 1:20, we only know in the way that demons "know": a knowledge shorn of honor, gratitude, and, most important, love.[32] Hence the truths that the created order proclaims—namely, that we are made—seem inaccessible to us, unnatural as we are due to sin.

What is natural to primordial creation, despite its suffering the deleterious effects of our rebellion, is what has always been—namely, a song of praise. Creation's praise is largely inaccessible to us now, isolated as we are from it in light of our sin. Hearing its praise to its Creator is accordingly not natural either, given our inversion of the Creator/creature relationship. In Christ and the Spirit do we see ourselves as creatures whose reason for being is a song of praise to the one in whom we live, move, and have our being. Through Christ and the Spirit do we exercise our natural powers rightly. This is news to us. Such good news speaks of truths inaccessible to us, acquired through revelation in faith; once acquired, however, we see how natural such truths are, how they indeed speak of a new relationship between God and the covenant partner in which God indwells him or her, thereby rendering the covenant partner newly compatible with him.[33] Indeed, the covenant partner enjoys a great gift in the form of a relationship with the covenant making, keeping, and perfecting God—a relationship that utterly exceeds the relationship with God enjoyed by the primordial creation.

The created order's praise is intuitive to it and natural to it. The human song of praise is different, however, in that unlike the primordial creation's praise it involves both intellect and will, Word and Spirit. Likewise, human

[32]See Jas 2:19-20: "You believe that God is one; you do well. Even the demons believe—and shudder. Do you want to be shown, you senseless person, that faith apart from works is barren?"
[33]See Jer 31:33: "But this is the covenant that I will make with the house of Israel after those days, says the LORD: I will put my law within them, and I will write it on their hearts; and I will be their God, and they shall be my people."

praise is distinguished from the primordial creation's song of praise. This distinction is clarified when we invoke the language of revelation. Revelation serves us in a primary sense, creatures in a derivative sense, insofar as Christ died for us—Adam's progeny—and in so doing liberated created goods from the effects imposed on them by our sin and death. We are released from sin and death and given over to a greater glory, the glory of seeing face to face. Revelation—the coming of God in Jesus Christ and the Spirit—naturalizes, indeed humanizes by reconciling, reforming us in a way that involves more than we can ask or imagine. Because of what Christ has done we can no longer "cease from my [God's] presence" (Jer 31:36).

To summarize what we mean by creation's openness, the creation's cause—God—is present to what he creates as its cause, and what is caused naturally sings praise to the one who is without cause. Our problem is not that we cannot know our cause, for surely we do in some sense. The Psalter recognizes this, and what it counsels is the cry "teach me your statutes" (Ps 119:68). Only when we learn to cry out can we be said to be on the way to knowing truly, which is to say naturally. When we sing the Lord's praise, knowledge that was once mostly inaccessible to us because of our sin—namely, our being created—becomes natural to us. We join with the trees of the field in singing our Creator's praise. If this is indeed the case, we need to turn our attention to the nature psalms, investigating just what these psalms teach us about praise of their cause.

NATURE PSALMS

The "nature-psalms"—the term is Barth's—teach us about how natural is the creation's praise of its Creator. Referring, for example, to Psalms 69:34; 148:4; or most famously Psalm 19:1-6, Barth avers that "it is highly contestable whether these passages, like others in the Psalms and Job which refer to the rest of creation represent or reveal an abstract natural theology." What Barth means is that these psalms do not sing praise to a neutral God, a God other than "the one who called the fathers, and revealed Himself to His people at Sinai." In other words, the nature psalms do not offer praise to an ephemeral deity. That is true. All that God has made—"the cosmos and therefore the upper cosmos"—declares God's praise, and such praise, as we have noted, is natural to them.[34] As Augustine says, "they cry aloud that they are made, for they suffer change and variation. . . . They also cry aloud that they have not made themselves."[35] In this sense, then, nature serves us by declaring its createdness even as it serves God by declaring his praise. The "highest heavens" are made in such a way that they do not begrudge their maker praise. The exuberance of their praise—which they always offer—indicates how "their principle," the Lord God, is infinitely greater than them, transcending "them out of all proportion."[36]

If the "heaven and earth praise him, the seas and everything that moves in them" (Ps 69:34) praise him without interruption, then there is no such thing as pure nature, that is, nature abstracted from its vocation of praise. The praise that heaven and earth offer—their voice of praise—and the knowledge that their voice imparts is, to be sure, "meagre."[37] The beauty, goodness, and being of heaven and earth are radically distinct from God's. As Augustine comments, "Thanks to you, we know this; and yet our knowledge is ignorance in comparison with yours."[38] How do we know that their witness is meager, something that even created things do not know? We know this because of revelation, which denotes a superior kind of knowledge of truths inaccessible. Nonetheless, the meager knowledge of God that the created order imparts is good because in this life our intellect knows things via sensibles, including, not surprisingly, God. When we look on the heavens, we cannot look past them to the one who made them. In Thomas's words, one's intellect "is utterly unable to rise so as to behold such things as transcend all proportion to the senses."[39] Yes, we cannot "behold" the Maker through what has been made, but we can know in a "meagre" way that he is.

Furthermore, the testimony of heaven and earth is never independent of the greater testimony, the covenant promised to Abraham and revealed at Sinai and consummated at the cross. The Psalter never encourages any disconnection between the two forms of testimony because the heavens and

---

[34]Barth, *CD* III/3, 446.
[35]Augustine, *Conf*, 11.5.
[36]Aquinas, *SCG* 4.1.
[37]Aquinas, *SCG* 4.1.
[38]Augustine, *Conf*, 11.5.
[39]Aquinas, *SCG* 4.1.

earth are never simply the heavens and the earth. Their voice is, following the pattern of the Psalms, never abstracted from the voice of the law, through which God's glory is also revealed. The creation and the law extol, in two different modes, the glory of the one Lord.

The knowledge of faith, the second form of knowledge, is, as we have seen, different from the knowledge acquired sensibly. The first form of knowledge is one that rises through what is made. The second kind of knowledge is through hearing. The latter involves divine truth that surpasses human intelligence, available to us by revelation as received in faith. Again, "the knowledge of God by faith comes down to us by divine revelation" through hearing the Word of God.[40] There are not two kinds of knowledge, strictly speaking, but rather one: there is knowledge from below (that is, created things, the heavens and the earth) and from above (via faith through revelation). That said, the one is distinct from the other, though there is not any incompatibility between the two. We do not learn of Trinity and incarnation through the heavens' declaration, but we do learn that we are made. Indeed, we learn through revelation what the heavens do not know—that is, how deficient they are in comparison with God's beauty, goodness, and being.[41] But again, we do learn from them that they (and we too) are created, summoned, as it were, into being by God, the same God who was reconciling the world to himself in Christ and who is present to his people now in Word and Sacrament.

Conclusion

In this chapter I have articulated the theological basis for created goods. God's goodness is radically generative of other goods, created goods, who naturally know themselves to be of the Lord God. We looked at how creation's praise is automatic, indeed intrinsic to it. Simply by virtue of their being, created things declare—in a manner appropriate to their mode—the Creator's praise. We noted that sin does not affect them as it does us, who on this side of the great trespass and in the devastation no longer know naturally. Instead, our rebellion against nature renders its testimony largely inaccessible to us. Only through grace are we able to receive the fullness of nature's testimony.

---

[40]Aquinas, *SCG* 4.1.
[41]See again Augustine, *Conf*, 11.6.

The doctrine of creation is the most appropriate place in which to think about the goodness of God, for it furnishes the context for articulating the difference between God's goodness and the goodness of creatures. But it highlights not simply the difference, for we also saw how God's difference from what is not God is actually the foundation for the latter's praise of and participation in God. "I will sing to the LORD as long as I live; I will sing praise to my God while I have being" (Ps 104:33). Analogical language was shown to be helpful in expounding how goodness is said of God and creatures, but of each in a radically different way. God is the pure act of being, dependent on nothing in order to be the goodness he is, whereas we, who are God's likeness, have no being or goodness apart from our cause. The Lord causes us in such a way that we might really and thus naturally relate to him as our only good.

Looking ahead, we think through the nature of evil as that which hinders God's good creation from achieving its end. Evil counsels resistance toward God's statutes. Evil's nothingness is what renders it so perniciousness. Evil's "agency" is, as we shall see, indicative of its privative character. I argue that in these dark days we must imitate the good that is God, and in so doing recognize and enjoy the help of the angels.

SIX

Goodness and Evil

T HE TASK OF THIS CHAPTER is to think about evil in relation to
God, taking seriously the fact that it is nothing—and that its agency
expresses the awful truth that it is nothing—but lies.[1] Accordingly, I argue
that evil is known as evil only with respect to God, in particular, God's
goodness, its epistemic principle. Evil and the devil as its great champion
are intelligible only in relation to what they lack. They are absurd, unable,
and unwilling to join with the communion of the saints and the angels in
testifying to what is real and true.

Consideration of the angels is an important dimension of our account of
goodness and evil. I ask, how does the preeminent goodness of God inform
discourse about the nature and offices of the angels? In what sense(s) do the
angels serve the good that the Lord is? As we shall see, I reflect on their
devotion to the Lord God as a good that ought to be imitated. We, like them,
have life to the extent that what is in us is of the Lord. After describing angels,
I proceed to think about how the Lord is inherently desirable and to be
imitated by the faithful. I reflect on how what is true of him in a transcendental sense is to be the basis of our desire and what we imitate. In all of this,
I do not stray from the first principle, the preeminent goodness of God. In
not deviating, I hope to show how every facet of Christian theology is
Christian to the extent that it abides with its principle and ever-present presupposition. I demonstrate the architectonic priority of what God is for
every dimension of Christian theology.

---

[1]See Jn 8:44: "When he lies, he speaks according to his own nature, for he is a liar and the father of lies."

THE PROBLEM OF THE WILL

Our first task in thinking through the nature of evil in light of the preeminent attribute of God is to ask what Psalm 119:68 teaches us about God's relationship to evil. The first thing to note is that the locus of the psalmist's prayer is the will; he needs to be instructed otherwise than he would naturally instruct himself, left to his own resources. This is because he as a sinner does not respond to God, indeed has no desire to do so. His nature as one created in the image and likeness of God is not the problem. As Griffiths notes, "anything is good to the extent that it exists."[2] The problem arises from the distorted character of his will. Accordingly, we begin this direction by distinguishing theologically between our nature and our will. Without such a distinction in play, we risk fleeing from theology to an account of evil determined by what seems natural to us, which is, as we shall see, quite devastatingly unnatural.

We, as with God, have a nature and a will. Unlike God, in whose nature understanding is convertible with will, our understanding and our will are not simultaneous. Indeed, we do—however absurdly—often will what is contrary to our nature as those created and upheld by God. When we do evil—Thomas uses the example of adultery—"it is not the nature but the will that is evil in adulterers."[3] Using language that is quite surprising, Thomas argues that God's cooperation "with adulterers in the action of nature involves no contradiction."[4] God may be said to cooperate with those who will evil in for example committing adultery, insofar as the nature that wills evil is caused and preserved by God. We at no point have existence apart from God. The will is at fault, not nature. Because we live and move and have our being in God, God is said to cooperate with us at the level of nature but not, as Thomas argues, in terms of will when the will does evil.

God is what is most real—independent reality, if you will—whereas we are real only in relation to God. We are the creature, not the Creator, and therefore are not indefectibly good. Why must we keep referring to this basic truth about God? Because evil, unlike God, is "not a real essence."[5] Evil

---

[2] Paul J. Griffiths, *Decreation: The Last Things of All Creatures* (Waco, TX: Baylor University Press, 2014), 131.
[3] Aquinas, *SCG* 2.87.
[4] Aquinas, *SCG* 2.87.
[5] Aquinas, *SCG* 3.7.

does not have being because it does not have essence. Evil cannot be said to be, to have being and therefore any goodness. Being, however, is, as Thomas avers, good and, as such, is what all things desire insofar as they are. Nothing desires its own destruction. In that sense, God cooperates with adulterers insofar as the nature that commits that evil act does not exist apart from God, even though it wills and acts apart from God. What that nature wills is evil, not the nature itself. If this is true, then, evil does not come from good but can only "exist" in light of the good. Thus "it is impossible for a being, as such, to be evil."[6] To put this in more colloquial terms, there is no such thing as "radical evil." Were that the case, there would be another "deity" competing with God, something or someone who, along with God, has being. But that is false: the God we meet in the Scriptures has no competitors; evil cannot be ascribed any ontological weight. Hence we see evil's privative character: it is lies all the way down.

Nonetheless, evil wills exist. How so? The will becomes evil insofar as its object is other than "the end and the good" that is God.[7] Evil's existence—I use the word *existence* circumspectly—is, accordingly, of an accidental character. God does not cause evil, and so its status must be accidental. The will that is evil is, however, born by a nature that is good, for a thing just by being is itself good. Indeed, I might be an adulterer. The society I inhabit may be profoundly promiscuous, permissive, indeed idolatrous, all of which happens to be true. On both levels, the individual and the societal, which can, of course, be distinguished but never ultimately separated, the subject that wills evil—in this case myself—is a good. The I who engages in evil—adultery—is "a cause of something, not *per se*, but accidentally."[8] How so? My being or nature, even as I will evil, nonetheless cooperates with God insofar as it exists at all only in relation to God, however much my willing may take me away from God. The evil that I do does not have any ontological ground. It is, instead, only accidental, parasitic, and absurd.

The cry of the adulterer—or more simply, the sinner—to be taught God's statutes is a cry that makes him or her better, more actual. When I cry out to God to be healed of that which entangles me and from which I cannot

---

[6] Aquinas, *SCG* 3.7.
[7] Aquinas, *SCG* 3.8.
[8] Aquinas, *SCG* 3.13.

extirpate myself, I am met by God and his goodwill to me. Those who cry out are good insofar as they *are*, but become better—more themselves rather than less—insofar as they continue to cry out to God via the statutes and finds themselves being drawn away from what is evil toward what is good, namely, God. The cry to be taught depends on God, who is "the good whereby each thing is good."[9] The cry is a good. It is elicited, however, by something even better, the law, whose source is that which is best, God. By God do we tend toward God, and by God—in whom we have our being—do we become better than we were, assuming that we join in the psalmist's cry. In other words, reformation of life is necessary for us, not for God. God needs to be taught no thing, whereas, of course, we do, that one thing being the law, whose fulfillment and end is Jesus Christ.

Such reflection is crucial to a theological account of evil. Without a rich account of God's nature in play, thinking about evil is inevitably confused. We must make clear at every point that evil is not God's competitor, and that, sinners that we are, we are good insofar as we exist (sin being an accident) but that our will is corrupt. The context for understanding evil is therefore God, and evil can only be described as evil by a heart being taught otherwise. Such judgments regarding evil are on this side of the fall not natural to us. They are the fruit of a renewed intelligence, one set on the path of the good. Put again, the law encourages godliness, and that is God's work all the way down. Intimacy with the Lord is not simply an epistemological prerequisite for describing evil. It is in fact a necessity. To be sure, we recognize the devastations the malformed will brings about because of "what the LORD has revealed."[10] More than that, however, the extent to which we recognize evil's utter repugnance to the Lord is a function of our appetite for the Lord, of a renewed will for God. Increased intimacy with the Lord helps us to see things as they are and teaches us to long for things to be as they should.

LAMENT AS RESPONSE TO EVIL

Evil's principle of intelligibility is God. Evil is understood via God. This we must keep on saying. In a book such as this, focused as it is on God's attributes, we cannot at any moment depart from God and the Scriptures that

---

[9]Aquinas, *SCG* 3.17.
[10]Griffiths, *Decreation*, 35.

speak of God. The presence of evil, whether in an individual or structural sense or in some combination thereof, naturally raises the theodicy question, indeed the character of evil's "existence" and the manner of its defeat. Why indeed, we ask, are our wills so perverted and the fruits of such perversion allowed to run seemingly rampant? What do the many laments in the Psalter teach us about evil?

Our ways and deeds are quite often wicked. This should surprise no one. Our doing evil, however, does not render us evil. As Thomas writes, "the subject of evil is a good."[11] I am a good, though I do not always do good, and I am good in reference to a goodness that lies outside myself, namely, God. I am caused and kept in relation to a goodness that is not ultimately my own but God's: "the good of all things depends on him."[12] Even the will that is evil and deformed is not radically—in an ontological sense—evil. An evil will is not dependent on but independent of its very good, which is God. An evil will resists its cause, which is the Lord, in favor of itself. Accordingly, the question in the devastation is: Can the will actually will what is good and obey God's commands?

Well, the psalmist does cry out: he desires to be taught, to wait on and be nourished by the Lord's loving instruction in the form of the law, the statues. Such a cry is, you might say, also properly described as a lament. The lament over one's ignorance of the statutes may by grace become a habit and in turn yield virtue in the form of a teachable heart. Calling on God—the action itself is important—generates habits. Calling on the Lord who will answer, incline, and hear is to be our habit always. Calling on God to show his steadfast love to those seeking refuge from their enemies and ruin is the habit of the holy. "Wondrously show your steadfast love, O savior of those who seek refuge from their adversaries at your right hand" (Ps 17:7).

Such a cry is entirely natural and in accord with the grain of the universe, meaning that it participates in the only true direction and end available to us, the Lord God.[13] Indeed, the doctrine of providence provides further context, theologically speaking, for our understanding of evil.

---

[11]Aquinas, *SCG* 3.12.
[12]Aquinas, *SCG* 3.17.
[13]See further Aquinas, *SCG* 3.17: "Therefore all things are directed to one good, God to wit, and their end."

God conserves that which he has made in order that it might be made to conform to his purposes for it. God delights in bringing into being a teachable spirit, such a spirit being most natural to whom the psalmist is created to be. All of us are made for God, for knowledge and, ultimately, love and sight of God and of all things in relationship to that God; but sight is not—for the most part—for this life, for in this life we believe in things we cannot see.

In the devastation, we think it natural to be wicked, to live independently, to seek perfection in relation to ourselves. We do not do good, no, not one of us, because we love ourselves and not God, not ourselves in relation to God and our neighbor also in relation to God. As effects of an agent (God) who is supremely good, we tend via the corruption of our will to ourselves. The result of such tending is that we become less, more and more unnatural— stupid, as it were, accordingly a much lesser good "since a thing is good forasmuch as it is perfect."[14] In other words, we die. Because we do not do good, we cease to be, having moved ourselves "entropically toward nothing."[15] Evil leads to death, which is, of course, the last enemy our Lord Jesus defeats.

If such is the case, then, the first step toward our last end is lament. To lament is to repent; specifically, to lament our inversion of the Creator/ creature relationship, which begins with our return to "the first truth, namely God," the Lord God who is "the last end of all man and of all his deeds and desires."[16] Sinners that we are, however, we resist our last end and first cause in favor of ourselves. What are we to do? We cry out that God might teach us his statutes and thereby heal us of our propensity to invert and reverse the Creator/creature relation.

Lament also has what might be called a social and cosmic dimension. David frequently laments the evil that others do to him and that wicked others bring on God's people. Lament includes not only the call for personal change but also the evils that others perpetrate. Indeed, lament is an expansive category, taking up not only personal and social but also natural evil. In terms of the latter, we lament the fact that the natural world is victim to our fallenness and so often works against human flourishing. This is what

---

[14]Aquinas, *SCG* 3.24.
[15]Griffiths, *Decreation*, 133.
[16]Aquinas, *SCG* 3.25.

is sometimes called "natural evil." Earthquakes, for example, the shifting of the tectonic plates beneath our feet, which can be so destructive of human life, are evil insofar as they indicate a cosmos off kilter, one that often "works" at cross purposes to the general well-being of humanity. Earthquakes are worth mentioning because unlike other instances of natural evil, for example floods, whose frequency and intensity can sometimes be traced to anthropogenic climate change, earthquakes have always been, though Jesus himself indicates that their increase and perhaps ferocity are indicative of the pains to be suffered on the eve before he comes again (Mt 24:7-8).

Having said that, sin in the form of moral evil cannot be taken too seriously, as if it were the last word about us. Our Father in Christ, who is good and does good, is sovereign over evil, moral and natural. Our doing what should not have been done and our not doing what should have been done are met at every point by his will to initiate, maintain, and perfect covenant fellowship with us. Our Father comes to us in Jesus Christ, suffers our disobedience and death, destroying and overcoming it in his Spirit. In him we are declared (justified) and made righteous (sanctified). This is the indicative—what is—that includes an imperative, namely, to repent—"teach me your statutes" (Ps 119:68).

Another way to approach the Psalter's many laments is to think of them as the fruit of the indicative, of the acclamation "you are good." The cry indicates that things are not as they should be. The cry also indicates a renewal, the mortification and vivification of the flesh. Again, the cry is most natural, for it is about the restoration of our happiness, our "last end which man desires naturally."[17]

To tie this together, if the object of the psalmist's cry is God, to be taught the laws by which God is known as God, then evil represents the suffocation and obliteration of that cry. Evil silences the cry. But because God is and does good, evil has no positive reality of its own in relationship to him. Evil is not a profoundly corrupt form of that which was a divine likeness. Evil simply *is* not; again, the devil can only lie. This is, I think, why Thomas's account of evil locates evil in the will, not nature. When we cry out, however inchoate and inarticulate it may be, we indicate the desire of the intellect for

---

[17]Aquinas, *SCG* 2.48.

what is not false. Whereas when we forget to cry, we hanker after what does not exist, for what is in no way, shape, or form "a divine likeness." Evil marks, in other words, the radical contraction of the self, the withdrawal of the self from itself, others, and God. The eyes of an evil heart only see and understand in relation to themselves. However, the *"good, as such, is self-diffusive,"* giving rise to other goods, which is why God loves diversity and multiplicity, whereas the only "thing" that evil extends and propagates is death.[18] Accordingly, it makes good theological sense to situate talk of evil in light of ends. The statutes direct us to our last end, God, whereas evil degenerates intelligence because it has no principle and therefore no future and no end. Evil causes the collapse of intelligence and understanding, "not *per se*, but accidentally."[19] Lament, however, reverses by grace the degeneration that accrues to the self turned in on itself.

What About the Devil?

What then of the Satan, the devil, the adversary, the one who exemplifies and encourages the fall of some of the heavenly host? Are we able to describe, biblically speaking, what he is? Is he a personal agent, and if so, may he be adequately described via a "privative" account of evil? Is the notion that "evil is not a real essence . . . for which no causal explanation is possible" transparent to biblical teaching regarding the principalities and powers, diametrically opposed as they are to all that God is and does?[20] In short, I think that it is fitting to say that evil—and the Satan as its embodiment and champion—exercises an agency that is false, and in its falsity is utterly malicious, lacking reality of any kind.[21] Because the devil does not submit to God's rule and give glory to the Lord, he is not real, certainly, in the sense that God is real. The devil is not real because he is not caused: he has no beginning, no positive reality, and therefore cannot receive any last end from God.[22]

The devil exemplifies what is proper to our devastation in that he refuses to live as a creature of the living God. His agency is therefore accidental. The

---

[18]Aquinas, *SCG* 3.24.

[19]Aquinas, *SCG* 3.14.

[20]Aquinas, *SCG* 3.7; Griffiths, *Decreation*, 135.

[21]In Job 1:6 the article *the* appears with the word *Satan*.

[22]In this regard, Griffiths writes: "Demons, in their legion, are, then, discarnate beings impelled toward nothing." *Decreation*, 132.

Satan causes, to be sure, but only accidentally.[23] Put differently, what he spawns (evil) is that which does not live in relation to itself but only in relation to some good to which it is inimical. Evil is parasitic, absurdly so. Evil proliferates, yes, but what it proliferates is not of itself but only accidental. Evil is not its own principle, but rather is intelligible only as the shadow side of what it seeks to defile. Evil spreads only by defiling, always looking for the next thing to devour.

To put this another way, good and evil "cause," but in profoundly different kinds of ways. In the case of evil, evil has no essence. Therefore, it has no being, *is* not good, and cannot as such effect good. Evil cannot cause; it can only corrupt. The Satan can only destroy the effects of the cause to whom he is accidentally related, namely, God. Quite the opposite with the good: creaturely good has being because it is in God and is a likeness of what God is in an essential sense. God has being in respect of his essence, which is subsisting being itself. There is no distinction in God between what he is (being itself) and what he has (goodness). Thus God causes what he is: a diversity of created goodnesses; whereas the evil one does not cause but only steals, corrupts, lies, and destroys. He has no intelligibility in relation to himself; he only—by his very nature—decreates. Satan thieves and wreaks havoc in relation to that which is good, and were there nothing truly good, he would not be. His proliferating energies are purely negative, entirely parasitic.

Here we see one of the fundamental differences between human and angelic rebellion. Rebels that we are, we can nonetheless by grace join in the psalmist's prayer for reform and renewal. We can learn with him that we are not God but have life only in relation to God. Angelic rebels do not have this prayer available to them. The angelic rebellion—the demonic—does acknowledge God, but to it is never given the possibility of reform.[24] Angelic rebels are only able to acknowledge Christ—they "know" who he is—but they cannot ever learn to love him; they cannot be redeemed. Their fate is depicted in Revelation 20:10.

If this is true, we see how God—and not we ourselves—can use evil for good.[25] Our sin is the occasion for something good, namely, the cry to be

---

[23]See further Aquinas, *SCG* 3.14: "Therefore evil is a cause of something, not *per se*, but accidentally."
[24]Jas 2:19: "You believe that God is one; you do well. Even the demons believe—and shudder."
[25]Rom 8:28: "We know that all things work together for good for those who love God, who are called according to his purpose."

taught good. This is true of the human, not the angelic. Human tragedy is, as with the angelic, circumscribed. Unlike the angelic tragedy, however, the human tragedy is subject to something new, namely, God's coming among us in torah and temple, fulfilled in Jesus Christ. The human may (by grace) cry out; the demonic cannot. The latter can only "acknowledge" and "believe"; they may never "love." Lament, in other words, is not a possibility available to the adversary and his servants, but it is to us.

Interestingly, the heavenly hosts who have not succumbed to the tempter operate only in the mode of praise. The life of the heavenly host is marked by ceaseless praise. That will be true of us in the life to come, wherein we share in the heavenly liturgy within the renewed cosmos, seeing all things in God and face to face.[26] But for now we, for the most part, live in lament, even though our lament is sometimes transfigured into extroverted and exuberant praise. Our fall occasions something good: the cry of lament that is also a form of praise, which is the genuine experience of the Creator/ creature distinction. Redemption is possible, for our damage is not irreversible.[27] "O Israel, hope in the LORD! For with the LORD there is steadfast love, and with him is great power to redeem" (Ps 130:7).

WHY DO WE DESIRE EVIL?

Evil is that from which we must be delivered. We desire life, which is itself a good and concomitant with being, but we do so on our terms, thereby corrupting the gift of life, which leads to our death. Evil, because it is not a real essence, cannot be perfected, whereas we who are evil—think of Luke 11:13—may be perfected because we are never truly evil. Instead, we, who are evil's subject, are good insofar as we have being and therefore a share in what is good. Yes, we commit iniquities and become iniquitous, but to us is the good of forgiveness directed. That good is focused on human creatures. Put differently, we try in vain to secure a good—that is, life—but in a way that is not good. We want life on our terms. We desire being but only in relation to ourselves, which is an expression of a depraved will. Accordingly, we do not will what is our end, the good that is God. We depend on ourselves, not on God, which is not good. Whatever seeks to be *per se*, autonomous,

---

[26]See Griffiths, *Decreation*, 52.
[27]See ibid., 142.

declines, whereas what is directed not to itself but to God (its cause) does not enjoy anything *per se*. Rather, it enjoys good in relation to the common and supreme good, which is God, and in so doing remains good.

Said differently, we want to possess and not participate in the good. We desire to possess, that is to say domesticate, God and not participate in God as those whose being is participated and caused. Such a sad state of affairs is due to sin. Sin dulls understanding, diminishes recognition of what is real. Sin discourages appetite for anything other than darkness, the void, and nothingness. How then can we long for something that opposes us? Why is that possibility available to us? That we could desire unreality is "definitional for us, created as we are *ex nihilo*."[28] This is, of course, not to say that sin is "definitional for us," only that its possibility is. We are created *ex nihilo* as those who could "extricate themselves from participation in the LORD."[29] Indeed, we do, tragically, extricate ourselves. That is evil. Evil's only real existence comes from turning away from the Lord. Such turning is, moreover, "typically proliferative: turning toward nothing is a habit that ordinarily increases in range, intensity, and depth over time."[30] The good seeks to increase; tragically, so too does evil. Malevolence by its very nature seeks its increase; a cold heart is contagious and desires to increase its range.

If such is the case, then, one should argue that things are getting worse. The longer the Lord Jesus waits to return, the greater the proliferation of sin, and the more urgent is the theodic question. Natural evil (e.g., earthquakes) and moral evil (e.g., gluttony) will only increase until Jesus comes again in glory to judge the living and the dead. And yet the Christian faith never withdraws from celebrating evil's nonbeing, its destruction, and the soon-to-be-revealed day when Christ's destruction of evil will be manifest and he hands over the kingdom to the Father so that he might be "all in all" (1 Cor 15:28).

Why do we desire the increase of evil? In short, it is because we are bored. Our boredom is the fruit of our disordered desires. As a result, our appetite becomes remarkably analogous to evil's appetite, inexhaustible and insatiable: we cannot rest. Evil is frenetic in its advance toward nothing. To be

---

[28]Ibid., 135.
[29]Ibid., 137.
[30]Ibid., 142.

sure, evil is by its very nature proliferative, but it is never generative. Its range increases, drawing more and more toward nothing. What it cannot do, however, is generate: that would presuppose an actual existence on its part. Instead, evil implies a radical diminution of the self in relation to other selves and to God, a hastening toward nothing; whereas God as goodness itself is ultimately fecund, generative of manifold likenesses of his goodness that continue, by his grace, to generate more goodness. Evil cannot rest, cannot be at peace, and that is because it is nothing. Instead, it can only corrupt, hurry forward in its separation from God toward hell, which is its end. Because it comes from nothing it advances toward nothing, "nonexistence," its destiny is hell.[31] Of course, evil is not in hell, but unrepentant sinners, the fallen angels, and the devil are, those who permanently and irreversibly separate themselves from the Lord. Evil's character is personal. The devil and his demons do not simply bear evil but instantiate and personalize evil. Our will becomes evil when it acquiesces to their corruption, participating in it. Like them, we lose being; we become shadows of what we once were, lusting after a repose that will never come.

Nature cannot overcome and destroy evil. Evil must be destroyed by what exceeds nature, indeed the Creator of all things. The law, pointing to its fulfillment in Jesus Christ, anticipates evil's destruction. The statutes place the sinner on the way to righteousness, whose ultimate content is Jesus Christ. The law bears Christ, the one who will show forth evil's baselessness by his triumph over it. The law comes from God, who is goodness itself and who desires to instruct us in goodness that we might come to more deeply participate in it. The law has God as its ground, whereas evil has nothing as its ground and end. The law does not teach itself but teaches God, whereas evil does not teach anything but only clings to what it hates, cajoling toward the nothing from which it came. Evil is without beginning and so without any end. It knows only nothing; it realizes nothing, lacking any reality before God. We, however, come from God and are given the gift of the law that teaches us to wait on the Lord, who is our only hope.[32]

---

[31] Ibid., 150.

[32] I am not convinced, as is Griffiths, that we should "hope even for the salvation of Satan." See *Decreation*, 147. Jesus died and was raised for us, i.e., human beings: for us and for our salvation. That, I think, excludes us from thinking that the devil's salvation, as with his demons, is something for which we should hope.

Only to human beings, indeed God's people Israel, is the gift of loving divine instruction given. Think, for example, of Psalm 18:20-26, one of the greatest thanksgiving psalms. David recognizes the reward of God for fleeing from evil. That reward is, Thomas comments, "ineffable joy, and increase of grace, which come from the keeping of God's commands."[33] So Psalm 18:24 proclaims, "Therefore the LORD has recompensed me according to my righteousness, according to the cleanness of my hands in his sight." Reformation of character is only available to them through the gift of the law. Accordingly, creation doctrine, which is itself derivative of the doctrine of God, is the natural theological home for thinking in a godly manner about evil. Evil is from nothing, lacking a cause or first principle, using all its power to return to nothing, whereas the created order is from God, who never ceases to be present to it as its cause, converting us and perfecting all things in the goodness that is its source and end.

To conclude, explaining our desire for evil, absurd as it is, never takes us away from a steadfast focus in the goodness that God is. Evil is shown to be nothing, and the desire for it ridiculous, given how it never leads to our increase but only our decrease as we journey further and further from our Creator. God is definitional for evil, and the same is true of the desire for evil. By virtue of our createdness, the possibility exists that we might desire our dissolution.

DESIRE AND IMITATION

When we desire evil, we desire what condemns us; in desiring evil, we imitate what is not God, which leads to our dissolution. In this section we consider the desire for God and how desire for God works in relation to imitation of God. Indeed, to desire God is to imitate, and we cannot imitate what we do not know and, ultimately, love.

We are to imitate what the mighty acts of God express, that is, their transcendental basis. Accordingly, we do not imitate God's omnipotence but we do desire to imitate his absolute attributes, for example, righteousness and wisdom. Here we see once again the importance of unfolding what God is. We are to imitate, but not in any unqualified sense, what God

---

[33]*In Ps* 18, trans. Hugh McDonald.

is. The attributes that tell us about the Lord's manner of existence—for example, his omniscience—are not to be imitated; they are incommunicable. Rather, the focal points are those attributes that speak of his existence itself. The Christian praises, desires, and imitates the great goodness of the Lord.

Let us look for a moment at Psalm 18:19, wherein David praises the Lord for his deliverance: "He brought me out into a broad place; he delivered me, because he delighted in me." What does it mean to speak of the Lord delighting in David? The Lord's grace liberates David, but not in a way that isolates his merit. God delivers because he delights in David, more specifically what in David is true of himself. In a seemingly offhanded comment, Thomas says, "the most powerful cause of liberation . . . [is] his [God's] will." Citing Ephesians 1 in support, it is God's will that works all things— "according to the good pleasure of his will" (Eph 1:5). God's works are works of his will. God works via his will "and not by necessity of nature."[34] This we have noted before. Metaphysics are never very far away. This is the setting in which we are to think about human merit. Accordingly, the good we do follows grace. There is a strict asymmetry between the Lord's will and human merit. Yet there is human merit; God's deliverance and the merit that follows do not cancel each other. God ascribes merit to whatever is in us that is of himself. The Lord "knows" us insofar as what is in us is of him.

Let us think deeply about that in which human merit consists. First, it is a matter of keeping "the ways of the LORD" (Ps 18:21), what Thomas calls "the working of good, and [second] in the avoidance of evil." So David says, "I . . . have not wickedly departed from my God" (Ps 18:21). Again, the psalm does not suggest that David's "righteousness" according to which the Lord rewards him is anything other than what the Lord has worked in him. Thomas, following Psalm 18, insists that we are rewarded according to the merits that God himself works in us. Our life of discipleship as Christians is a life marked by a lessening of what is of ourselves and a heightening of what is of the Lord.

In considering evil, its personal character and agency, our (absurd) desire of it, and the desire for and imitation of God that cures us of evil, we need to also reflect more deliberately on the angels. What is it that their

---

[34]Aquinas, *SCG* 3.2.94.

help in relation to the saints expresses regarding God's goodness? And how do their offices shed light on the character of opposition to God in light of God's goodness?

The Help of the Angels

A life that ponders the steadfast love of God—"We ponder your steadfast love, O God" (Ps 48:9)—and a life that perseveres in God is one that enjoys the help of God. Sometimes that help takes angelic form. "The Collect for the Close of the Day" from the Book of Common Prayer puts it this way— "let your holy angels dwell with us to preserve us in peace."[35] The collect sets us on the right path insofar as it draws attention to some of the angelic offices, including those dwelling with and preserving the faithful in the peace of Christ.[36]

In an account of evil that takes its cues from the goodness that is God, we are obliged to consider how angels precede, accompany, and victoriously ward off all that would obscure our being directed toward the goodness of the Lord.[37] We must, in other words, consider the help the angels provide. While I am not convinced that Barth's dialectical account of heaven and earth quite gets at the heart of the matter—I fear it is too contrastive of heaven and earth—Barth's account of the angels nonetheless offers much guidance for noting their help in relation to God. Of particular value is Barth's sense that "in angelology too the theological question is a spiritual one."[38] He writes, "even in this matter of angels we must dare to trust the Holy Spirit."[39]

Importantly, Barth recognizes that indifference to angels, wherever it occurs but especially in dogmatics, denotes a spiritual problem. That problem is a lack of trust in the Spirit. And it is at this juncture that we may connect Barth's judgment with the Psalter. The Psalter assumes the presence and work of the heavenly host in promoting God's purposes and

---

[35]From "An Order for Compline," in The Book of Common Prayer (New York: Church Hymnal Corporation), available at www.bcponline.org/DailyOffice/compline.html.

[36]See Barth, CD III/3, 383.

[37]The language here is Barth's. See Barth, CD III/3, 375.

[38]Barth, CD III/3, 404.

[39]Barth, CD III/3, 403. Such trust is decidedly lacking in eighteenth-, nineteenth-, and early twentieth-century Protestant thinking on angels, which Barth caustically calls "the angelology of the shrug of the shoulders." See Barth, CD III/3, 488.

in worshiping his name. Where the Psalter is most instructive is that it reminds us that all theological questions are fundamentally spiritual ones, including that of the angels. Barth's description of "the nature of heaven . . . as this counterpart of earth . . . the sum of all that which in creation is unfathomable, distant, alien, and mysterious in creation" explains the spiritual character of seriously theological questions.[40] It would be all too easy to ignore what "is unfathomable," that is, "the invisible creaturely reality of heaven in relationship to earth."[41] Our ignoring or dismissing such, however, is due to spiritual apathy on our part. We do not see the "honor" of God indwelling the creaturely world—"this . . . theatre of His glory"—because we have not been trained to receive it.[42] We are not spiritual enough. We receive, in part, God's honor when we, as God's people, open ourselves to the knowledge and love of God in Christ that the angels preserve in us. "The love of God suffices to strengthen man's mind in good," and that strengthening assumes angelic help.[43] To be sure, this help is episodic in relationship to the unwavering help that is God, but is nonetheless a factor in the grace that is our end. God's goodness, which is his great love for us, strengthens us in the good he is through a variety of means, and not in the least the angels.

In greater detail, the Psalms teach us—Psalm 49 is particularly edifying in this respect—about the angels' ministry via the illusory nature of riches. The Psalms encourage the faithful to make judgments that are, according to the rules of earth's inhabitants, foolish. Those who "count themselves happy—for you are praised when you do well for yourself . . . will never again see the light" (Ps 49:18-19). The rich do not recognize another "sphere" that is not in any sense their own.[44] But the faithful do. God is good in such a way that he supplies us with messengers who serve the history of our salvation "incidentally but genuinely" by opening the eyes of our heart to the heavenly sphere that accompanies and precedes us.[45] It is this sphere that serves to preserve us in the deep truth that "trust in . . . wealth" and

---

[40]Barth, *CD* III/3, 422.
[41]Barth, *CD* III/3, 424, 425.
[42]Barth, *CD* III/3, 431.
[43]Aquinas, *SCG* 2.3.158.
[44]Barth, *CD* III/3, 425.
[45]Barth, *CD* III/3, 411.

"abundance of . . . riches" (Ps 49:6) are useless in the life that lasts forever and "never see[s] the grave" (Ps 49:9).

The angels serve us as well as their Lord in a thoroughly self-effacing way. "Where an angel appears and is and speaks and works, God Himself appears and is and speaks and works."[46] We may think of them only in their relationship to God, which is in terms of their "nature and manner."[47] That said, we may "find the most unexpected traces of the way in which the angels have been present . . . in the heavenly power of their witness and promise."[48] Traces, yes, experiences, no. Insofar as we obey the Lord's "spoken word," inasmuch as we bless the Lord, there is a "conjunction" between ourselves and the angels.[49] "Bless the LORD, O you his angels, you mighty ones who do his bidding, obedient to his spoken word" (Ps 103:20). When we do the Lord's bidding we should find "the most unexpected traces" of the angels' presence, speech, and action. We are blessed with them. The names available to us in the Psalter of the angels include "heavenly beings" (Ps 29:1), "holy ones" (Ps 89:5), and "the gods" (Ps 82:1); these "are always and everywhere present," not in and of themselves but as witnesses in terms of "function and service" to God, as both a collective and as individuals.[50]

If such is the case, then, we see how an account of angels and their "unexpected traces" must proceed from God. We cannot account for them in relation to their opposition but rather in relation to God. They do in heaven what will one day be done on earth by all, and on account of God, whose "own speech and action on earth" they are given to share.[51] Such a thoroughgoing theocentrism is necessary if we are to stand under the biblical testimony and stand with the angels. The angels are heralds of the mystery of salvation who serve us in that by strengthening us in the good that is salvation's basis.

PSALM 91:9-13 AS TEST CASE

These particular verses, housed in the midst of a psalm celebrating God's protection, reinforce many of the things that Barth says. The angels

---

[46]Barth, *CD* III/3, 480.
[47]Barth, *CD* III/3, 478.
[48]Barth, *CD* III/3, 462.
[49]Barth, *CD* III/3, 474.
[50]Barth, *CD* III/3, 462, 459.
[51]Barth, *CD* III/3, 480.

belong to the Lord; they are his. They make known his help; they do not offer their own help. They present his goodness and not their own. As Barth says, they are "pure witnesses" who represent him to us.[52] Even "the angel of the LORD," whom we meet, for example, in Psalms 34:7; 35:6, is "a perfect mirror of God."[53] The angels do bear us up, but they do so only in relation to God. That is their service. Our witness, as frail as it is, to the supreme goodness of God assumes their witness. Again, Barth describes the angelic witness as "the necessary presupposition for the human witness"; our witness, whether we know it or not, being executed in their company.[54] Again, we do not seek their hands, though it is their hands that bear us up. We do not seek refuge in them, though they represent the refuge that is God to us. The Lord delivers through them, though we only know the Lord as our deliverance. "Those who love me, I will deliver" (Ps 91:14).

The obvious corollary in the minds of many when we speak about the angelic, is, of course, the demonic. This is not good. Why is it "quite inappropriate to speak of God and the devil or angels . . . in the same breath"?[55] The Psalms, though in them references to the angels are few, reinforce what the rest of Scripture teaches, namely, the ambassadorial character of the angels. The simple reason boils down to how much greater is God in his infinite goodness than what is opposed to him, however strong (though absurd) its opposition might seem. Interestingly, the Psalter's treatment of the "enemies" is profoundly instructive for "demythologizing" the devil and demons.[56] The overwhelming testimony of the Psalter discourages anything that valorizes the opposition to God and ontologizes it.

To take one example, see Psalm 54:5, 7, "He will repay my enemies for their evil. In your faithfulness, put an end to them. . . . My eye has looked in triumph on my enemies." David's enemies in Psalm 54 are Ziphites who told Saul, "David is in hiding among us." David's enemies here, the Ziphites and Saul, are not to be equated with the demons in any straightforward

---

[52]Barth, *CD* III/3, 486.
[53]Barth, *CD* III/3, 490.
[54]Barth, *CD* III/3, 499.
[55]Barth, *CD* III/3, 520.
[56]I do not mean this in the Bultmannian sense. Rather, my aim is like that of Barth's, namely, to remove falsehood from our understanding of them.

sense. Yet David's "curse" with respect to his enemies—"put an end to them"—is instructive, nonetheless, for understanding the demonic. As we have seen, evil, the Satan, and the demonic are not created. They lack being, any positive reality. "Their origin and nature," Barth observes, "lie in nothingness."[57] David's enemies are very real: on the one hand they want him dead; on the other hand, they are entirely false. "Nothingness," ultimately, "is falsehood."[58] David's enemies are falsely real precisely because as with the demons, "they can only hate God and His creation."[59] David's enemies seek his life because "they do not set God before them" (Ps 54:3). David's enemies are thus like the demons; for both, the truth of God is not present. Again, "they do not set God before them." Such is the nature of the demonic. It exists only where "the truth of God is not present and proclaimed and believed and grasped," whereas the angels are ambassadors of what is the truth of God, strengthening and serving those who proclaim, believe, and grasp it.[60]

Thomas, furthermore, is sensitive to how David's pleas for God to "put an end to them" are at odds with "the expression of Christ, who says: 'pray for those who persecute you.'" Thomas describes David's curse as a kind of spiritual denunciation.[61] "When sinners cease to sin, at that time they die and they cease to be sinners. And this is something to be prayed for continually."[62] David prays for his enemies' destruction, yes, that they would cease to exist as sinners. Such a prayer is fitting and in accord with the grain of the universe, precisely because it does not grant the opposition ontological weight. The angels have ontological weight as created goodnesses, unlike evil. David's curses on those who "do not call upon God" (Ps 53:4) thus make sense against the theological backdrop Barth's account supplies and of, by extension, God's goodness. David takes the promise of God

---

[57] Barth, *CD* III/3, 522.
[58] Barth, *CD* III/3, 525.
[59] Barth, *CD* III/3, 523.
[60] Barth, *CD* III/3, 529.
[61] Aquinas, *In Ps* 54, trans. Gregory Sadler. This is but one of the complex ways in which Thomas understands imprecatory language. The psalmist may be speaking prophetically or according to God's justice. The positive desire of the latter is that God's justice be fulfilled in terms of the rectification of the sinner. As Torretta notes of Thomas on the imprecatory Psalms, "punishment in its threat and its actuality is an indispensable part of mercy." See Gabriel Torretta, OP, "Rediscovering the Imprecatory Psalms: A Thomistic Approach," *The Thomist* 80 (2016): 23-48, on 46.
[62] Aquinas, *In Ps* 54.

more seriously than the insolent and ruthless who seek his life. It is the truth of God that enables David (and us) to see how groundless is the enemies' faithlessness when compared to the goodness and truth of God, of which the angels are ambassadors.

In sum, what is of God shares, in a manner befitting its mode, in God. The angels are of God and thus serve his purposes, whereas the demonic is not and does not. The enemies of God are those humans and angels who do not set themselves before God. Evil's nature thus lies in relation to its vision. Evil is what declines from God, whereas we are truly good insofar as we love the Creator and rejoice in his saving work on our behalf. When we accept and rejoice in what he has done, we see that we have nothing apart from him and desire that there be nothing of us that is not of him who has what he is from no one.

CONCLUSION

In this chapter I have shown how God's attributes are the context by which we understand what is not God. What is not God makes sense only in relation to God: the Creator is the principle of that which is created. This is especially true of evil—not because it is created but because it is a "reality" that confronts creatures, one that is not explainable apart from God. Accordingly, I reflected on its accidental character, unfolding how it is not caused but is, rather, a parasite, lacking any reality of its own, exercising a kind of agency that is nonetheless proliferative. The devil cannot make but can only destroy. I argued that when we take time to consider God, we see how false is the devil's nature, how antithetical he is to God's truth and goodness.

We also thought about the role of desire and how in desiring God we come to imitate that which God is. One who is being taught good is one who is learning to see, and the one whom one eventually—eschatologically—sees is God. "Whoever does evil has not seen God" (3 Jn 11). Sight is, however, the mode of apprehending intrinsic to the next life. In this life, we know and walk by faith; occasionally, though, we are given glimpses of the one we shall see insofar as our hearts are pure and avoid evil.

Looking ahead, we shall discuss how God communicates his goodness "according to likeness," which results in a great diversity of forms belonging to the nature of goodness itself.[63] It belongs to the nature of God as goodness itself to communicate itself to created things. We shall explore this majestic truth as we reflect on the loving divine instruction of the Torah as the principal fruit of the communication of goodness.

---

[63] Aquinas, *SCG* 1.50.

SEVEN

Teach Me Your Statutes

O UR CONCERN IN THIS CHAPTER will be to unfold something of the moral character of God's goodness. I consider what the cry to be taught (Ps 119:68) teaches us about God's goodness and ourselves in relation to that goodness, how that goodness shapes us as God's people. I argue there is no gift more appropriate to or consistent with God's goodness than the gift of the law. God cannot be recalled to what he is, for God is always good; but we are not, and God in his infinite goodness recalls us to himself through the law. As we shall see, sin distorts our being in such a way that we neither resemble our cause nor desire our true end. We need to be governed. Thankfully, our principle and cause—the Lord God—does not allow our disobedience to have the last word. God is a conserving cause, renewing us in relation to himself through the instrumentality of the law. God contains us, as it were, in himself through the gift that is the law. The law derives from the Lord's will that "man adhere to God."[1] In encouraging adherence to God, the law encourages love of the same. I show throughout the chapter how the law is given that we might love its giver. The cry of the psalmist offers a wonderful platform for further considering the moral dimension of God's goodness.

PSALM 19 AND GOODNESS

Psalm 19 teaches us about the two different ways in which God instructs us. God teaches us by things general and things specific. Through things general

---

[1]Aquinas, *In Ps* 19, trans. Hugh McDonald.

and specific, God commends himself to us by virtue of what Thomas calls God's own "erudition," of which Psalm 19 speaks eloquently.[2] Just so, God instructs all people everywhere by his works, though in different ways. First, God commends himself in a general way, "relating equally to all" through the created order.[3] Thomas cites Romans 1:18 in support of this. In terms of the second way, the Lord God conveys himself "through law-giving, which is only to the faithful."[4] Put again, the heavens' message relates equally to all, though not "the law of the LORD" (Ps 19:7). The law is given by God to the faithful to lead them to God.[5]

Importantly, Thomas does not let his twofold account of the means by which God commends himself loose from God. In discussing the sun, its tent in the heavens (see Ps 19:4), he says that we "must understand two things about God." First, there "is the glory of God, in which glory he is glorious; second, his works."[6] The latter, as we have just seen, whether they are his general works or his specific works addressed to his covenant people, are instruments of his commendation, functioning in different ways for different audiences. The works of the Lord, either general or specific, rest on and express what is first, the glory and fullness of God. All of God's works attest God. Discussion of God's works always begins with God.

The heavens do not tell of themselves but rather of God. That is what they do: declare God's glory. God is glorious (in part) because the heavens do not have dominion over him; rather, he has dominion over them and their fruits. The heavens are caused, but God is not; God is free in relation to his creative acts. As Thomas notes, "*he is free who is cause of himself.*"[7] We see here how created things teach us about the one who extols himself through them.

God can and does reveal himself in general and in specific ways because he is glorious. Psalm 19 begins with a general work, God's first work in following Scripture's narrative pattern, creation itself. This is followed by a specific work, that is, law giving in relation to the faithful. In terms of Psalm 19:1-6, you have the general; in terms of Psalm 19:7-10, you have the specific.

---

[2] Aquinas, *In Ps* 19.
[3] Aquinas, *In Ps* 19.
[4] Aquinas, *In Ps* 19.
[5] See Aquinas, *SCG* 3.2.115.
[6] Aquinas, *In Ps* 19.
[7] Aquinas, *SCG* 3.2.112.

The latter has a different purpose from the former. Law, specifically, "is directed to love" of God.[8] Again, "the chief intention of the divine law," Thomas notes, is "to adhere to God by love."[9] We would not say that creation is more to be desired "than gold, even much fine gold" (Ps 19:10), but we would say that of the commandments. We say it of the commandments only because they intend that we "adhere to God by love."[10] In adhering to God by love via the commands, we become good. This is not to say that we are the active agents—that we make ourselves good—but rather that God is the one who "makes men good."[11] The Lord God makes us good through what lies outside us, the law. He restores us in goodness through our obedience to him via the law.

In sum, by beginning our exploration of the moral character of God's goodness with Psalm 19, we are reminded of how the law, as a distinct and specific good, commends God and is most consistent with God. While the heavens attest God, they do not incite love for God or commend adherence to God as does the law.

A MORAL GOOD

God is not only a generative but also a conserving cause. By conserving creatures in relation to him as their cause, God, moreover, perfects them. Such conserving on God's part shows us what kind of good, indeed what kind of cause, God is. We see that God is the kind of good who is present to what he causes. The Lord is present to us as our governor. The statutes are the means by which God governs us, inciting us to flee the corruption that comes into us when we rescind from our proper nature.[12]

The law is a good consistent with God's goodness. God is not the kind of cause that disregards what he has made. Rather, he governs us, encouraging our welfare, through the law. Because the law is a good consistent with God's goodness, we ought not to think in competitive terms about God's relationship to creatures, especially when it comes to thinking about the creature's obedience to God. The creature's obedience—which is also a distinct

---

[8]Aquinas, *SCG* 3.2.116.
[9]Aquinas, *SCG* 3.2.116.
[10]Aquinas, *In Ps* 19.
[11]Aquinas, *SCG* 3.2.116.
[12]See further Aquinas, *DN*, 284.

good—is her own and yet a gift from God evoked by God's law. Her desire to learn the statutes is her own, even as it comes to her from God. The reason that she can and does cry out to God is that God converts her to her ultimate good, which is God himself. Of course, the desire with which she desires to be taught derives from the fact that she is an effect whose cause is *per se* desirable. But that is not to detract from how God conserves her by governing her through the law and as such encourages her obedience.

Accordingly, when we talk about the attributes of God, we do not disregard morality. Human beings, who proceed from God as his likeness and who are their Creator's similitude, are to be moral, to strive for moral fitness. We are to resist sin and therefore do good by obeying the law. As Pieper notes, "all obligation is based upon being," the being of God who is the pure act of being itself, and who in turn creates beings who are compatible with himself. God is the foundation for morality, "the foundation of ethics."[13] God helps the psalmist via teaching him obedience, teaching him obligation based on his cause.

The help God supplies shows us something about God. God is in no need of teaching, whereas of course the psalmist is in need of teaching and healing. The psalmist is on the way, so to speak, toward finding himself in God, but God is not on the way to finding himself in another. There is nothing in God that could potentially defer to sin. God is an indefectible good. We, however, are defectible, but, again, God is not. God is the norm, the good, recalling us to himself in a way that is utterly consistent with his goodness. That way is the law. Without the statues as our lamp and guide, we are like wild beasts that do not know themselves in accordance with reality itself, the Lord God. Without the statutes, our minds and hearts cannot be aligned with reality as with the good.

Let us briefly recount the point of this short but crucial section. The law, as a moral good, possesses its character as such from God. God is the kind of cause who conserves what he causes, not allowing it to languish in its own acts of self-making and preservation, which are really acts of unmaking. The law befits God's goodness. God is the kind of good who gives good things to those who need to be recalled to his goodness. We turn now to thinking

---

[13]Josef Pieper, *Living the Truth: The Truth of All Things: Reality and the Good*, trans. Stella Lange (San Francisco: Ignatius Press, 1989), 111.

through how it is that the law actually teaches us what is good via considering its threefold character.

THE THREEFOLD LAW

The law is about three things. The three dimensions of the law speak to God as the one who has caused something that indicates him—"The law of the LORD is perfect" (Ps 19:7). In Thomas's *In Ps* 19, he maintains that the law is perfect, yes, because God is perfect, and perfect in its combination of "testimonies, judgments, and precepts." First, the law is a testimony to wisdom; it is the Lord's teaching and his truth, for it is from the one who is wisdom itself. The law is entirely trustworthy, ordering us toward life with God. "God," Thomas writes, "gives us testimonies in order that his authority take root in our hearts." Second, the law contains judgments. Thomas has in minds texts such as Exodus 22, which talks about what to do with one who has stolen a cow or sheep. He also cites texts such as Isaiah 26, which talk about the right path of the just to walk. The law's judgments encourage God's people in ways that are holy and good. Third, Thomas describes the law in terms of precepts, which he describes as "things that are to be done; as if we are held to do that exactly."[14] The law prescribes certain acts, forbidding others.

The law as a combination of testimonies, judgments, and precepts is "more to be desired . . . than gold, even much fine gold" (Ps 19:10), precisely because of "its sweetness and joy."[15] Its sweetness and joy derives, not surprisingly, from God. Accordingly, the virtue on the human side most appropriate to the law is humility, for humility befits the divine goodness. A willingness to be taught wisdom, to adhere to God's judgments, and to follow God's precepts heightens, rather profoundly, our appreciation of the radical distinction between God and creatures. The law teaches us that we are not God's equals but rather God's beloved creatures, those who are always God's debtors.

The statutes' function is this: to teach us that "the LORD is God" (Ps 118:27). Psalm 105, the great recital of God's faithfulness to Israel, ends by explaining the rationale for God's great deeds of liberation, namely, "that they might keep his statutes and observe his laws" (Ps 105:45). In keeping his statutes

---

[14]Aquinas, *In Ps* 19.
[15]Aquinas, *In Ps* 19.

and laws, we learn that the Lord is God and to adhere to him. The law teaches and explains the Creator/creature distinction to us. Its pedagogical function is to awaken us to the Lord through its perfect combination of testimonies, judgments, and precepts.

CAUSALITY AND THE LAW

God's works manifest his attributes. Creation, for example, attests God's aseity, his ontological self-sufficiency. God, who is unmade, is free to make what is made. The giving of the law tells us something true of God's self. What, specifically, does it say to us? It communicates that God is good. No other attribute is more consistent with the gift of the law than God's goodness. The law is good precisely because it instructs us in faithfully apprehending our createdness. Without the law, we would remain woefully ignorant of our being made and of the shape of life that our being made entails. God, of course, needs no law, for God knows himself truly. We, however, need help, profoundly so, and the help that God gives us is the law.

The law evokes knowledge of who we are before God, that is, creatures; creatures know themselves in relation to another, whereas God does not know himself in relation to other things: there is no law above him. But again, God knows himself in relation to himself and knows other things only insofar as they relate to him. This is why we say, for example, that God does not know sin. God cannot know what is antithetical to God, whereas we so often desire what is antithetical to our flourishing as creatures, dwelling on what is inimical to our creatureliness.

We do not truly know ourselves in relation to ourselves. This is what the law communicates. We are, rather, dependent creatures, unlike the Lord, who needs no other to know himself. The Lord God does not act by anything outside himself, for he is pure act and so acts by his essence. The same is not true for us. We need law, for without law we are imprisoned by our attempts at self-mastery. Discipleship is a matter of seeing ourselves as God's and so recognizing that we have nothing worth having outside him or what is ordered to him. The law nurtures an excentric existence, oriented to the one who has no need of anyone or anything else in order to know himself. In obeying the statutes, we learn that we are caused, that we are not the sheep of our pasture. What the cry tells us about God is that he is our cause and that through acts of penitence, prayer, and praise, we awaken to our cause, who is goodness itself. Moreover, the acts by which we learn that we are the Lord's are themselves "caused." We obey the law in the Lord, who fulfills the law through us. The law to which the psalmist refers has thus a kind of mystical horizon. The law of Moses anticipates or prefigures the law of Christ. Moses' law bears Christ, and it demonstrates Christ. It is an instrument through which God draws us to intimacy with himself.

The law lovingly instructs us in our cause and thus in seeing ourselves as caused and made. The law orders us to our end: God. The law is not an end in itself. It has no power to cause what it commends. The law is a tutor that evokes love of and reverence for its source. This is why the law is said to be good. God causes good things, things that are compatible with and befitting to him. The law is good, pleasing, and perfect, then, not in itself but in relation to God. It is incumbent on us to be mindful of how the law commends its cause. The law extols what is good, though it does not make us good. The law serves to orient or reorder us to our only good, but again it does not rectify us in relation to the good as does Jesus Christ.

Another way to think about God as the cause and the law as caused is to note how we receive understanding of the good through things. We receive understanding of our cause in relation to things. The law is a conservative principle, pointing to God, who wills that we be conserved in relation to him. We do not create, sustain, and conserve ourselves. Quite the opposite: only in relation to the Lord God do we know as those who are created and conserved.

The law can become a stumbling block—as was the case for the Pharisees—if it is not loved in and through God. The law then becomes an idol, treated as if it were uncaused. God is a productive good, creating us from nothing, and a conservative good, conserving us in relation to himself through the law. We are to love what is good—"Oh, how I love your law! It is my meditation all day long" (Ps 119:97). Why? Because it teaches us that we are not our own but belong to another, who forever belongs to no one and who teaches us this truth by teaching us his law.

Is Obedience Natural to Us?

Having wrestled with what the law teaches us about God and ourselves as caused and conserved by God, we are in a position to consider the cry itself.

We ask in this section about why the cry is so unnatural to us as members of Adam's helpless race.

Our creaturely goodness—indeed, our being—is, as we have noted, "by participation," had in relation to another, that is, God, who is unparticipated being.[16] Any good that we may do is from another, that is, God, which is not to suggest that there is any competition between our doing good and God gifting us with the capacity to do good. The challenge arises in accounting for this in Thomistic terms with respect to whether "the common view of the learned [that] maintains that everything that is tends to the good" works, biblically speaking.[17] The "common view" to which Thomas refers is that of Aristotle in his *Nicomachean Ethics*. Does the creature, as God's "likeness," have, as Aristotle avers, "a natural inclination toward what it pursues," namely, God?[18] Is it natural to us to tend toward God? The answer is yes and no. Though it is natural for us to tend toward God, we are in an unnatural state, having reversed in Adam the Creator/creature relationship. As a result, it is natural to us to tend toward ourselves. Sin turns us in on ourselves, away from God and the neighbor, such that we are "prone to hate God and our neighbor."[19] Sin renders natural a way of being that is profoundly unnatural. If the common view that Thomas may be said to endorse is correct, namely, that we tend naturally toward God, then what remains of the psalmist's cry "teach me your statutes" (Ps 119:68)? The cry assumes that he cannot do what is natural. The cry is a stark acknowledgment of how distant is his heart from God. The psalmist needs God's naturalizing help. The presence of the cry indicates such help. The psalmist does begin to tend toward God, but this tending is entirely God's doing insofar as it is God working in and through him so as to turn the psalmist toward himself.

Much of the import of Thomas's treatment hinges on the designations "natural" and "natural inclination." Does the cry represent a "natural inclination"?[20] Yes, it does, insofar as we, naturally speaking, are from another—"the first good."[21] What is natural to us as created beings is what

---

[16]Aquinas, *Hebdomads*, 43.
[17]Aquinas, *Hebdomads*, 40.
[18]Aquinas, *Hebdomads*, 38.
[19]HC, q 5, response.
[20]Aquinas, *Hebdomads*, 38.
[21]Aquinas, *Truth*, 21.4.

aligns us with who we were created to be. Inclinations natural to us derive from the one in whom we, as beings, participate simply by existing. But because sin is from nothing and leads to nothing, it destroys everything that is. Satan only lies, for that is his nature. Sin reduces us to nothing. The more we embrace sin, the less we are. Sin profoundly distorts and corrupts what is natural in such a way that it seems "natural" to us to think and act as if we are our own Creator.

Another way to think about the psalmist's cry in a Thomistic direction is with reference to our dependence on God. To depend on God is the most natural thing for us to do. Accordingly, it is unnatural for us to abscond and to assert our independence from God, though, of course, we do! It befits our creatureliness to depend on the principle whereby we are produced and conserved in being. Our creatureliness—as creatureliness—implies a natural relation to God. "To be created is to be made," writes Thomas; creation denotes "a kind of relation."[22] We are indeed naturally related to God by virtue of being made, and obedience is natural to our relationship with our Creator, for in obeying we live as those who are made.

The principle of creation, God, is "in the creature as its subject."[23] This is, I think, the ultimate ground for maintaining "that everything that is tends to the good."[24] The created order has the Creator as its principle, and the Creator does not will that what is created succumb to the cancer of sin and death, for he remains its subject. Accordingly, the created order cannot be understood without God, for God is present in it as its subject. If so, then, the notion of "natural inclination" is not alien to the psalmist's cry, for such a cry is the most "natural" cry on the part of one for whom God is its subject. If the category "natural" need not be understood naturalistically—that is, without reference to God—then Thomas's basic point, as undergirded by Aristotle, illuminates the psalmist's cry. The psalmist recognizes just how unnatural it is to refrain from the cry, sinner that he is, and to resist tending toward God. Natural life recognizes its existence in relation to another.

The Lord God is most natural to us as our subject. Created things are made in such a way that they "are directed to one good, God to wit, as their

---

[22]Aquinas, *SCG* 4.48, 2.18.
[23]Aquinas, *SCG* 2.18.
[24]Aquinas, *Hebdomads*, 30.

end."[25] God is our natural end, an end agreeable to whom we are as God's
creatures, and we experience God's direction in the law. To say that we
possess a "natural inclination" toward God and that we "are directed to one
good, God to wit" are, I think, complementary statements, insofar as we also
lean on the doctrine of providence. Let me explain. The doctrine of providence is an extension of the doctrine of creation and has its logic therein.
The doctrine of creation articulates nature's basis, its productive principle.
Providence is intrinsic to the doctrine of creation insofar as it unfolds creation's conservative principle. "Nature . . . does not direct to an end but is
directed."[26] Our being directed Godward is simply a function of God's
presence as our subject. Teaching on our createdness is inadequate if it does
not also include teaching on our directedness, which is precisely where we
locate God's gift of the law. God does good in relation to us by directing us
to himself through the law.

Psalm 27:4 illuminates this. "One thing I asked of the Lord, that will I
seek after: to live in the house of the Lord all the days of my life." In rumi-
nating on this text, Thomas unfolds the relationship between the perfection
of the psalmist's desire and its cause in God. God causes us and is the source
of everything in us that agrees with him. God is perfect and as such is perfect
love. David desires as he does in Psalm 27:4 because of God, who is perfect
love, and who as such "gathers together the powers (of a person) into a
single whole and moves it toward the things loved."[27] David is said to be a
lover of God—"One thing I asked of the Lord" (Ps 27:4)—but David's being
a lover of God is all because of God. There is (again) not any competition
here. David loves God in God; any good that David has is in God and is
God's. David moves toward God, seeks God, in and by God, and all that
through God's law. Divine love, Thomas notes, "makes the whole man tend
toward God without wavering."[28] Insofar as we tend to God by God, through
receiving in faith God's direction in the law, we are naturalized.

Having considered how obedience is the most naturalizing thing we could
ever do, we are in a position to deepen our inquiry into what the law teaches

[25] Aquinas, *SCG* 3.17.
[26] Aquinas, *Truth* 22.1.
[27] Aquinas, *In Ps* 27, trans. James Miguez.
[28] Aquinas, *In Ps* 27.

us of God and ourselves in relation to him by considering what obedience to the statutes achieves. David's cry is an indication of the extent to which "we can fail to be good with accidental goodness, which is absolute and unqualified goodness."[29] God cannot cease to be good, but we can, because absolute goodness is accidental to us. We may live as unrepentant sinners even as our existence *qua* existence and our being as being is good and indicative of an implicit desire for God himself. So Thomas states, "Complete or absolute goodness increases and diminishes and disappears entirely in us, but not in God."[30] Even those who cry out will all too often hanker after what is false, which is a salutary reminder, again, of how different is our goodness from God's. Obedience to the law adds goodness to our essence; obedience increases goodness in us. Inasmuch as we obey, we are more, rather than less, good. Of course, we do fail, and we do disobey, but when we obey we increase. Such an increase is accidental. Insofar as I obey, I am more myself—more "Chris"—rather than less, but God is never less nor more God. God always is. In sum, the cry reflects, however provisionally, our correspondence to and imitation of one whose being is identical with goodness itself. Our obedience adds something to us that was not there before, namely, goodness in a qualified sense, but even as those who obey, the Creator/creature distinction is always intact with respect to God's unqualified goodness. God does not increase in goodness as we by his grace become better.

LOVING GOD THROUGH GOD'S LAW

We love the law in God, who in return loves the law not in relation to anything else. Rather, God loves the law, as with all things that come from him, "for the sake of God's own goodness."[31] There are created things precisely because of God's love of his own goodness. This is the foundation of the doctrine of our creation and preservation. In this section we think about how God is loved through what is from nothing. The law does not come from us but is of God, who speaks it into being in his encounter with Moses—"I am the God of your father, the God of Abraham, the God of Isaac, and the God of Jacob" (Ex 3:6).

---

[29] Aquinas, *Truth* 21.5.
[30] Aquinas, *Truth* 21.5.
[31] Aquinas, *DN*, 376.

In learning to love the law, we learn to love God as its source. The law participates in God as its source. In fact, we cherish the law because it participates or shares in the goodness proper to God himself. It is not fortuitous, then, that God's law is acclaimed in the Psalter over and over again as good. It is good because it befits, is appropriate to, and is consistent with his goodness.

The key is to love the law in relation to its source. The law's goodness is derivative of God insofar as the law in not good through itself but by virtue of its similitude to God's goodness. The law perfectly participates in goodness as law. Accordingly, the end of the law is that we might more perfectly participate in the divine goodness and love the same.

The fact that there is a law is (again) testimony to the conservative character of God's goodness. "For it belongs to the Good to produce and conserve good things."[32] The days of creation point to the generative character of God's goodness, the law to the conservative character of it. By loving the divine instruction that is the law, we are conserved, brought by his grace to our senses. In setting God before us, the law serves as an instrument by which our intellects are united to God. This is a good thing. The law creates a good that was not there before, namely, an intellect on its way toward the good from which it has defected. The good that is obedience points to a basic metaphysical principle intrinsic to an account of God's goodness. Being is determined, for Thomas, "after the Good, since the Good in some ways extends itself to more things."[33] Thomas's point is that the good "extends itself to existents as well as to non-existents."[34] God, as goodness itself, is creative of new goods, in this case the good that is obedience, which itself rests on a good, the law. A good that did not exist before (obedience), that was "in potency to *esse*," now exists, demonstrating the extent to which God's goodness is prior even to being itself.[35] What was not there before— that is, a person wanting to be taught God's statutes—is there now. A new good is brought into being from the uncreated good that is God.

The law is not its own end. Just as it has a beginning, it has an end, which is God. Accordingly, the statutes are not God but are in the service of God,

---

[32]Aquinas, *DN*, 411.
[33]Aquinas, *DN*, 431.
[34]Aquinas, *DN*, 432.
[35]Aquinas, *DN*, 432.

recalling us from sin and pointing us to their source. Of course, the law does not have the power to draw us to its source apart from the source itself—the Trinity. However, because the law bears Christ, and it is he who fulfills it for us, the law does in Christ serve as an aid in our conversion and recollection to God. Ultimately, it is Christ's law, and in being taught it are we taught him and to exist in him, through his Spirit. The God to whom the law belongs causes what he is—goodness, life, beauty, love, holiness, and so on—to increase and flourish in us so that we, as his effects, might share in what he has.

The law is thus a profound gift for us. Without God, who "is superabundantly full," we are empty, turned in on ourselves, given over to nothing, participants in our own decreation.[36] Our intellects recede from God, making us unwise. Sadly, we would rather stand outside God, ignoring the law that takes us outside ourselves, reminding us of God.[37] The law is gift precisely insofar as it disrupts and destabilizes our sinful efforts to know ourselves in relation to ourselves rather than God, who knows himself in relation to no other. What a blessing, then, it is to be known by God as one who seeks to be taught by God.

Expressed in the register of the Psalms, the law converts us to God not through any agency of its own but rather through awakening in us a hunger and thirst for God, which itself comes from God. This would, of course, not occur if the law were not of God, and we (creatures) were not God's likeness and similitude. The law teaches us desire and love of the Lord God, whose image we are. Indeed, we are not made to desire what is alien to us. It is natural to us to desire God, and such desire has a proper cause, the Lord God.

Another way in which to bring the law's source—the immeasurability of God—into greater focus is to ask the question: Does God prepossess what the law brings about? Does God, for example, prepossess obedience? Indeed, if "all effects preexist virtually in their cause," is it right to argue that faith preexists in God, who is its cause?[38] Faith, as the highest form of obedience, is of God; faith is a gift of God. But does God prepossess it? No, it would be a mistake to read either obedience or faith back into God, for they imply a lack that is not true of God. Through the obedience of faith we are

---

[36] Aquinas, *DN*, 457.
[37] See further Aquinas, *DN*, 460.
[38] Aquinas, *DN*, 503.

reordered to God, but such reorientation never applies to God, who is always faithful and good. Obedience is a gift from God, but God cannot be ever said to obey, as if there were another to whom God was bound.

Put another way, God, in prepossessing infinite goodness, desires us in relation to himself; in loving himself, the Lord God loves us. The obedience that our cry expresses is God's work all the way down; but we would not say that obedience itself is what God prepossesses. Obedience is a created good whose foundation and presupposition lies with God. God is its basic principle—as is the case with all creatures great and small—but we would not say that these things are "prepossessed" by God. What we would say is that God prepossesses the good they express.

In sum, God commends himself to us through the law so that we might love him. The law commends his goodness by conserving us in relationship to our one and only good. What the law does not do is declare and make us good. Again, it displays the good but cannot make good, for that is, finally, the work of Christ. In this last section we examine the relationship between the law in its threefold form and Jesus Christ.

THE LAW AND JESUS CHRIST

This basic truth taught by Ephesians 2 is that Jesus Christ eliminates and defeats the hostility between Jew and Gentile through the blood of his cross. Such hostility is not done away with by Gentiles converting to Judaism but by Jesus' sacrificial death.[39] So Ephesians 2:15 insists, "He has abolished (*katargeō*) the law with its commandments and ordinances, that he might create in himself one new humanity in place of the two, thus making peace."[40] Paul teaches that covenant relationship with God is no longer secured by fidelity to the Mosaic law but rather by Christ's cross. And yet, in many places in Paul's corpus—and I am assuming Pauline authorship of Ephesians— he goes to great lengths to explain why Jesus Christ does not abolish the law; for example, the profound sequence of Romans 3:31–4:25: "Do we then overthrow the law by this faith? By no means! On the contrary, we uphold the law" (Rom 3:31). Why, then, does Paul use the word *abolish* in

---

[39]See Peter S. Williamson, *Ephesians*, CCSS 3 (Grand Rapids: Baker Academic, 2009), 71.
[40]According to BDAG, "make the law invalid" is a most fitting translation, as are "make ineffec-
tive" and "nullify." See καταργέω, 525.

Ephesians when in other letters he champions the notion of the law as gift and, as noted in Romans 7:12, as "holy and just and good"? What are we to make of two seemingly contradictory statements about the law? And how do these statements relate to the psalmist's unreserved delight in and love for the law?

The first thing to be said is that the problem is not with the law itself but with sin. Sin distorts the law. The psalmist delights in the law and longs to be taught its statutes precisely because he, like Paul, acknowledges the law as a gift of a generous God. The law holds the promise of life and as such is to be loved in the light of God. The law bears Jesus Christ; it has its center in him who does not supersede the law but fulfills it. The law, however, is not life itself; it has a promissory character. It points us to the one who is and communicates life itself—Jesus Christ. In other words, the law attests our end but cannot unite us to our end because the law is subject to corruption by sin.

If such is the case, then, what is good and a gift becomes, tragically, an agent of hostility between Jews and Gentiles. The Jews capitulate to sin's destruction of the law, allowing the law to produce enmity between them and Gentiles. Sin causes Jews to separate from Gentiles so as to deprive them "of access to God through the Scriptures."[41] Sin takes the law hostage, preventing it from fulfilling its proper function in God's economy, namely, that of pointing to Jesus Christ. Incredibly, Jesus abolishes the law held hostage by sin, which is the only law that we know. In so doing, he frees the law so as to enable it to fulfill its proper purpose of witnessing to him. The problem is not the law but, as Fowl notes, "sin's influence."[42] What Christ abolishes is the only law that we know, that is, a law held hostage to principalities and powers inimical to it and more powerful than it. Hence Paul describes the law's ministry in 2 Corinthians 3:7 as "the ministry of death."

Thomas, commenting on Ephesians 2:15, adds further insight. He helps us to see that one dimension of the law is actually abolished, namely, the ceremonial, referring to it as "old."[43] When Thomas talks about the old law

---

[41]Frank Thielman, *Ephesians*, BECNT (Grand Rapids: Baker Academic, 2010), 170. Cf. Eph 2:12.
[42]Stephen E. Fowl, *Ephesians*, TNTL (Louisville: Westminster John Knox, 2012), 94.
[43]Thomas Aquinas, *Commentary on St Paul's Epistle to the Ephesians*, trans. Matthew L. Lamb (Albany, NY: Magi Books, 1966), chap. 2, lecture 5, dhspriory.org/thomas/Eph2.htm#5.

in negative terms, he has in mind other New Testament texts such as Acts 15:10. Accordingly, Thomas thinks that the old law is nullified because of "the great number of legal injunctions it contained, so many that men could not possibly keep them all." The many legal injunctions could not be kept because the old law "did not confer grace through which men would have been assisted in fulfilling the law."[44] In other words, the law commands too much and does not supply enough. This means that there are two problems with the law: first, it is distorted by sin through no fault of its own; second, it does not assist one in obeying what it commands, especially its "legal injunctions." Nonetheless, the old law has "permanent goodness," for when it is embraced in faith, it is the means by which Christ recalls us to himself.[45] As Thomas notes, "Every law aims at establishing friendship either between man and man, or between man and God."[46] The law's abiding goodness has to do with its intention and end, namely, friendship with God. "The chief intention of the divine law is to establish man in friendship with God."[47] The law awakens that desire for friendship. "I do not call you servants any longer . . . but I have called you friends" (Jn 15:15).

The new law and its precepts are superior to the old, argues Thomas, because the new "regulates what must be done by giving commands, and it aids in fulfilling them by bestowing grace." The new law of the new covenant—the law of Christ—commands just as does the old, although the new law has far fewer commands. Unlike the old, however, it gives the strength to do what it commands. The old law is but a shadow "made void by the perfect. . . . This happened by the decrees, referring to the precepts of the New Testament through which the law was annulled." Importantly, Thomas is not arguing that the old law in its entirety is invalidated, only "the ceremonial precepts of the Old Law as they were in themselves."[48] The moral dimension of the law, which is the second table of the Decalogue, remains a valid source of holy teaching.

---

[44]Ibid.

[45]Matthew Levering, *Christ's Fulfillment of Torah and Temple: Salvation According to Thomas Aquinas* (Notre Dame, IN: University of Notre Dame Press, 2001), 22.

[46]Aquinas, *ST* 1.2.99.1 ad 2.

[47]Note that the chief end of "human law is to create friendship between man and man." See Aquinas, *ST* 1.2.99.2.

[48]Aquinas, *Ephesians*, chap. 2, lecture 5.

In a rather startling turn of phrase, Thomas also says that the new law—
that is, the precepts of the New Testament—is accompanied by "the Natural
Law."[49] The precepts of the new covenant do not compete with "Natural Law,"
which is synonymous with the moral law, the foundation of right living as
encapsulated by the Decalogue. If Thomas is correct in his reading of Ephesians 2:15, as I think he is, then he subtly alters the picture given to us by
leading contemporary commentators on Ephesians such as Fowl. What do
I mean? For Thomas, the ceremonial (and judicial) law is abolished, not the
moral commands. The latter "were not destroyed by Christ but fulfilled in
the counsels he added and in his explanations of what the Scribes and Pharisees had wrongly interpreted."[50] The ceremonial, however, is only abolished
because Jesus "fulfilled them with regard to what they prefigured," that is,
interior cleansing by his blood.[51] Thomas's division of the law makes good
theological sense, for what Christ commands—the precepts of the New Testament—are precepts that he through the Spirit gives us the power to obey.[52]
Jesus Christ fulfills the commands of the new covenant in and through us.
We observe the law in him who fulfilled it for us.

That said, would it be fair to say that the psalmist only delights in what
Thomas calls the "moral" as opposed to the "ceremonial" law? I do not think
so. The psalmist seems to delight in the totality of God's law. Thomas's distinction between the "ceremonial" and the "moral" would not have been
intelligible to the psalmist.[53] Nonetheless, such a distinction is theologically
useful because it helps us to make sense of both the positive and negative
comments that New Testament authors make about the law. In addition, the
psalmist loves the law, as we should, because it bears Christ's and the Spirit's
voices, evoking friendship and intimacy with them.

We hear Christ speak through the law, and we obey it in him. Proper
obedience to God's law "is best understood and practiced in Christ. . . . [He

---

[49]Ibid.

[50]Thomas has in mind texts such as Mt 5:17, 20, 43-44. By moral commands he means, for example, the command to act justly, to love your enemies, etc.

[51]Aquinas, *Ephesians*, chap. 2, lecture 5.

[52]Ibid., chap. 2, lecture 3.

[53]See further Aquinas, *ST* 1.2.101.2. Thomas argues that the ceremonial "pertains to the divine
worship," that is, as "determinations of the moral precepts whereby man is directed to God, just
as the judicial precepts are determinations of the moral precepts whereby he is directed to his
neighbor."

is] the telos of the Torah."[54] The call to be taught God's law is thus the call to be taught Jesus Christ. Jesus Christ teaches us the law, which is himself; he is "the filter" through which the law of Moses passes.[55] In receiving the statutes, we receive Christ and fulfill the only law there is, that is, the "law of Christ" (Gal 6:2), which is concomitant with what Thomas calls the moral law. The law, as is the case with the temple, has its intelligence in Christ. In keeping the law, we are keeping company with Jesus Christ. He abolishes the only law we know—that is, a law held hostage to sin—and liberates it in such a way that it can truly fulfill its purpose as an agent of promise and as the light that directs our path in obedience to him.

In sum, God gives the law (in all its moral, ceremonial, and judicial dimensions) because he is good. It is a gift consistent with and befitting his goodness, especially its conservative character. We love the law because it is God's. We love the law, moreover, because the law of Moses indicates our Savior Jesus Christ truly though obliquely and extrinsically. Although the law does not heal our souls of the sting of sin, it does point to and bear him who does. The law sets us on the path toward God and is fulfilled—not superseded—in Jesus. In loving the law, we love Jesus Christ; in being conformed to Christ, we honor the law.

CONCLUSION

In sum, what we have done in this chapter is expound the moral dimension of God's goodness via the psalmist's cry. We have statutes by which to cry because God is a conserving good. Not only is God productive of good but is conservative of created goods, especially we who have fallen so far from him. The overarching principle expressed in this chapter is that the works of God—in this case, the giving of the law and the incitement of the cry to be taught—express God's goodness. God's goodness is moral, we noted, because it preserves. It bears on us and commends itself to us through a particular good, the law. Just so, when we consider God's care for his wayward creatures, we give thanks for the law. The law enables us to see that our life

---

[54]Fowl, *Ephesians*, 95. Fowl makes the interesting observation that "pagans must come to understand themselves as Gentiles." However, he also notes that change in terms of self-understanding is required from Jews as well.

[55]I owe that turn of phrase to Thielman, *Ephesians*, 170.

is had in loving obedience in relation to our Creator, the God and Father of our Lord Jesus Christ.

The Thomistic notion that divine (though really all) attributes are signified according to works holds great promise for understanding the relationship of goodness and the law. Such a notion helps us to receive the Psalter's witness to God via Psalm 119:68. If the works of the Trinity are indivisible, as they are, then works such as providence demonstrate the indivisible being of God. Rather than thinking that the triune persons expound attributes, Thomas argues that works expound attributes, which are, of course, accomplished by the three. The attributes of God are common to the deity of God, simple and indivisible as it is, and we understand these attributes according to works, indivisible as they are.

Through obedience to the law, we live as God's beloved children. The law, as the fruit of his goodness, commends goodness, helping us to see that we have no other good apart from God. Accordingly, knowledge is precious and so must be taught. The law is not a part of the natural furniture of the human, though, as we saw, obedience to it naturalizes us. The law is a gift from outside, providing knowledge of God that far exceeds what is natural to us on this side of the fall, though again it does not teach us anything unnatural. I have argued that the law, because it ultimately belongs to Christ and bears Christ, enables us in the devastation to attain in his Spirit heights incommensurate with our natural abilities. We do not come to see God as he is in himself through the law, but we are given to know and love him through it.

Looking ahead, we ask about the goodness of Christ's person and how it is that he communicates goodness to us, declaring and making us good. We also look at what Christ's person as true God and true man infers for understanding the difference between the Creator and created things.

EIGHT

Goodness and Jesus Christ

I N THIS CHAPTER I CONSIDER the goodness of the one person of
Jesus Christ, truly divine and truly human. I hope to show how teaching
on the divine goodness and more broadly the doctrine of God's attributes
informs an account of Jesus Christ as one Person subsisting *in* two natures.[1]

I intend to circle around two texts in particular, one from the Psalms,
"My God, my God, why have you forsaken me?" (Ps 22:1) and another from
the Gospels, namely, Mark 10:18, "Why do you call me good? No one is
good but God alone."[2] These two texts will focus our treatment of three
complex themes intrinsic to Christology. First, there is the structural matter.
In what sense is incarnation a work most befitting divine goodness as its
fundamental principle? Second, we consider how "Scripture ascribes passion
and death to God's one and only-begotten Son."[3] Third and last, I describe
how some things said of Jesus Christ are more becoming to one of his two
natures without for a moment compromising their union in his very person.
In all this, I hope to show the extent to which Christology cannot be uncoupled from the doctrine of God.

GOODNESS AND INCARNATION

The incarnation is a work of God. This is obvious, but the theological sig-
nificance of the word *work* is not always appreciated. After all, a work is a

---

[1] I italicize the *in* to obviate any sense in which the presupposition *through* could be used. The one
person of Jesus Christ does not subsist through anything.

[2] The parallel text is Mt 19:17.

[3] Aquinas, *SCG* 4.34.

work of someone who is something. In this first major part of the chapter we contemplate how a work is related to the essence and identity of the one who undertakes it.

A work is something external to the divine life itself. To use Thomas's language, it is an "effect." The origin of the incarnation as an effect lies in the depths of God's being. Indeed, we have, in this regard, to think about two things. The first has to do with why God communicates and reveals himself to human beings. The response is simply that goodness is by its very nature communicative. The second thing to say is that the incarnation as a work befits God's goodness, the goodness common to Father, Son, and Spirit. Incarnation is a temporal extension of the Son's eternal procession from the Father. The Son shows us that his goodness is from the Father. The ground and principle of the Son as sent is his procession from the Father, just as the ground of the Father's sending is his being the begetter, and all that in the goodness belonging to them.

Emphasis on the incarnation as a mission that accomplishes the work of salvation, whose foundation is the Son's procession, points to the Son's immutability. "No change took place in God's Word Himself, but only in the human nature assumed by the Word."[4] The work of incarnation does not change the Son. Incarnation expresses rather what and who he is. The incarnation does not make him better, more divine than he was before, but the incarnation does make human nature better. The Word does not gain anything in terms of what he is or who he is. We instead are the recipients of his "most effective existence" all the way down.[5] The Son—who is wholly good in relationship to the Father and their Spirit, who never diminishes in goodness, who never ceases to be good—assists us, rather, out of his supreme goodness.

GOODNESS AND PSALM 22:1

If such is the case, then, how might Psalm 22:1 deepen our sense of the incarnation as a work expressive of the goodness of the Son? Psalm 22:1 is the cry of dereliction of the Son of God, who from eternity bears the name of Jesus Christ. It is the cry of one person, Jesus Christ, "God's own and

---

[4]Aquinas, *SCG* 4.49.
[5]Aquinas, *SCG* 4.54.

only-begotten Son."[6] It is he, who is true God, who becomes human, assuming "the likeness of sinful flesh" (Rom 8:3). Accordingly, he is not turned into a human but becomes human. He cannot cease to be the goodness he has always been, the goodness common to him and his Father and their Spirit. He also cannot cease to be the Father's only begotten. To be sure, the Son, the Word, assumes "an earthly and passible body."[7] However, he—the Son—assumes that without his essence or his originating relation to the Father being altered. He remains the one he has always been, the beloved Son of the Father, sharing in all that is the Father's as the Son. He is, from his birth to his death to his resurrection, one person who subsists in two natures, each remaining whole.

Thus as we think about Psalm 22:1, it would be a profound mistake to contrast the goodness of the Father with the goodness either of the Son or the Spirit. One cannot suggest that the one who dies ceases to be the Father's Son. One essence is common to the three and subsists in them. To be sure, the incarnation is a work appropriated to the Son, a work that discloses his sonship via the Father. Just so, Scripture would not have us say that the cry of dereliction pertains to Christ's human nature. The distinct will and operation of each of his natures does not mean that there are different operations. Christ's "rational soul and human flesh" are true of his human nature, yes, and his soul and flesh are entirely compatible with, though distinct from, his "perfect divine nature."[8] Nonetheless, both natures are in and united by his one person.

Thus the one who cries out on the cross is God's eternally beloved Son. Psalm 22:1 reminds us that the Lord Jesus dies bearing his own Word, that Word he first spoke through David. Jesus knew that David was writing about him. Jesus also knew the trajectory of the psalm, Psalm 22:5, for example, "to you they cried, and were saved." The Lord knows that salvation, not dereliction, has the last word. This is to say, in a more systematic idiom, "Holy Scripture, without making any distinction, ascribes divine things to the man; and to God, things pertaining to the man."[9] Because the one who

---

[6]Aquinas, *SCG* 4.34.
[7]Aquinas, *SCG* 4.30.
[8]Aquinas, *SCG* 4.39.
[9]Aquinas, *SCG* 4.39.

cries is God's Son, he cries as the forsaken one. The cry pertains to God because he (the Son) subsists in his human nature. The cry is the cry of God the Son, fully divine and human.

One of the reasons that there is no conflict with respect to the "distinct will and operation" of each nature is because of the pure actuality and aseity of the Son.[10] Because he is complete goodness, born eternally of the Father, he does not subsist through anything. Because he is complete in himself, the Lord Jesus bears what is not good in his unblemished humanity to such an extent that he became sin. He would, of course, not be our salvation if he were not all that the Father and Spirit are. The Son became sin, and the Son died, yes, as the Son. No more than this may we say. Our salvation is in his one person; reconciliation is effected in his one person, not in his natures, subsisting as it does in two natures. Put again, the one person subsists *in* and not *through* the natures. Were he to subsist through them, he would no longer be sovereign over his own person. He would no longer possess the one essence common to him, the Father, and their Spirit. Even as Jesus dies, he never ceases to be God's Son. Even in his death, he is all that the Father and Spirit are, supreme goodness. His person does not cease. The Lord does not cease to be good even as he bears the curse of sin and death. The death of this man would not be good were he not the supremely good Son of God. The goodness of the Lord, lasting as it does forever, does not cease, even on Good Friday.

The unity of essence, indeed what is identical to that essence, has once again a profound effect at this juncture in our inquiry. Goodness is never ceasing "by reason of the unity of the essence."[11] Jesus is crucified as a common criminal on a first-century instrument of Roman imperial torture as the one Son of the Father. This we must never forget. Our salvation is effected in the person who is eternally united in essence with the Father and the Spirit.

Where does this leave us? In short, let us not forget the Lord Jesus, to whom belongs the one essence common to the Trinity and who never ceases to be born of the Father even in death. The ground of the hypostatic union is the person who is one with the Father and Spirit and who proceeds

---

[10] Aquinas, *SCG* 4.36.
[11] Aquinas, *SCG* 4.25.

eternally from the Father's being, begotten and therefore sent. The cry denotes dereliction, yes, but not alteration of what and who he is. He, as
goodness itself, assumes our passible body and all the cries concomitant
with it so as to render us incorruptible and heavenly. Scripture ascribes to
the Son things that pertain to humanity, namely, suffering and death, and
the reason why these things are destroyed is that it is God the Son who bears
them in the fullness of what and who he is, together with the Father and the
Spirit.

GOODNESS AND MARK 10:18

Having considered the principle of the incarnation in terms of divine
goodness and how the cry of dereliction manifests what the Son is and who
he is in relationship to the Father and Spirit, we are now in a position to
briefly explore with respect to Mark 10:18, "Why do you call me good? No
one is good but God alone," how certain scriptural texts are more befitting
of either his humanity or his divinity.

The divine nature of our Lord is "greater" than his human nature, for his
human nature, sinless though it is, is not—by nature, if you can forgive the
pun—incorruptible and heavenly, as is the case with his divine nature. That
is not to denigrate his true humanity, for it is our nature that needs to be
rendered good in an indefectible sense, as is true of God. In other words,
there is an asymmetry between the two natures, the greater being the divine.
The Son of God subsists in and through two natures, and so in his divinity
is personally united with humanity. You could think of it this way. The humility exhibited by Jesus in relation to his Father "is becoming to Him in
His humanity." The Lord Jesus displays his humility, for example, in his
obedience to his Father's will even unto death. "Humility," however, "is not
becoming to God, who has no superior." One nature is thus superior to
another, though one is not in competition with the other. It is enough to say
with Thomas that the "virtue of humility" exhibited by Christ is "becoming
to Him in His humanity."[12]

Jesus' humility is entirely compatible with his supreme goodness, yes,
but should not be said of his divinity, the Son of God's subsistence in "two

---

[12]Aquinas, *SCG* 4.55.

distinct unmixed natures."[13] This means that one must avoid collapsing the Person into the natures and instead consider the natures in relation to the person to whom they are united. Natures belong to one person, and that person subsists in them, as the goodness he is, together with the Father and Spirit.

To push this further in relation to Mark 10:18, God (the Father) alone is good, yes, because the Father has his being from no one—that is, his innascibility—whereas the Son has his being and thus his goodness from him, from the Father. Because the Son is begotten of the Father's substance, he is all that the Father is but as Son. If one of the key underlying dogmatic principles of Psalm 22:1 is the unity of essence, for Mark it is the procession of the Son from the Father. The Lord Jesus has his goodness from the Father alone, and the Father from himself alone.

If so, then, I think we are in a better position to receive the fullness of the biblical testimony to Christ's person. The reason that there are glimpses of his omnipresence, omniscience, and omnipotence in the Gospels is that nothing prevents him from expressing in his humanity what is proper to him by dint of his unity of essence with the Father and Spirit. Because the Son is unchangeably good, he suffers no loss of goodness even as he in his incarnate and humiliated state says that God alone is good. It is the Son who, though equal to God, humbled himself. If we do not take the "alone" of Mark 10:18 seriously, we detract from the extent to which the mission of the Son and its culmination in his work of reconciliation on the cross uniquely expresses what is common to the Father, Son, and Spirit.

CHRISTOLOGY AND THE CREATOR/CREATURE DISTINCTION

What has been said with respect to these important passages merits our stepping back, as it were, and considering how they inform a central concern of the book, the Creator/creature distinction. How does Christology illuminate the similarity and ever-greater dissimilarity between Creator and creature?

Let us note, first, Jesus' life. The life of the man Jesus is one of uninterrupted praise, obedience, and love for his Father, the God of Israel, with whom he is one, together with their Spirit. This man, consubstantial as he is with the Father and the Spirit, shares our existence as true human. He

---

[13] Aquinas, *SCG* 4.39.

assumes our existence, unites our fallen humanity to his perfect humanity and divinity, and all that in his one person. More specifically, Christ's knowledge of his own deity, his life with the Father and Spirit, is "immediate" and "intuitive knowledge."[14] Such knowledge is natural to who he is as a human, hypostatically united as he is to the eternal Son. Creation's "knowledge" of its Creator is similarly immediate and intuitive. In some instances in the Psalms, for example, Psalm 148, "sun and moon . . . and shining stars" (Ps 148:3) are called to praise; in other instances, most famously, Psalm 19, "the heavens are telling the glory of God" (Ps 19:1). In either case, what is most natural to the "heavens" and the "sun and moon" is praise. Created things naturally praise their maker. Their cause is present to them in such a way that the most fitting thing the heavens and the earth can do is sing their Creator's praise. In terms of the man Jesus, the most knowledge he has—the most immediate—is that "of his own filial divine nature and will."[15] It is entirely natural to him to see and do only that which the Father sees and does. His humanity as evidenced throughout his ministry, passion, death, and resurrection is entirely transparent to who he is as the Father's only begotten Son. He exists in his cause, the Father, in unimaginable intimacy, just as his Father exists in him, eternally.

Creation, similarly, is transparent to God. There is nothing in the created order that would cause it to resist declaring its createdness. This is true given that something that proceeds from God could not oppose him from whom it proceeds, for it exists in him. Expressed in a more Thomistic idiom, effects are known only in relationship to their cause and express naturally, in a manner befitting their various modes, their cause. Moreover, the Creator is present to what is created as its Creator, its very subject. The triune Creator is radically transcendent to what he creates—Creator and creature do not share in something common to them—and also intimate to it. The Creator is present to what is created as its preserver, what Ephraim Radner calls "directional presence."[16] Creation's praise of its Creator, as so wonderfully depicted in the Psalter, is entirely fitting given its createdness.

---

[14]Thomas Joseph White, OP, *The Incarnate Lord: A Thomistic Study in Christology* (Washington, DC: Catholic University of America Press, 2015), 237.

[15]Ibid., 247.

[16]Ephraim Radner, *A Time to Keep: Theology, Mortality, and the Shape of a Human Life* (Waco, TX: Baylor University Press, 2016), 68.

Even more, intimacy with the Creator is the fulfillment of creation. In the end, when sin and death have been manifestly vanquished, transparency will be superseded by the most unimaginable intimacy. Accordingly, responsible talk of God in relation to Christology includes talk of God as creation's origin, as its preserver, and as its fulfillment *in* Jesus Christ. Just as Jesus Christ is the one who completes torah and temple, he, as the agent of creation, is the very fulfillment of the created order. He is the one through whom all things were made and the one for whom all things were made. And yet, we would not say that all things are "from" him, for Scripture uses "from" only with respect to God (the Father). The Son is (again) the agent of creation and the one who is to "have first place in everything" (Col 1:18). That said, the Father has (eschatological) priority insofar as "when all things are subjected to him, then the Son himself will also be subjected to the one who put all things in subjection under him, so that God may be all in all" (1 Cor 15:28).

If such is the case, then, we see how the goodness of Christ informs how Creator and created things differ from each other. The Father, as we have seen, is present to all and indwells the community of the baptized through Jesus and the Spirit. When the end comes, the Father will be "all in all." All that exists will be "in" God, and God will be "in" all that exists. The beatific vision that Jesus possesses by nature—that is, immediate knowledge of God—will characterize by grace the life of glorified humanity. Indeed, God will be immediately known in relation to all things, all things declaring his praises in Jesus. Seeing him as he is and all things in him will be our bliss to all eternity. The creation will no longer groan "in labor pains," for its Creator will be "all in all," again not simply present to all, but "all in all" (Rom 8:22; 1 Cor 15:28). What was immediate and intuitive to Jesus will be immediate and intuitive to all created things, in a manner appropriate to their mode of being.

Jesus' life thus provides the template for discerning how the goodness common to the three will be common to created things. Created things are naturalized by his goodness. He enables them to imitate without interruption the mode of being that characterized his own earthly life, namely, total openness to his Father. In the life of the world to come, nothing will impede created things declaring and rejoicing in their createdness. They will, in other words, be perfectly united with their Creator but not absorbed, as it were, into him. They will remain distinct but in nonetheless unimaginable intimacy to the living God as they direct their praise to the Father through the glorified flesh of the Son in the Spirit.

Next we consider how the maintenance of this distinction is a work that is also proper to the Spirit. We take up how the Spirit, as the Spirit of the Father and Son, strengthens our intimacy with God and with all that is true of God's substance.

PNEUMATOLOGY AND THE CREATOR/CREATURE DISTINCTION

In *Trinity*, Augustine reminds us that what is identical with the divine substance is identical with the three persons. Goodness is predicated of the three, qualitatively—the Father, Son, and Spirit. The Father is not "better" than the Son; the Spirit is not "better" than the Father or Son. And yet each is distinguished from the others by opposing relations of origin. The Spirit proceeds as love, the love of the Father for the Son and the Son for the Father. As Thomas notes, "the name *Love* in God can be taken essentially and personally."[17] God is love in an essential sense, and the Spirit is love in an essential and personal sense. Following John 17:26, the Spirit is love proceeding.

Why mention this in a section on the pneumatological dimension of the Creator/creature relation? Precisely because the Spirit, resting as the Spirit does on Christ, enables us to live as creatures of the Son. The Spirit's gift of life, indeed of the life of Jesus Christ, is always "Son-shaped."[18] The Spirit is never, in either theology or economy, detached from the Son. As Thomas says, the "Holy Ghost is said to rest in the Son as the love of the lover abides in the beloved."[19] Just as the Spirit's distinction with respect to the Son is not compromised by his unity with him, the particular work of the Spirit among us, the Spirit's mission, is not any less the Spirit's because it is Son-shaped.

The Spirit's work is essentially that of giving—indeed, filling us with what he is: love. The Spirit gives us the love he is together with the Father and the Son. In so doing, the Spirit communicates goodness. The goodness of the

---

[17]Aquinas, *ST* 1.37.1.
[18]Gilles Emery, OP, *The Trinitarian Theology of Thomas Aquinas*, trans. Francesca Aran Murphy (New York: Oxford University Press, 2007), 271.
[19]Aquinas, *ST* 1.36.2 ad 3.

Spirit is most manifest through the gift he gives, which is the ability to love the Son and through him the Father. When we love the Father through the Son in the Spirit, we receive the Spirit's own love, through which he communicates goodness to us.

The Spirit is the great gift of God given in time. As Thomas states, "*Gift* is the proper name of the Holy Ghost."[20] The gift of the Spirit is love, the love by which we love him and our neighbor in him, which is the very form his goodness takes when communicated among us. Following Augustine, this is intimacy with God: that we love him who has not acquired the goodness with which he is good.[21] Love rests in and delights in its object. Though we often find ourselves in the midst of many earthly travails, by virtue of our baptism we rest in the Son through the Spirit, who himself rests in the Son and in him, the Father. The language of love is important to maintain, not only because of the dominical command (Mt 22:37-39), but because it is by the Spirit that we love the Father and the Son and thus have our destiny as creatures fulfilled.

Just as Christology may never be separated from pneumatology, so pneumatology may never be separated from Christology, to say nothing of the Trinity. Unimaginable intimacy with our Creator in the life of the world to come is the fruit of his goodness, whose form is love. This is the distinct point that our brief gesture toward pneumatological teaching introduces—namely, his goodness communicated among us "renders us able to love."[22] The Creator/creature distinction, in other words, is fully manifest in love. Intimacy's highest form is love. The Holy Spirit is love, the love by which we love the Father and the Son and through them the neighbor.

The love the Spirit compels will, in this life, have a cruciform shape. Our salvation is enjoyment of God's goodness, but the form that enjoyment takes on this side of glory is cruciform. We love him in a manner that corresponds to the form of his love for us. He pours out his Spirit on the cross, and that same Spirit leads us to his cross, to suffering "for a little while" (1 Pet 5:10). The cross of the Lord Jesus reconciles us to the Father, who sends his people out to love him in the crucified one and in the Spirit. Just

---

[20]Aquinas, *ST* 1.37.1.
[21]See Augustine, *Trinity* 15.2.
[22]Emery, *Trinitarian Theology*, 256.

so, the Spirit enables us to love through mortifying in us all that falls short of the goodness with which he is. The Spirit declares us good in Jesus Christ and makes us good in him, and the form of his making is cruciform. As Jesus says to Peter, "someone else will fasten a belt around you and take you where you do not wish to go" (Jn 21:18). We may not wish to go to the cross. But that is where we must go if we to be cleansed, made new, rendered able to love.

The Spirit will lead us to enunciate the Creator/creature distinction in unity with the Psalms, especially those prayers of deliverance from enemies. Think of Psalm 13: "How long, O LORD? Will you forget me forever?" (Ps 13:1). The great dissimilarity between God and the creature does not negate the similarity between the two. That similarity assumes an "ever greater distance," but there is no contradiction between the Creator and the creature.[23] "How long shall my enemy be exalted over me?" (Ps 13:2). The psalmist knows how unnatural, how contradictory his predicament is. The Lord is not one who forgets forever. It would seem that the way he often teaches us that he does not forget forever is through the enemy's exaltation. The enemy's exaltation, however, is occasion to cry, "Consider and answer me, O LORD my God!" (Ps 13:3).

The Spirit as the love and gift of God draws forth—sometimes even wrenches—the confession "I trusted in your steadfast love" (Ps 13:5). God, who is the same always, is the basis for the psalmist singing because even as he cries, "How long must I bear pain in my soul?" (Ps 13:2), he knows that he will shout to the Lord "because he has dealt bountifully with me" (Ps 13:6). Even the prayer "Will you forget me forever?" is a function of God's bountiful goodness.

The living out of the distinction is the work of the Spirit. The Spirit's work expresses, temporally, who the Spirit has always been in relationship to Father and Son, and what the Spirit is as absolute goodness itself. Intimacy with the Spirit, the indwelling of the Spirit, will in this life bear fruit. It will bear fruit via a costly intimacy, an intimacy whose form may very well indicate great dissimilarity. "How long will you hide your face from me?" (Ps 13:1). That dissimilarity does not preclude fellowship, indeed, communion.

---

[23]Erich Przywara, *Analogia Entis: Metaphysics: Original Structure and Universal Rhythm*, trans. John R. Betz and David Bentley Hart (Grand Rapids: Eerdmans, 2014), 426.

The Spirit is "within in such a way that he is without."[24] The Spirit cries in and through us but always as one who is supremely above us. We are not our salvation. But we do rejoice through the Spirit in our salvation, the Lord, who is, as Paul says, the Spirit (2 Cor 3:17). The Spirit "encompasses in such a way that he penetrates: thus he presides in such a way that he upholds; thus he upholds in such a way that he presides."[25] That is what it means for us to be bound to God's goodness through the Spirit.

CONCLUSION

In this short but challenging chapter we have considered how there is "no loss of dignity" in the Son's becoming human.[26] We saw how his death saves us from sin and death "by reason of the perfection and unchangeableness of the divine goodness."[27] Indeed, the incarnation and atonement are rooted in the doctrine of God. Everything doctrinally speaking proceeds from God—notably, divine goodness—that is, from Father, Son, and Spirit. I have sought to demonstrate how in assuming our death, the Son suffers no diminution of goodness. Because he does not subsist through his two distinct natures but in them, he remains himself—the Father's beloved—even as he suffers, cries out, and dies.

The salvation he achieves for us is simply "the enjoyment of the same goodness" common to him and the Father and the Spirit. It is the incarnation of the Son that communicates goodness to us.[28] The incarnation is effective, then, because of its "principal agent."[29] The Son is perfect and unchangeably good, together with the Father and the Spirit, and he, in turn, declares and makes us good. Without an appreciation of the unchangeable goodness of God, the incarnation is without rationale or ground. The incarnation assists as it does by reason of the divine goodness. Moreover, without an account of the processions up and running it would be too easy to read Mark 10:18 as denoting a kind of ontological subordination of the Son to the Father. The Father is good in a different way from the Son insofar as he has

---

[24]Ibid., 522.
[25]Ibid., 527.
[26]Aquinas, *SCG* 4.55.
[27]Aquinas, *SCG* 4.54.
[28]Aquinas, *SCG* 4.55.
[29]Aquinas, *SCG* 4.56.

goodness from no one, whereas the Son, I argued, has goodness from someone, the Father, but they are not two goodnesses—"the Father and I are one" (Jn 10:30). The oneness of Father and Son also provided room for us to think through how christological teaching informs the Creator/creature distinction. To be a creature is to exist intimately with the Father, indeed to be one with him in the Son, but like the Son remain distinct from him even in the midst of unimaginable intimacy with him.

Let us now give some thought to our beatitude, to our perfection in the goodness that our Lord imports to us and in accordance with which he remakes us. As we shall see, our perfection has to do with God, whose goodness is perfection and who would have us make pilgrimage toward his perfection.

NINE

Perfection

D IVINE GOODNESS IS PERFECTIVE. It has the character of an end, the end being God. God has made us in such a way that we might commune with him, and perfectly. In this chapter I discuss the perfect and perfective character of divine goodness, in particular what divine goodness implies for the shape of the life in the world to come. I think through some of the dimensions of the goodness of God relevant to the day when he will be "all in all" and "in all" (1 Cor 15:28; Eph 4:6).

In particular I ask, what is divine happiness or blessedness, and how does it express divine goodness? Thomas provides a crisp sentence that I shall inhabit in the pages to come: "Happiness is simply the perfect good."[1] Happiness is God, the perfect good. I take up divine happiness as equivalent to divine goodness, articulating how the happiness of God makes happy in this life and immeasurably so in the next. Thus this chapter has two concerns: first, mapping why happiness is perfect goodness and, second, identifying why goodness is necessarily perfective and what that implies for our pilgrimage toward perfection.

GOODNESS AND SIGHT

We begin our inquiry in this chapter by considering how our minds are brought to God. Thomas tells us about two ways, "one way by God himself; in the second way by something else."[2] In terms of the first way, the Lord

---

[1]Aquinas, *Compend* §9.
[2]Aquinas, *Compend* §9.

Jesus has made God (the Father) known and seen, for one knows and sees the Father in the Son. We are never given unmediated access to the Father in this life; instead it is through torah and temple, as fulfilled in the Son, that we are given to know and love him. Knowledge of God that is christologically mediated is knowledge of God himself. We know God (the Father) through God (the Son, the Lord Jesus) and in God (the Holy Spirit).

The second way that we are brought to knowledge of God as one who makes himself known in Christ and the Spirit is through faith. In this life, we do not know God in a direct sense—as does the Son the Father—but through faith, that "something else." What is the relationship between sight and faith, in this life? In this life, we see by faith. Surpassing "natural reason," Thomas teaches that "the vision of that spiritual lovable object which is God, is impossible to us in the present life except by faith."[3] We see by faith. Sight apart from faith, as is the case with knowledge, is blindness; but seeing in faith is the way of happiness and enjoyment of God. When Paul states in 2 Corinthians 5:7 that "we live by faith, not by sight" (NIV), he is not opposing the two. His point, rather, is that sight without faith is not truly sight. To walk in faith is to see. Why is this important to highlight at the start of our discussion? Because our knowledge and sight of God in this life is indirect, that is, through other things. The principal thing is faith, which is a matter of seeing with the eyes of the heart. Moreover, our hearts and minds are in this life directed to God by Word and sacrament, as received in faith. The life of Christian discipleship is a matter (in part) of experiencing ever-greater intimacy with the Lord of the life to come. His goodness works in just this way, not only conserving but perfecting us in this life in the glories of the life to come.

What is the character of our seeing, and why do the Psalms and the New Testament—especially the Johannine material—privilege the motif of sight? Why is God's goodness to be seen? And why is seeing superior to knowing? It would seem that sight has a kind of expansiveness that knowing does not. When we see, we are said to know truly. But we would not say the reverse. Sight is the consummation of knowledge, the very perfection of love. Indeed, sight eclipses knowledge. How does this work with respect to the beatific

---

[3]Aquinas, *SCG* 3.2.118.

vision? The vision involves our intellect, and the intellect's seeing is superior to its knowing. Again, this is not to divorce knowledge and sight but to think about sight as perfecting knowledge. In a dense statement, Thomas notes, "the more one sees God, who is the source of goodness, the more necessary it is to love him, and so also the more one will desire to enjoy him."[4] To see is to love, and love increases desire for the one who is our joy. Love is the perfection of knowledge, sight the fruit of pure love. To know is to desire and to see what is known. In New Testament discourse, one can know without loving, but one cannot be said to see without at the same time loving. Accordingly, *sight* is the most comprehensive term available to us by which to describe the heavenly union of the created intellect with God. Indeed, sight and love are mingled together. The more that we see, the more we love.

How then do we hold fast in this life to our happiness, which is our good? Our happiness is a matter of holding fast to God, our "proper good." Commenting on Psalm 33:12, "happy is the nation whose God is the Lord," Thomas notes that holding fast to the Lord, having him as our God is, in this life, a matter of "intellect and will," indeed "the mind." Accordingly, it is not a matter of the senses "because we have this in common with the brutes." Holding fast involves the intellect "through contemplation and knowing."[5] Holding fast is a matter of the mind inasmuch as it contemplates, knows, and loves. We hold fast via intellect and will so that we might see, and we seek to know and contemplate so that we might behold.

In the vision of God, "the divine essence is both the object and medium of the vision."[6] We see God—the object—through God, and through God we will see all things in relation to God. This is heaven. It is God who always makes us like God, who enables us as creatures to share in all that he is. We become, in a memorable turn of phrase, "participators of His bliss: since God understands His substance by His essence, and this is His bliss."[7] Thomas's point is that in the life to come the intellect shall understand by the form of the divine substance itself. We shall share in his bliss, seeing ourselves (our substance) by our essence (our existence), which is God.

---

[4] Aquinas, *Compend* §9.
[5] Aquinas, *In Ps* 33, trans. Alexander Hall.
[6] Aquinas, *SCG* 3.51.
[7] Aquinas, *SCG* 3.51.

How does the bliss of the life to come relate to this life? Interestingly, Thomas points to Psalm 17:15 in describing how "justice" (*iustitia* in the Vulgate, Ps 16:15) or "righteousness" (NRSV) is intrinsic to the vision he cites in relation to Psalm 15:1-2: "Who may dwell on your holy hill? Those who walk blamelessly, and do what is right." Justice, righteousness, right conduct—these are the means through which "one arrives at the vision of God."[8] Without justice, there is no vision. Do justly and walk humbly, and you shall see. Through godly conduct in this life, one is set on the path toward the vision, "your glory in which are all good things."[9] Notice, further to this, the language of seeing. Sight is the manner in which the divine goodness is most fully received.

God is the active agent of the vision, its medium and end. This is what we mean in part by the perfective character of God's goodness. God is not simply our end but the means by which he becomes our end. He gives us a new disposition. That said, we must cultivate that disposition. This is important to think about. There is "diversity in the divine vision," meaning that divine delights are disproportionately allotted to those who in this life assiduously store up treasures in heaven.[10] Some will even judge the angels, though that will not be a source for heavenly envy! Those who see the most in the life to come are those who in this life acquire the strongest appetite for God. They are, in the life to come, raised to the greatest degree so they may see God's substance. Again, those who see most clearly are those who have been rich toward God in this life. Those who see supremely love what is seen and hence possess him as their end.

As creatures created in God's image and likeness and reconciled and redeemed by the image of God, Jesus Christ, our intellect and will are those dimensions of our creaturely being that are the seat of the vision. Intellect and will are consummated in sight. Love for God in the next life will never cease. The vision cannot change, for we could not will otherwise, nor would we want to will otherwise. As Thomas writes, "the will of those who see God cannot be perverse . . . [and] the will of the just will be unchangeable to evil."[11] Stated differently, the vision is immaculable, "incapable of self-performed

---

[8] Aquinas, *In Ps* 16, trans. Stephen Loughlin.
[9] Aquinas, *In Ps* 16.
[10] Aquinas, *SCG* 3.58.
[11] Aquinas, *SCG* 4.92, 93.

and self-inflicted sin."[12] There will be no sin in the life to come, the possibility of such having been forever vanquished. "It is impossible for the beatific vision of God ever to cease."[13] Why? Thomas answers that "the nearer a thing is to God who is utterly unchangeable, the less changeable and the more enduring is it."[14] We will not only be near but will possess what we see, receiving a kind of permanency unknown to us in this transitory life. God, as goodness itself, lacks nothing. We, who shall see him intimately—as he is—will be near him, and he will be in us.

Such possession is not to be understood in terms of our having God on our own terms. Instead, there is in heaven "no space for first-person awareness."[15] God will be in all, meaning in part that our entire mode of being will be receptive and that what we receive from God will be so utterly ours that we—without being aware of ourselves—may be said to possess it. We will live forever as those who possess life that is not their own, unable to defect and abscond from it. But more than live, we will see; indeed, we shall live by seeing. Seeing God, seeing the glorified flesh of Christ at the heart of the heavenly city, is the means by which we "attain to true beatitude, when . . . every desire is satisfied, and when there is a sufficiency of all good things."[16]

In sum, the language of sight is most serviceable for describing the means by which we apprehend our happiness in the life to come. We shall see what we do not very clearly in this life see, which is all things perfectly ordered to God as their last end. God is the perfective good. The doctrine of the last things rests on this premise. In this life we must be taught, for our desires are disordered. But when everything is near to God, as everything shall be in the life to come, all things shall be marked by endless praise. There will be nothing that is not of God, nothing that will not be from God and thus toward God. Every human shall be good, not by way of likeness, as is the case with this life, but by way of vision. We shall see, and what we see we shall participate in. All that we are (our intelligence, will, soul, and body)

---

[12]Paul J. Griffiths, *Decreation: The Last Things of All Creatures* (Waco, TX: Baylor University Press, 2014), 269.

[13]Aquinas, *SCG* 3.57.

[14]Aquinas, *SCG* 3.62.

[15]Griffiths, *Decreation*, 238.

[16]Aquinas, *SCG* 3.58.

shall attain "its ultimate perfection by its proper operation."[17] No operation
of ours shall be incongruent with what we see. We shall be perfect, see face
to face. Everything will be unsurpassably intimate with the Lord. We will
never want anything other than what we shall have, which is the Lord God.
As the perfect good, he will be our bliss, world without end.

THE CREATOR/CREATURE DISTINCTION RENEWED

If sight is the consummation of knowledge, what are the implications for the
Creator/creature distinction in the life to come? What is the relevance of the
distinction? In heaven, we are not collapsed into God, subsumed, as it were,
mingled in relation to him. The Creator/creature distinction remains intact
as ever in the life to come except it is not at that time subject to violation and
devastation. This is precisely why Thomas says "that God must be everywhere and in all things."[18] He will be in all things, and all things will be in him
in unsurpassing intimacy as their very cause. Accordingly, the doctrine of
creation and providence have ongoing salience for understanding the life to
come. God will continue to do good in relation to what is not God. There will
be nothing that has life outside him. Heaven's intelligibility thus has its roots
in the doctrine of creation and providence. In Thomas's memorable phrase,
commenting on Psalm 11:4, "heaven is the cradle in which God sits."[19]

The utter simplicity of God is important for understanding heaven, what
Griffiths calls "the LORD as our timespace."[20] The doctrine of God, of what
and who God is, makes its presence felt through all the doctrines of the faith,
of which the doctrine of the life to come is but one. Put tersely, in the life to
come "He [God] is all everywhere."[21] Nothing in the life to come will remain
distant to God, who "is all everywhere." Everything said, done, and seen will
be in him, present to him as what is only through him. Having said that,
Thomas is not suggesting that we are conflated with God. God is all everywhere, yes, though the same is not true of us; our exaltation in God does not
come at the expense of the integrity of our humanity. For example, we do
not become ubiquitous. Our bodily integrity remains.

---

[17] Aquinas, *SCG* 3.64.
[18] Aquinas, *SCG* 3.67.
[19] Aquinas, *In Ps* 11, trans. Stephen Loughlin.
[20] Griffiths, *Decreation*, 216.
[21] Aquinas, *SCG* 3.67.

In the life to come we remain localized; our resurrection bodies are bodies existing somewhere and not everywhere. We are not everywhere because God is all everywhere. The Creator/creature distinction is not blurred. The distinction, rather, is perfected, restored to its proper shape. All that exists in the life of the world to come will be in God as its active cause; every human person will be conscious of its absolute dependence on God. But more than that, we will not only know ourselves in dependence on God, but (following Thomas) God will be in us, indeed, "in all things as active cause."[22] One of the marks of our bliss in the life to come will be a conscious sense of our being caused by one who is in us without his being affected by us. More radical than seeing ourselves in God will be God in us, without, again, being mingled with us. This is what, I think, the notion of active causality honors in terms of the doctrine of the last things. God is in us: that is the first thing that needs to be said, and as a result, we are in God. The order matters. Our sense of who "we" are will, as a result, be fundamentally overturned. The only awareness we will have of ourselves in heaven will be as those in whom God is, those who are maximally intimate with the Lord, and who see and experience all things in the Lord.

"We will see him as he is" precisely because of his being in us (1 Jn 3:2). His goodness, beauty, and radiant splendor shall be ours. Because God has no parts, he shall be completely in what he is not, creatures animate and inanimate. The Holy Trinity of Father, Son, and Spirit shall be all in all but, of course, in a way that honors the primacy of the Father when it comes to the "all in all." Think again of Ephesians 4:6. The Father does not have a body, whereas the Son has a body. Therefore, one has to ask whether we will be able to see the Father. Asked differently, how shall we see one who is without a body? It may be fair to say that we will not so much see the Father in the life to come but shall instead see him in all things as their active cause. Sight of the Father in the life of the world to come will be sight that incorporates all things, insofar as he shall be seen as he is in a diversity of things. The clarification "all things" matters profoundly. To see the Father as he is will be a matter of seeing him in all things. The one who is alone good shall be seen as such in many things; seen as he is, not apart from all things but in all things.

---

[22]Aquinas, *SCG* 3.68.

What about the Son? How will he be seen? He will be seen bodily, to be sure, but will he not be seen as he is in all things, as is the case with the Father? Not quite: the Son will be at the center of all things seen. Just as the Father will be "in all things as active cause," so the Son will be seen as the orienting center of all things.[23] Because the Father loves the Son, one of the fruits of the Father's presence in all things shall be his directing of them toward the praise of his beloved Son, who is the center of all things. The Son will not be in all things, but he will be seen and, as such, worshiped and adored, by all things.

What is common to the Father, the Son, and the Spirit by dint of their one essence shall be common to all things in a mode appropriate to their being, but what is particular to each of the three shall not be in all things. It would, for example, be unintelligible to think of the Father's innascibility—his personal property of being from no one—as communicable. Because the Father shall be seen as he is in all things, all things shall see, adore, love, worship, and be maximally intimate with the Son and in him the Spirit. All things, furthermore, shall never cease to see and adore the Son because from him will flow the Spirit without measure (cf. Jn 3:34; Rev 22:1). What sees him shall receive his Spirit, the Spirit that flows from him and the Father throughout eternity. In the life of the world to come, therefore, we shall not see the Spirit. The Spirit remains Spirit, invisible. But in the Spirit we shall see the Son; in the Spirit we shall see the Father in all things, just as all things will be oriented to the Son.

Does God's nature there remain "invisible"? Not quite. I think the creation healed and restored will exercise something of a mediating function in the life to come. The invisible nature of God will be clearly and unambiguously seen in what he has made. What he had made will be utterly permeable to him. The center of creation redeemed will be the flesh of Christ. At the same time, the Father will be in all, all flesh will see him face to face, in all.

If such is the case, then, I think we are in a better position to receive Scripture's testimony to the creation's praise of its Creator. "The trees of the field shall clap their hands" (Is 55:12) because God will be in the trees as their active

---

[23] Aquinas, *SCG* 3.68.

cause, in a way that he cannot now be, given the trees' "bondage to decay" (Rom 8:21), activated as it is by our fallenness. The trees will no longer suffer as a result of our "project of self-extrication from the LORD" precisely because God will be in the trees as their active cause.[24] The creation groans now in travail because God is not in all things as he shall be in all things. Created things sense that their current state is not their natural state. It is not the trees that need to be taught God's statutes, for the trees have never sinned, whereas we have. In the next life, however, we will no longer need to be taught, for we shall experience, as do the trees here and now in a proleptic sense, God in us and thus ourselves in God. The song of the trees shall, moreover, be sung in one direction, toward the lamb who was slain. All things shall see him and sing his praises precisely because the Father shall be in all things, and all things shall receive and welcome the Spirit of the Father and Son.

The life to come will represent the perfection of the distinction. Nothing shall be mingled with God, nothing shall in any way cause God to be. God remains, as God always has, unchangeable. Aseity doctrine, even here, informs what we say about the life of the world to come. All things shall know themselves as actively caused, as ontologically dependent creatures, whatever their mode of creatureliness may be. Humans, who alone out of all creatures (with the exception of the fallen angels) have sinned, shall no longer need the statutes. There will be no law, no statutes in the life of the world to come. Law will have passed away, for the conditions under which the law was given shall be no more. Nothing shall want to or shall be able to extricate itself from the Lord. The aims of the statutes—principally, love of the Lord your God and of your neighbor in God—will accordingly be natural to us. The statutes assume our dislocatedness, a dislocatedness that shall be no more. The statutes anticipate a vision that shall be radically realized in the life of the world to come.

In the midst of the devastation, we see God nonsensorily, for the most part anyhow. In the life of the world to come, we shall see sensorily, not with the eyes of the heart but with the eyes as representative of our whole being and without the help of the former things, that is, the law. So too with many other things necessary for our intimacy with the Lord in this life,

---

[24]Griffiths, *Decreation*, 237.

things intrinsic to our seeing on this side of glory: the Scriptures as a whole, the chalice and the paten, the baptismal font, indeed the church.[25] In the life to come, we shall see transparently, with our eyes, with the intellect and the heart. We shall be seen and known by God, and insofar as we are known shall we be loved: "anyone who loves God is known by him" (1 Cor 8:3). There will be nothing in us that is not of God, not known by God, not participant in God. All that we are shall be transparent to the one whom we see and by whom we see all things, all creatures animate and disanimate healed by the Lord's glory.[26] What we shall see shall constitute us evermore. There shall be no lament, for all things shall have attained God's likeness. And nothing shall defect from what it has attained—hence again the surety of the vision.

The immensity of the experience of God's goodness in the life to come shall be such that the appetitive and the affective are perfectly united. We will never cease to want God, and in desiring God, to love God. There shall be rest forevermore. Our proper actions in the life of the world to come, not just our being but our actions, shall be entirely receptive to God. There is, in this respect, a progressive character to our intimacy with the Lord in the life to come, ever-increasing delight, world without end. Our life with him is glorious and indestructible from the moment it begins in earnest when we are judged and raised with Jesus to life eternal. We will only receive in heaven from the Lord, becoming more and more actual in relation to him.

To sum up, the Creator/creature distinction shall be perfected. We shall never be distant from the Lord in the life of the world to come. We are not pure act, as, of course, God is, and never shall be. We always have life in relation to the Lord God, though not he us. Intimacy with the Lord, ever-greater intimacy world without end, assumes less and less distance from him as we come to see more and more clearly. But we shall neither be absorbed into him nor mingled with him; we shall be like the Lord, without, as it were, being annexed into him, and thus shall see him. We will be completely like him, without being swallowed up by him. As Thomas says, "the last end of every creature is to attain God's likeness."[27] The last end of every creature is

---

[25]See further ibid., 308.
[26]See further ibid., 313.
[27]Aquinas, *SCG* 3.1.73.

for that creature, in all its fullness, to share in the Lord's goodness, participant in a manner befitting its mode of being in what is common to the three.

GOODNESS AND LIKENESS

The hope of heaven is that we and all other creatures with us will be immaculate, that is to say unblemished, by anything relating to the devastation. This new relation to God's perfect goodness shall nullify the entropic character of creaturely life, whether that is of plants or animals, things animate or inanimate. When things attain God's likeness, they attain the immutability proper to God in a mode appropriate to their givenness—hence the compatibility motif, once again.

Creatures shall be healed of all that ravages them. Creatures shall enjoy a surety in terms of their being, as God does in a primary and utterly exclusive sense. Another way to say this is that what is attributed to God shall be true of all creatures in the mode of likeness. All creatures shall be like God insofar as they receive from him goodness, life, being, impeccability, eternity, etc. All things shall be like God in being good, in having life, in not being subject to change, in enduring forever. What Griffiths calls "the repetitively static and endless peaceful participation of redeemed and healed creatures in the glory of the LORD," in short, heaven, derives its static and endlessly peaceful character from what God is.[28] "Static" denotes an incapacity to change: there shall be no potential for a fall of any kind, as everything shall be intimate with the Lord, having attained his likeness, lacking nothing.

The deep Sabbath rest of heaven (Heb 4:9-11) is intelligible in relation to the perfective character of God's goodness. Because God's goodness is naturally diffusive and communicative, all creatures shall communicate to one another the goodness they receive from God, communication being intrinsic to their perfection. All shall be made beautiful in relation to God and experience that beauty in relation to other things, receiving it from God as if it were from one another. This again helps us to see that heaven, while being "repetitively static" on one hand, will not be without ever-fresh wonders. The lives of all things shall unfold into ever-greater intimacy with the Lord, world without end, as things communicate to other things the

---

[28]Griffiths, *Decreation*, 313.

goodness they receive from God. God's goodness shall not only sustain every creature in being but mutually constitute every creature. Every creature will communicate to other creatures the good it receives from God as it directs its praise to Christ's glorified flesh.

How might this help us to indwell the Psalms? Psalm 35:10 is especially relevant to answering the question. What we mean by "likeness" is illustrated brilliantly in Thomas's treatment of Psalm 35, the second of the great psalms that tell of Christ's passion. In Psalm 35:9-10, we have David's exaltation of God's deliverance followed by his reverence of God. Not surprisingly, Thomas reads Psalm 35:9 in a robustly christological way, the deliverance and salvation achieved as belonging, first and foremost, to Christ, and in him to the church. But our real concern is with the reverence he offers to God, as a fruit of the Lord's deliverance, in the form of "O LORD, who is like you?" (Ps 35:10).

In what sense do we share in the likeness of the Lord, especially if there is nothing comparable to the Lord? Thomas's response is important and interesting. His commentary on Psalm 35 responds "by saying that things are said to be similar which have the same form and character. But similitude is two-fold."[29] Our similitude in this life with respect to God does not have to do with a common nature between us and God. God and humans are not different forms of the same nature. That said, "similar things are said of God and of man, namely by remote participation of the latter [i.e., man] in the former [i.e., God]." Notice the order: human beings are said to remotely participate in God, though the reverse is not true. For example, existence is common to both but in a radically dissimilar way. Existence is a likeness; those in the grave do not praise the living Lord. While both God and humans exist, we (humans) exist "by participation, and likewise concerning other things. And for that reason, this similitude is of dissimilar things."[30] Thus when we join in the psalmist's cry—"O LORD, who is like you?" (Ps 35:10)—we join in a cry that helps us to understand in what sense we are God's likenesses. God is not like us, but we are like God, that is, imperfect and remote participations in things such as existence that are true of God's very essence.

---

[29]Aquinas, *In Ps* 35, trans. Stephen Loughlin.
[30]Aquinas, *In Ps* 35.

One day, however, we shall be vindicated, and our tongues "shall tell of your righteousness and of your praise all day long" (Ps 35:28). This day is the day of heaven, the time of endless praise marked by immeasurable joys. Our future good—God, who is also our present good—will have been obtained. We shall not cease to be dissimilar to God; we shall remain remote participants, to be sure, and yet as such, God will be our all in all. The joy of sharing in God's greatness shall not come at the expense of our creatureliness. We cry through eternity, "O LORD, who is like you?" (Ps 35:10).

Thinking about the bliss of the life of the world to come is necessary, moreover, if we are to appreciate the use of the Psalms in preparing us for that life. The psalms of lament and praise—which is basically the whole Psalter—assume the devastation, the double fall, as it were; the Psalms make sense only against that background. When all things are healed, we shall no longer need the Psalter, for we will no longer be taught God but shall be known by God and so shall love God forevermore. We will sing, chant, meditate, and say the Psalms, individually and corporately, no more. The inversion of the Creator/creature relationship that the Psalms assume will be an artifact. This is not to say that the refrain of, for example, "give thanks to the LORD, for he is good; his steadfast love endures forever" shall not be on our lips all of our days (Ps 118:1). However, in the life to come, this shall not be a refrain, for we will be more in act—actual—than we have ever been; that is to say, we will be more in God than we have ever been and more related to what is nonhuman than we have ever been, to say nothing of each other.

There will be praise forevermore, but the not the praise of the pilgrim whose praise is intermingled with weeping, embracing lament, and confession. There will be supreme harmony between what we are, what the world is, and God, for all things will have attained God's likeness, centered on the flesh of Christ, who is God's image; God (the Father) will be "in all" (Eph 4:6).

Here we see, I think, the function of the doctrine of God's attributes (and especially God's goodness) when describing heaven's perfection. Christian teaching on heaven is derivative of God. Our end as creatures makes sense only in relation to God, who wills that every creature attain his likeness and thus as the creature it is, attain what he is. Every creature is to attain, as the creature it is, his goodness, beauty, happiness, and love. Thus we have the perfection of the Creator/creature distinction.

CONCLUSION

In this chapter I have thought through some of the implications of the "in all" of Ephesians 4:6 in relationship to the perfective character of God's goodness. As we have seen throughout the book, the Psalms do not separate the created order from God. They remind us that God is not only above all but through all and in all. The life of the world to come is a perfect life because God (the Father) will be "in all" without reserve. There is a sense in which that is true now, but only partially, because many things—most especially Adam's descendants—do not recognize that, indeed do not see that. In the life to come, all things will see themselves in relation to God. This does not mean that all things will be absorbed into God. Instead, there will be maximal intimacy of all things with God, and with Christ at the center, God will be seen as God, face to face, invisible as he is, through the instrumentality of all things. This is the renewal of the Creator/creature relationship and its perfection in vision. The happiness of heaven is seeing God in all. God will be seen as God through what he has made, and everything made will gaze on and sing toward Christ in the Spirit, to the glory of God the Father, world without end.

Conclusion

I HAVE ENJOYED WRITING THIS BOOK. It has given me the opportunity to think through some of the assumptions and implications of the Psalter's presentation of God. What is most important to the Psalter is God. Much modern theology has neglected God in favor of God's acts. Karl Barth, to his immense credit, took time, dogmatically speaking, to think through the attributes of God, though in a way that aligned with his particular and not always satisfying form of christocentric thinking. In this book I have taken a somewhat different tack from Barth, indeed a more Thomistic one. I have distinguished between things said of God's essence and things said of the three in relation to one another. This is salutary because it follows Scripture's lead in speaking not only about who God is but about what God is, his attributes, most especially his goodness. Accordingly, I have spoken in a Thomistic way—though with heavy doses of Augustine—about goodness as God and as convertible with the pure act of being that God is.

I have also talked about goodness as something that God does. The goodness that God is structures his acts in relationship to us. We noted how various works of God, whether they are of nature or of grace, express the great truths of God's attributes and who God is. In this last chapter I tie the threads of this study together with a view to their bearing on devotion toward God. I discuss how the doctrine of God must be lived, focusing on the role not only of devotion but also of experience, gladness, and grace. The point is to show that contemplation of God demands a deep renewal of the heart and mind. Prayer and praise are, I show, the prime modes of relation to God.

I pursued this line of inquiry because much modern theology seems to sit fairly lightly on the question of what kind of person you must be on your way to becoming in order to faithfully contemplate and bear witness to what Scripture teaches about the oneness and threeness of God and of all things in relationship to him. Dogmatic work demands an ascetic disposition, an abundance of good deeds, a prayerful openness to being shown things that may only be glimpsed when 3 John 11 is internalized. "Whoever does good is from God; whoever does evil has not seen God."

Modernity cannot accept "the givenness of things."[1] The modern does not recognize that "vast stretches of reality . . . are absolutes, not relative to conceptual schemes," whereas Scripture teaches that things are indeed given and given for a reason, namely, that they might delight in and praise their Creator and, moreover, teach us to do the same.[2] Were we more sensitive to the presence of the supernatural in and toward what is natural, we would see things as they are, that is, as created and thus having their being in God. The doctrine of revelation would accordingly occupy a smaller place in our dogmatics in favor of a more exalted place for the goodness of created things in relation to their Creator, to whom they are similar in the midst of ever-greater dissimilarity.

Criticisms of modernity aside, the point is to be theocentric, attentive to the Lord God, through whom our "cup overflows" (Ps 23:5). God is inebriating. Dogmatics, following the lead of Scripture itself, ought to demonstrate enrapture. If "there is nothing better than God," as Thomas insists, then theology ought to proceed in a manner, to use Augustine's gastronomic metaphor, that belches forth God's goodness.[3] Christian theology ought to work according to the impulse of God's supreme goodness, be filled with his love in order that it may speak according to grace. Without his love and without being captive to his goodness, it will be but a resounding gong and a clanging symbol.

The Christian ought not to be afraid of being "commingled with God."[4] I have throughout the text emphasized the importance of experience, indeed

---

[1]This is the title of Marilynne Robinson's most recent collect of essays, *The Givenness of Things: Essays* (New York: Farrar, Straus, and Giroux, 2015).
[2]William P. Alston, *A Sensible Metaphysical Realism*, Aquinas Lecture 65 (Milwaukee: Marquette University Press, 2001), 19.
[3]Aquinas, *ST* 1.25.6.4; Augustine, *Psalms* 5:87; Ps 102(103):3-5.
[4]Aquinas, *In Ps* 9, trans. Gregory Sadler.

the experience of God "who is a better spiritual thing."[5] When the Christian is not herself commingled, she can neither see nor enjoy well divine things. Indeed, only to the extent to which her soul is "commingled" is she able to turn from what is filthy to what is "clear and bright."[6] Heaven is said to dwell in her. The Lord makes his heaven in her. Theology's task is to help the faithful receive the Lord's making of heaven within.

Indeed, theology is undertaken by we who are very small before a God who is very great and does not think it beyond himself to bind himself to us who are so weak. Theology shares in the fruit of the incarnation, the conversion of humanity to God. It passes on the fruits of its contemplation for the edification of the faithful. We now reflect on the most salient characteristics of a theological intelligence being renewed in relation to the goodness of the Lord, beginning with devotion.

GOODNESS AND DEVOTION

Psalm 27:7: "Hear, O LORD, when I cry aloud, be gracious to me and answer me!" What is the import of this call to unfolding the doctrine of God? The answer, in short, is much. So Thomas writes, "Devotion is the reason that someone is heard by God. Devotion is a cry of the heart, which rouses God to hear."[7] The interior cry of the devoted heart is a bulwark against idolatry, for absconding from God in favor of gods of our own making. The first commandment, "You shall have no other gods before me," is terribly relevant to describing God. How do we know that we are speaking of the one true God and not an idol? Well, in part, because we are devout: "'Come,' my heart says, 'seek his face!'" (Ps 27:8). If we harbor sin in our hearts, we are unfit to see his face. Mortification of the flesh is intrinsic to the systematic-theological task. Accordingly, the theologian must pray that what she says of God is worthy of God. The only way in which one says things that are more rather than less worthy is via scripturally anchored devotion. Devotion is an important sense through which God's goodness is unfolded.

Matters of devotion are related to matters of sight. The goodness of the Lord will, so the psalmist believes, be seen "in the land of the living"

---

[5]Aquinas, *In Ps* 10.
[6]Aquinas, *In Ps* 10.
[7]Aquinas, *In Ps* 27, trans. James Miguez.

(Ps 27:13). We cannot see what is in God and things in reference to God unless our intelligence is being renewed with respect to the goodness seen in good things. Another way to say this is that the goodness of the Lord is to be seen in "those things that are in the Lord."[8] Devotion as expressed in Psalm 27:7 enables the theologian, indeed the people of God, to receive scriptural teaching regarding the goodness of created things as participatory in the supreme goodness of their Creator. We do not have in the Psalter a systematic treatise on the attributes of God, but we do have something better: a vision of the goodness of the Lord that teaches the blessed of all those things the Lord is and of how he is the goodness of created things.

To put this slightly differently, theology—with the doctrine of God's attributes as its center—fulfills its vocation when it begins and ends in ascription. Those among us called to the systematic-theological task ascribe— together with all God's people—glory and strength to the Lord. Theology's task is, in effect, to present the metaphysics of ascription. Theology reminds the faithful that the Lord is not in need of our worship, but that we are in need of him as "the origin of all our good and the end to which all is to be referred." Just so, "we can add nothing to God: and so we ought to glorify him."[9] Here we see how all teaching on God is moral. Because nothing can be added to God, we ought to worship and obey him.

Having said a few words about how the divine goodness assumes and engenders devotion, we now turn toward consideration of its experiential character.

GOODNESS AND EXPERIENCE

Experience matters. As Thomas comments on Psalm 34:8, the psalmist "urges experience. . . . He extols others . . . to experience friendship with God."[10] If theology's task is to say something about the divinity and identity of the one God and of things as they proceed from him, such saying demands friendship with the one about whom the theologian seeks to speak faithfully. Friendship with the Lord is a matter of tasting and seeing his goodness. The one who does not taste cannot know, to say nothing of see.

---

[8] Aquinas, *In Ps* 27.
[9] Aquinas, *In Ps* 27.
[10] Aquinas, *In Ps* 34, trans. Gregory Froelich.

Knowledge follows from experience; goodness must be tasted before it can be described. Experience of the divine goodness is an ongoing condition for the very possibility of the doctrine of God, for seeing his goodness.

This is an important insight into the nature of doctrine. When we teach, for example, about the doctrine of providence as an extension of the doctrine of God, it would be wise to begin instructing the saints in the fear of God. The providence of God cannot be explained without the fear of God. "O fear the LORD, you his holy ones" (Ps 34:9). To teach well, then, the doctrines of Christian faith, theology must respect the rules of the spiritual world, wherein tasting anticipates sight, wherein living and experiencing God's goodness precedes presentation of the same.

The relationship between taste and sight is important for the systematic presentation of God. Our doctrine of God's attributes begins with taste and ends in sight. Systematic-theological understanding is deeply spiritual and indeed ascetical in nature. This is important to acknowledge because theology may suffer a kind of spiritual death. Why? Because it is very hard for sinners to do theology. Though the life of grace "is the best since it comes from God," it contains many afflictions.[11] To be sure, theology is about the greatest good—God. But God's goodness is such that it strips us of the comfort of things we tend to think of as our goods. The home for theology is the Scriptures as received in faith in the company of the faithful. Sin, however, makes such receiving very, very hard. The Psalter reminds us, in an uncomfortably powerful way, that the righteous will suffer many afflictions; theology, too, will suffer, but the Lord will rescue it, enabling it to edify the Christian community to the extent that it holds fast to his goodness.

Theology's home is the promises of God. There will always in this life be theology, tasting and seeing of the Lord's goodness. The Lord God will continue to make theology possible in and through "his holy ones" (Ps 34:9), though very most likely in ways that are more bound to the lived life of the Christian community than has often been the case (in Protestant modernity, anyhow).

"The LORD redeems the life of his servants" (Ps 34:22). It is through the Lord God only that theology will be able to bear a difficult yoke—divine instruction. Insofar as it does, it will be redeemed. Though it will—as with

---

[11] Aquinas, *In Ps* 34.

us all—chase from time to time after false gods, the Lord will redeem it, not allowing it to completely capitulate to forgetfulness and death. Theology must understand itself in and through the wonderful gift of the Scriptures, incorporate their idioms, internalize their movements. Insofar as it does, theology will know the protection and sustenance of the Lord and champion experience of the same.

Just so, this has been in many respects a book about how to "think God."[12] The dominant conversation partner has been Thomas, but a largely silent one has been Karl Barth. At many junctures, I have asked myself whether Barth's statement—"It is always an abstraction to think God apart from the fact that, as the One from and by whom the creature is, He is also its Lord . . . its Saviour, the God of grace and covenant"—is quite right.[13] I sense that there is an imbalance here. The works, the acts of God are, as Barth insists, that by which we are given to think God. This is true enough. But those acts and the goods they confer on us encourage us to think of God as the principle of those acts, as the fullness of being itself. The Scriptures are interested in both what and who God is as well as what God does. Moreover, they are deeply interested in the spiritual condition of the one thinking. The acts of God encourage contemplation of God's dignity, God's greatness— indeed the very heights of God's nature—as the ground of God's offices and experience of this. The Psalms work in just this way. They glory in God's greatness: "For the LORD, the Most High, is awesome" (Ps 47:2). The pattern of praise in the Psalter—Psalm 47, for example—is praise of God on account of God's being God, in this case his being awesome, and from praise of his nature to those signs that indicate it. The Lord is "a great king over all the earth" (Ps 47:2) and as such is my God. Tying thought of God so tightly to grace and covenant as Barth does short-changes, I think, attention to the ground of grace and covenant, "the LORD, the Most High," and the encouraging of experience of that ground. In other words, Holy Scripture unfolds both nature and offices, including therewith the experience of the former as made possible by the latter. But there is priority with respect to God's nature, God's own essence. The Psalms, as I have sought to argue, give much press to both dignity and works, but the weight is on

---

[12]Barth, *CD* III/3, 423.
[13]Barth, *CD* III/3, 423.

dignity. The antidote to neglecting God's dignity—divinity—is the pattern that many of the Psalms assume when they announce with such enthusiasm "that this is God" (Ps 48:14).

As we draw this brief section to a close, I have written so as to draw us to God, the great "I always am." The doctrine of God's attributes must avoid spiritual adultery, that is, twisting of sacred Scripture "into another sense, or to some other end" than as that which speaks of God and directs us to him.[14] The aim of all of this has been refreshment in the one who always is supremely good. It has been a work of praise—what Thomas calls "the devotion of praise," the offering of the mind to God. This book has sought to assist the reader in recognizing and experiencing the centrality of "that this is God" for the systematic-theological enterprise.

GOODNESS AND GLADNESS

The experience of God's goodness evokes spiritual gladness. In an arresting comment on Psalm 51:8, "Let me hear joy and gladness; let the bones that you have crushed rejoice," Thomas says that "spiritual powers . . . are increased through spiritual gladness."[15] To consider well the God we are given to know, taste, love, and see in Scripture requires considerable spiritual powers. Such powers, however, are not natural to us. Spiritual joy and gladness, which come to us entirely from God, give spiritual powers. Such power is necessary for contemplation and the passing on of the fruits of contemplation for the faithful. Systematic study of God and the works of God requires spiritual power—ultimately, the power of the Holy Spirit received in praise and prayer. We cannot underestimate this. There is much that we cannot see or say (that must nonetheless be seen and said) unless we hear the Scriptures with joy and gladness, unless our efforts to do theology out of our own moment and resources are abandoned.

Another way to say this is that theology is a spiritual undertaking, rooted in the acquisition of spiritual power, which we cannot receive without our becoming "learned in spiritual warfare."[16] Battle language appears, as is well known, throughout the Psalms. Recall, for example, Psalm 18:39. Therein

---

[14]Aquinas, *In Ps* 50, trans. Stephen Loughlin.
[15]Aquinas, *In Ps* 51, trans. Ed Redmond.
[16]Aquinas, *In Ps* 18, trans. Hugh McDonald.

David implores the Lord God to deliver him from his enemies and praises him when he does. Many modern readers bristle at this and are embarrassed by it. Why is David as a warrior-king exalted by the Psalter in this way? Why is the deliverance David seeks often related to military conquest and the annihilation of God's enemies? How, for example, are texts such as Psalm 18:34-42, "He trains my hands for war, so that my arms can bend a bow of bronze," God's Word? Thomas's thought is instructive. He recognizes the literal sense but does not think it exhaustive, for it gives way to the spiritual sense, which the literal itself presupposes. When Thomas reads of David being girded by God with strength for the battle in Psalm 18:39, Thomas points to its "mystical sense," stating, as we noted a moment ago, "we must be learned in spiritual warfare." Thomas continues, citing Sirach 11, that "many are the snares of the crafty one, which we cannot avoid unless we have the divine learning and help."[17]

Becoming learned in spiritual warfare is a matter of acquiring divine learning and experiencing divine help. Spiritual powers are increased through spiritual gladness, which itself is a fruit of "becoming learned in spiritual warfare." Instruction and experience are fundamental to warfare. We recall the great things that God has done so that we might be mindful of the great things he is doing and will do. Similarly, advancement in spiritual warfare assumes an experience of God's help. David's battles are, on one level, against flesh and blood but are, on another level, against an evil that is not concomitant with his enemies. There is an evil—the devil—who seeks to devour David (and indeed all God's people), against whom we have no recourse save God. Learning is a matter of experiencing God's saving help— "you made my assailants sink under me" (Ps 18:39). Learning of God is a matter of God's beating our enemies—sin, death, and the devil—"fine, like dust before the wind" (Ps 18:42). This we cannot do ourselves, but with God all things are possible. God gives increase in spiritual power insofar as we increase in gladness as acquired by proficiency in spiritual warfare.

Another reason why such learnedness is necessary is that it renders the Psalter a little less "familiar." We are at home with more sedate-sounding language such as pilgrimage rather than the charged language of warfare. If

---

[17] Aquinas, *In Ps* 18.

we follow the message of Scripture, however, our pilgrimage will assume at many points the character of a battle. The New Testament is permeated by references to the angelic and demonic, to the devil, Satan, the evil one. Again, for modern readers who assume a rationalistic view of the world, this is troubling. But for those seeking to become learned in warfare, it should not be. The principal weapons God gives us on our pilgrimage toward him are Word and sacrament. The Psalms, in language that is often violent—"I struck them down, so that they were not able to rise" (Ps 18:38)—are food and drink for our pilgrimage to the Lord God and warfare against those powers inimical to him.

Kathryn Greene McCreight makes this clear in her remarkable book, *Darkness Is My Only Companion: A Christian Response to Mental Illness.* Commenting on reading the Psalms devotionally, she writes,

> After all, the Psalms can seem bloodthirsty and violent at times. How can one read Psalm 137 or similar psalms devotionally unless by transmuting the Babylonian babies, or the enemies, into something else? So when I read the Psalms, my enemies according to the tropological sense were my mood swings, my brain chemistry, thoughts and feelings that were beyond my control. These were truly my enemies. Many people are repulsed by the warlike imagery of the Old Testament. But most of us have figurative, yet very real, enemies that we need to fight and bring to peace in the embrace of God.[18]

The moral (or tropological sense) means that the enemies we have (internal and external) can be subdued by us only in God. There is hope, however, because God promises supernatural strength such that "my arms can bend a bow of bronze" (Ps 18:34).

Disciplined pursuit of a biblically derived and spiritually robust doctrine of God involves battle against many enemies, enemies that will conquer us unless we become learned in spiritual warfare. Perhaps the first thing to go is gladness. The most bloodthirsty and violent psalms, such as parts of Psalm 18, give us permission to bring our enemies before God—in Greene Mc-Creight's case, her faulty brain chemistry—with a view to the promise of

---

[18]Kathryn Greene McCreight, *Darkness Is My Only Companion: A Christian Response to Mental Illness,* 2nd ed. (Grand Rapids: Brazos, 2015), 192.

victory: "You made my assailants sink under me" (Ps 18:39). Put differently, our pilgrimage is nourished above all else by the Word of God. One of the great enemies of the doctrine of God is indifference to the Word. The Word of God on its various levels—the literal, moral, and mystical or christological—equips us for warfare. Christ casts out his enemies "like the mire of the streets" (Ps 18:42). He does the same for us when we call on him. Teaching on God, to the extent to which it is teaching on *God*, will suffer many assailants. The enemy of the doctrine is fundamentally our own flesh, according to the moral sense "the movements of concupiscence that are within us." Importantly, Thomas reminds us that we will not gain victory over them in this life, but they may "continually grow weaker."[19] Though they will not be completely brought into submission—"as soon as they heard of me they obeyed me" (Ps 18:44)—their movements will weaken, that we can be assured of. God does indeed give us vengeance to subdue these movements. And insofar as they are subdued under us, are we able to "taste and see that the LORD is good" (Ps 34:8). Teaching on God may, by grace, resist the sirens of the flesh, giving way to taste and sight.

The doctrine of God is the fruit of a promise. Many things distract us; nonetheless, following the pattern of the Psalter, our inattention does not have the last word. Spiritual gladness in God, which leads to increase in spiritual power, is possible because of the promise of God. Temptations to think according to anything other than God dissipate under the promise of God to preserve a people who announce in ways that include the systematic-theological task "this is our God."

GOODNESS AND GRACE

I end with how grace expresses goodness. God converts us to himself. God is the active agent in our conversion in Christ through the Spirit. This we have seen all along. God is a perfective good. Psalm 32:8-9 is instructive in this. Psalm 32:1-7 bears the voice of David. The speaker, however, shifts in Psalm 32:8 to the Lord. The Lord reminds David that he "brings about the conversion of David by imposing his hand on him—the hand of the Lord."[20] The Lord knows that we are "in need of supernatural assistance," though he

---

[19] Aquinas, *In Ps* 18, trans. Hugh McDonald.
[20] Aquinas, *In Ps* 32, trans. Peter Zerner.

does not compel us to seek such, if we are to be converted to him.[21] Sin turns us away from our "last end, but also turns us unduly to other things as ends."[22] When we confess our sins, we do not make God aware of what he was not unaware of before; rather, we express our desire for "God to be aware of it, in order to forgive it."[23] The change takes place in us. Rather than wanting to be turned away from God, confession indicates our desire to be turned toward God and so to be forgiven. The doctrine of God demands such a confessional stance. God does not need to be made aware of what turns us from him, but teaching on God must be aware of the idols, anything that causes us to attend to what is other than our true end.

This discussion of God's instruction in Psalm 32:8-9 offers great insight into the nature of grace. God's instruction—indeed the statutes—is a work of grace all the way down. This is what Thomas calls "antecedent grace."[24] God's loving divine instruction in the form of the law is an example of that grace. The law is a gift, teaching us the way we should go, though not having the power to move us in the way that we should go. Thus the truth is that the good work of obedience is a work to which God moves our soul. Theology is a good work toward which God moves us. Inasmuch as our souls are moved to obey God's divine instruction, we experience "His protection."[25] The Lord counsels us with his eyes on us—"I will counsel you with my eye upon you" (Ps 32:8). Theology, too, lives by the same promise.

The end effect of grace is joy. The penitential psalms—of which Psalm 32 is but one—"begin in sorrow and end in joy, since it is penitence that accomplishes this joy."[26] In confessing our sin and engaging in penitential acts, we move from not only being "glad in the LORD" (Ps 32:11); we move, moreover, to the more exuberant and extroverted language of shouting for joy. Gladness ends in joy. Joy is for the "righteous" and the "upright in heart" (Ps 32:11). When our wills are conformed to God, we are glad, so glad that we shout for joy. This is grace, and theology may have a share in expressing, in a rather extroverted manner, the joy intrinsic to the subject matter.

---

[21] Aquinas, *SCG* 3.2.147.
[22] Aquinas, *SCG* 3.2.145.
[23] Aquinas, *In Ps* 32, trans. Peter Zerner.
[24] Aquinas, *In Ps* 32.
[25] Aquinas, *In Ps* 32.
[26] Aquinas, *In Ps* 32.

The pilgrimage and battle of which we have been speaking in this book may be described, to be sure, but ultimately divine goodness must be experienced and lived. Beatitude is for the just and upright. Beatitude requires or assumes a disposition, an upright disposition, if we would have our hearts and minds conformed to God. Theology is an act of praise, a form of praise and prayer, and without an upright heart, the theologian's work will cease to be theology, having promoted gods of his or her own making. Prayer and praise are the "lens" through which the doctrine of God must be addressed.

If theology as with praise "befits the upright" (Ps 33:1), then it is possible to do theology in a mode "full of the steadfast love of the Lord" (Ps 33:5). That fullness or repleteness, as Thomas notes in an extremely perceptive comment, is more a matter of "spiritual goods" rather than "temporal . . . more so since the coming of Christ."[27] He then cites Acts 2:4, the pouring out of the Spirit, Pentecost. The earth is subject to an abundance of spiritual goodness that is often manifesting visibly, for example, in the rain that falls on the just and unjust. Importantly, this is not to minimize human suffering. Rather, it is counsel for the upright. In the next life, we will not say such things, for heaven *is* the steadfast love of the Lord, of which there is nothing better. Heaven is the Lord himself, and all things existing—directly—in relationship to the Lord himself. This is our hope, and it is grace; and theology, if it be theology, nurtures that hope, encourages that intimacy.

Were there not grace, we would not be. The function of theology is to assist the faithful in remaining with the Lord himself. In our strange moment, when it would seem that, existentially speaking, chaos has never been more ubiquitous, there is God, theology's very subject matter. Accordingly, I conclude this book with almost a rebuke to myself. Why was I so slow in treating things that theology treats—for example, the works of salvation, the whole Christ—without referring them to God? The question of the Gospels, especially of the Fourth Gospel, is "Where do you come from?" Jesus, of course, says that he is from the Father, from God, with whom he is one.

I suspect I was so slow in part because I did not really know how to pray, or indeed want to pray, ordained minister though I am. Just so, it is in living the doctrine of God, at whose heart is the Creator/creature distinction, that

---

[27] Aquinas, *In Ps* 32.

one sees why Christ, by whom we are saved, gladly and delightfully orders himself to his Father, our Father, even unto death. We treat salvation, yes, the whole Christ, yes, these and many more things, but only "so far as they are ordered to God."[28] It is this robust, disciplined, and spiritually motivated theocentrism that matters for unfolding the great teachings of the faith. Without God's unity and the distinction of persons being placed front and center, which includes the procession of creatures from him, the other great teachings of the church catholic lack a home, especially in relation to the Old Testament. The christological concentration championed today reflects something of a distortion. We must treat the whole Christ, his person and work and his members, the church, his body, but not without these themes being ordered to God and being scripturally narrated from Genesis to Revelation.

If this book has any salience for the pursuit of a scripturally rooted reception of the glories of God, I would hope that it helps revitalize attention to the importance of attending to some classical and medieval distinctions in the doctrine of God, indeed how those distinctions encourage us to cry out to God that we may be taught him so as to love him, world without end.

---

[28] Aquinas, *ST* 1.7.

Bibliography

Aertsen, Jan. *Medieval Philosophy as Transcendental Thought: From Philip the Chancellor (CA. 1225) to Francisco Suarez*, Studien Und Texte Zur Geistesge-schichte Des Mittelalters. Leiden: Brill, 2012.

Alston, William P. *A Sensible Metaphysical Realism*. Milwaukee: Marquette University Press, 2001.

Anselm of Canterbury. *Anselm of Canterbury: The Major Works*. Edited by Brian Davies and G. R. Evans. Oxford: Oxford University Press, 1998.

Aquinas, Thomas. *Basic Writings of Saint Thomas Aquinas*. Edited by Anton C. Pegis. Vol. I, *God and the Order of Creation*. Indianapolis: Hackett, 1997.

———. *Commentary on St Paul's Epistle to the Ephesians*. Translated by Matthew L. Lamb. Albany, NY: Magi Books, 1966.

———. *Compendium of Theology*. Translated by Richard J. Regan. Oxford: Oxford University Press, 2009.

———. *Disputed Questions on Truth*. Translated by Robert W. Mulligan, James V. McGlynn, and Robert W. Schmidt. 3 vols. Indianapolis: Hackett, 1994.

———. *An Exposition of "On the Hebdomads" of Boethius*. Translated by Janice L. Shultz and Edward Λ. Synan. Washington, DC: Catholic University of America Press, 2001.

———. *On the Divine Names*. Translated by Harry C. Marsh. In "'Cosmic Structure and Knowledge of God: Thomas Aquinas' *In Librum beati Dionysii de divinis nominibus exposition,*" 265-549. PhD diss., Vanderbilt University, 1994.

———. *St. Thomas's Exposition of the Psalms of David*. Translated by various. Project coordinator Stephen Loughlin. Center Valley, PA: Aquinas Translation Project. Last updated September 4, 2012. http://hosted.desales.edu/w4/philtheo/loughlin/ATP/index.html.

———. *The Summa Contra Gentiles*. Translated by Fathers of the English Dominican Province. 4 vols. London: Burns, Oates & Washbourne, 1923–1929.

Arndt, William F., and F. Wilbur Gingrich. *A Greek-English Lexicon of the New Testament and Other Early Christian Literature*. 4th ed. Chicago: University of Chicago Press, 1971.

Athanasius. *On the Incarnation*. Crestwood, NY: St. Vladimir's Seminary Press, 1993.

Augustine. *Confessions*. Translated by Henry Chadwick. Oxford: Oxford University Press, 1992.

———. *Exposition of the Psalms*. Translated by Maria Boulding, OSB. 6 vols. Hyde Park, NY: New City Press, 2000–2004.

———. *On Christian Teaching*. Translated by R. P. H. Green. Oxford: Oxford University Press, 1997.

———. *The Trinity*. Translated by Edmund Hill, OP. Brooklyn, NY: New City Press, 1991.

Barnett, Victoria J., and Barbara Wojhoski, eds. *Dietrich Bonhoeffer Works*. 17 vols. Minneapolis: Fortress, 2014.

Barth, Karl. *Church Dogmatics*. Edited by G. W. Bromiley and T. F. Torrance. Translated by G. W. Bromiley et al. 4 vols. Edinburgh: T&T Clark, 1956–1975.

Blaising, Craig A., and Carmen S. Hardin, eds. *Psalms 1–50*. ACCS Old Testament VII. Edited by Thomas C. Oden. Downers Grove, IL: IVP Academic, 2008.

Botterweck, G. Johannes, Hans-Josef Fabry, and Helmer Ringgren, eds. *Theological Dictionary of the Old Testament*. Vol. 5. Grand Rapids: Eerdmans, 1986.

Brito, Emilio. "Deux Modèles du Dieu Unique: Thomas d'Aquin et Hegel." *Église et Théologie* 21 (1990): 33-64.

Brueggemann, Walter, and William H. Bellinger Jr. *Psalms*. NCBC. Edited by Ben Witherington III. Cambridge: Cambridge University Press, 2014.

Calvin, John. *Joshua and the Psalms*. Translated by Henry Beveridge. Grand Rapids: AP&A, n.d.

Chrysostom, St. John. *The Fathers of the Church: A New Translation*. Edited by Hermigild Dressler, OFM. Vol. 72, *On the Incomprehensible Nature of God*. Translated by Paul W. Harkins. Washington, DC: Catholic University of America Press, 1982.

Clarke, W. Norris. *The One and the Many: A Contemporary Thomistic Metaphysics*. Notre Dame, IN: University of Notre Dame Press, 2001.

Davidson, Ivor J. "Divine Sufficiency: Theology in the Presence of God." In *Theological Theology: Essays in Honour of John Webster* edited by R. David Nelson, Darren Sarisky, and Justin Stratis, 55-74. London: Bloomsbury T&T Clark, 2015.

Duby, Stephen J. *Divine Simplicity: A Dogmatic Account*. London: Bloomsbury T&T Clark, 2016.

Emery, Gilles, OP. "Essentialism or Personalism in the Treatise on God in St. Thomas Aquinas?" In *Trinity in Aquinas*, 165-208. Ypsilanti, MI: Sapientia Press, 2003.

————. *The Trinitarian Theology of Thomas Aquinas.* Translated by Francesca Aran Murphy. New York: Oxford University Press, 2007.

Fowl, Stephen E. *Ephesians: A Commentary.* TNTL. Louisville: Westminster John Knox, 2012.

Ginther, James R. "The Scholastic Psalms' Commentary as a Textbook for Theology: The Case of Thomas Aquinas." In *Omnia Disce: Medieval Studies in Memory of Leonard Boyle, O.P.* edited by Anne J. Duggan, Joan Greatrex, and Brenda Bolton, 197-216. Aldershot, UK: Ashgate, 2005.

Greene McCreight, Kathryn. *Darkness Is My Only Companion: A Christian Response to Mental Illness.* 2nd ed. Grand Rapids: Brazos, 2015.

Griffiths, Paul J. *Decreation: The Last Things of All Creatures.* Waco, TX: Baylor University Press, 2014.

Gunton, Colin. *Act and Being: Toward a Theology of the Divine Attributes.* Grand Rapids: Eerdmans, 2002.

Harris, R. Laird, Gleason Archer Jr., and Bruce K. Waltke, eds. *Theological Wordbook of the Old Testament.* Chicago: Moody Press, 2003.

Hart, David Bentley. "We Need to Talk About God." *Church Times* 12, no. 2 (2016), www.churchtimes.co.uk/articles/2016/12-february/features/features /immortal-invisible-the-doctrine-of-god.

Holmes, Christopher R. J. *Revisiting the Doctrine of the Divine Attributes: In Dialogue with Karl Barth, Eberhard Jüngel, and Wolf Krötke.* New York: Peter Lang, 2007.

Krötke, Wolf. *Gottes Klarheiten: Eine Neuinterpretation der Lehre von Gottes 'Eigenschaften.'* Tübingen: Mohr Siebeck, 2001.

Levering, Matthew. *Christ's Fulfillment of Torah and Temple: Salvation According to Thomas Aquinas.* Notre Dame, IN: University of Notre Dame Press, 2001.

Marshall, Bruce D. "The Absolute and the Trinity." *Pro Ecclesia* 23, no. 2 (2014): 147-64.

Mays, James L. *Psalms.* Interpretation: A Bible Commentary for Teaching and Preaching. Louisville: Westminster John Knox, 2011.

O'Rourke, Fran. *Pseudo-Dionysius and the Metaphysics of Aquinas.* Leiden: Brill, 1999.

Ortlund, Gavin. "Divine Simplicity in Historical Perspective: Resourcing a Contemporary Discussion." *IJST* 16, no. 4 (2014): 436-53.

Pieper, Josef. *Living the Truth: Reality and the Good: The Truth of All Things.* Translated by Stella Lange. San Francisco: Ignatius, 1999.

Plantinga, Cornelius, Jr. "Social Trinity and Tritheism." In *Trinity, Incarnation, and Atonement: Philosophical and Theological Essays,* 21-47. Edited by Ronald

J. Feenstra and Cornelius Plantinga Jr. Notre Dame, IN: University of Notre Dame Press, 1990.

Przywara, Erich, SJ. *Analogia Entis: Metaphysics: Original Structure and Universal Rhythm*. Translated by John R. Betz and David Bentley Hart. Grand Rapids: Eerdmans, 2014.

Radner, Ephraim. *A Time to Keep: Theology, Mortality, and the Shape of a Human Life*. Waco, TX: Baylor University Press, 2016.

Robinson, Marilynne. *The Givenness of Things: Essays*. New York: Farrar, Straus and Giroux, 2015.

Ryan, Thomas F. *Thomas Aquinas as Reader of the Psalms*. Notre Dame, IN: University of Notre Dame Press, 2000.

Sokolowski, Robert. *The God of Faith and Reason: Foundations of Christian Theology*. Washington, DC: Catholic University of America Press, 1995.

Sonderegger, Katherine. *Systematic Theology*. Vol. 1, *The Doctrine of God*. Minneapolis: Fortress Press, 2015.

Thielman, Frank. *Ephesians*. Baker Exegetical Commentary on the New Testament. Edited by Robert W. Yarbrough and Robert H. Stein. Grand Rapids: Baker Academic, 2010.

Ticciati, Susannah. "How New Is New Creation? Resurrection and Creation *ex nihilo.*" In *Eternal God, Eternal Life: Theological Investigations into the Concept of Immortality*, 89-114. Edited by Philip G. Ziegler. London: Bloomsbury T&T Clark, 2016.

Torretta, Gabriel, OP. "Rediscovering the Imprecatory Psalms: A Thomistic Approach." *The Thomist* 80, no. 1 (2016): 23-48.

Webster, John. *Confessing God II: Essays in Christian Dogmatics*. 2nd ed. London: Bloomsbury T&T Clark, 2015.

White, Thomas Joseph, OP. *The Incarnate Lord: A Thomistic Study in Christology*. Washington, DC: Catholic University of America Press, 2015.

Williams, Rowan. "Augustine and the Psalms." *Interpretation* 58, no. 1 (2004): 17-27.

Williamson, Peter S. *Ephesians*. CCSS 3. Grand Rapids: Baker Academic, 2009.

Wippel, John. "Aquinas's Route to the Real Distinction: A Note on *De Ente et Essentia.*" *The Thomist* 43 (1979): 279-95.

Wittman, Tyler R. "Confessing God as God: Thomas Aquinas, Karl Barth and the Relation Between Theology and Economy." PhD diss., University of St Andrews, 2016.

Name and Subject Index

Scripture Index

x 104:33, 107